Deleuze and Ethology

Also Available from Bloomsbury

Deleuze, Guattari, and the Problem of Transdisciplinarity, ed. Guillaume Collett
Deleuze and Guattari: Selected Writings, Kenneth Surin
Deleuze and the Schizoanalysis of Feminism, ed. Cheri Carr and Janae Sholtz
Space After Deleuze, Arun Saldanha
The History of Animals, Oxana Timofeeva

Deleuze and Ethology

A Philosophy of Entangled Life

Jason Cullen

BLOOMSBURY ACADEMIC
LONDON • NEW YORK • OXFORD • NEW DELHI • SYDNEY

BLOOMSBURY ACADEMIC
Bloomsbury Publishing Plc
50 Bedford Square, London, WC1B 3DP, UK
1385 Broadway, New York, NY 10018, USA
29 Earlsfort Terrace, Dublin 2, Ireland

BLOOMSBURY, BLOOMSBURY ACADEMIC and the Diana logo are trademarks of
Bloomsbury Publishing Plc

First published in Great Britain 2021
This paperback edition published in 2022

Copyright © Jason Cullen, 2021

Jason Cullen has asserted his right under the Copyright, Designs and
Patents Act, 1988, to be identified as Author of this work.

For legal purposes the Acknowledgements on p. viii constitute an
extension of this copyright page.

Cover design by Charlotte Daniels
Cover image © Natali Alba / Alamy Stock Photo

All rights reserved. No part of this publication may be reproduced or transmitted
in any form or by any means, electronic or mechanical, including photocopying,
recording, or any information storage or retrieval system, without prior
permission in writing from the publishers.

Bloomsbury Publishing Plc does not have any control over, or responsibility for, any third-
party websites referred to or in this book. All internet addresses given in this book were
correct at the time of going to press. The author and publisher regret any inconvenience
caused if addresses have changed or sites have ceased to exist, but can accept no
responsibility for any such changes.

A catalogue record for this book is available from the British Library.

Library of Congress Control Number: 2020941213

ISBN: HB: 978-1-3501-3379-2
PB: 978-1-3502-0400-3
ePDF: 978-1-3501-3380-8
eBook: 978-1-3501-3381-5

Typeset by Deanta Global Publishing Services, Chennai, India

To find out more about our authors and books visit www.bloomsbury.com
and sign up for our newsletters.

Contents

List of figures	vii
Preface and acknowledgements	viii
List of abbreviations	ix
Introduction	1
1 The problem: An ethology of sense	**17**
Introduction	17
Ethology	18
Uexküll and the functional circle	21
Hegel, Hyppolite and Deleuze: Difference and sense	29
Semiotics	33
Making sense: The simultaneity of a virtual whole and its actual parts	38
Conclusion: Sense and the formulation of problems	43
2 On Deleuze's Spinozism: Expression and sense-making in the logic of holism	**47**
Univocity	48
Immanence	51
Attribution, distinction and the constitution of substance	53
Attribution and the production of the modes	58
Modification as the expression of power	63
Conclusion	67
3 On Deleuze's Bergson: The transformation of the whole	**71**
Deleuze's Nietzschean critique of Spinoza	72
Bergson's critique of the possible and the real and the genesis of novelty	74
The dialectic of problems: The virtual and actualization	77
Multiplicities	79
The three syntheses of time and correspondence without resemblance	82
Conclusion: Syntheses and the renewal of holism	89

4	Images and affect	93
	Movement and distinction	94
	Images and representation	98
	The movement-image and its avatars	102
	Perception and action, problems and solutions	105
	Affection and the reciprocal presupposition of individuals and the whole	109
	Conclusion	112
5	Subjectivity, experimentation beyond the action-image and an 'art of living'	115
	Resisting the privilege of a human point of view: Bergsonism contra phenomenology	117
	Bipolar perceptions: Analysis, description and semisubjectivity	120
	Framing and the determination of problems	125
	Memory, perception and temporal series	128
	Signs and the differentiation of the image	134
	On the failure of the sensory-motor schema and an art of living	136
	Conclusion: The breakdown of the sensory-motor schema and experimentation	142
Conclusion		143
	Immanence and expression between causality and determination	144
	Towards a Deleuzian ethology	151
Notes		161
Bibliography		189
Index		198

Figures

1 Jakob von Uexküll's functional cycle (Reproduced with permission of Minnesota University Press) — 23
2 Bergson's 'second great schema', *Matter and Memory*'s famous cone with 'virtual circuits ... which contain all our past as [it] preserved in itself' — 127
3 Bergson's 'first great schema', the circuits of memory and perception — 132

Preface and acknowledgements

Like many first books, *Deleuze and Ethology* began its life as a PhD thesis. In this case, it was a study of the metaphysical significance of Gilles Deleuze's two-volume *Cinema* project. While *Deleuze and Ethology*'s transition from a PhD thesis to the present (hopefully improved) work has largely been a solitary passion project, there has been a handful of people who have aided its transformation: Greg Hainge, a supervisor who became a colleague and friend who has helped in many practical ways; Ronald Bogue and Greg Flaxman, my thesis examiners who offered unexpectedly generous encouragement to write this book as well as suggestions that have been key to its transformation; Lucy Russell at Bloomsbury who has been a kind guide through an unfamiliar process; and Jeff Moen at Minnesota University Press for granting permission to reproduce Uexküll's functional cycle. And, of course, Yasmin Marysia for keeping me sane and motivated through the years of *Deleuze and Ethology*'s production.

Deleuze once wrote that, even when working alone, one is never truly alone because we inhabit densely populated worlds. Of course, the world I inhabited while writing *Deleuze and Ethology* was populated by the philosophers and scholars who fill out this work's bibliography, and many more besides. However, one of the most joyful aspects of writing this book has been the chance to reflect on the extent to which my world is shot through with connections to the worlds of myriad species and beings – connections I might, unfortunately, ordinarily overlook. It was encounters with other species – while bird-watching, to be precise – and the sense that Deleuze's philosophy had something meaningful to say about how they negotiated their worlds that made me a Deleuzian. And, while working, it was the daily reminders that other beings simply going about their lives explicated Deleuze in startling ways that led to the transformative confrontation of ontology, ethics and ethology presented here. In this spirit, I would like to dedicate *Deleuze and Ethology* to the hope that philosophy's current interaction with ethology leads to a new metaphysics – a metaphysics whereby we embrace and prioritize our lives' entanglements with the myriad worlds around us.

Abbreviations

Citations of Spinoza's *Ethics* are abbreviated in line with convention:

E	Ethics
P	Proposition
D	Demonstration
S	Scholium
C	Corollary
A	Axiom
Exp	Explanation
Def	Definition
L	Lemma
Post	Postulate
Pref	Preface
App	Appendix
Def Aff	Definition of Affects

Roman numerals after E refer to one of the five parts of the *Ethics*, Arabic numerals refer to particular definitions, propositions, lemmas and so on. For example, EIP25S refers to *Ethics*, part one, proposition 25, scholium.

Introduction

In *Difference and Repetition*, Gilles Deleuze articulated a logic of individuals as embedded and entangled in their environments and determined reciprocally with the ongoing transformations of the worlds that surround them. He argues that the conditions of an individual's genesis cannot be reduced to the capacities and powers that inhere in it, and to understand why an individual being is the particular individual that it is, we must attend to the movements, processes and relationships – the 'kinetics of population'[1] – that constitute its milieu. The aim of this book is to unpack the metaphysical logic of this view and to offer an interpretation of Deleuze's project as ethological. This description of Deleuze's project as an ethology has its origins in a problem that is at the heart of the work done by the only ethologist Deleuze explicitly cites in a significant way, Jakob von Uexküll. It is unfortunate that, while Deleuze cites Uexküll's example of a tick's perception of its passing food, the full extent of Uexküll's importance has not previously been discussed in commentaries on Deleuze, for, as I will argue here, in this example we find an early instance of a problem that animates much of Deleuze's philosophical project.

In a number of places in his oeuvre, Deleuze cites Uexküll's most famous example, a tick and the way its orientation towards the world is defined by its affective capacities; however, I want to suggest that Deleuze's and Uexküll's common ground is much richer than this one case. In his *A Stroll through the Worlds of Animals and Men*,[2] Uexküll explicates a long-standing model for thinking about the structure of an organism's interaction with its environment. In *A Stroll*, Uexküll deploys a motif he developed elsewhere and describes these interactions in musical terms, so that animals and their environments are conceived in terms of the melodies they produce together. To develop this theme more specifically, Uexküll offers a model, a 'functional circle', to capture the structure of these interactions with respect to the meaning and significance that organisms have for each other. It is on this point that Deleuze and Uexküll converge.

This is not to suggest that Uexküll directly inspired or influenced Deleuze's project, however. Even when ethology is mentioned in Deleuze's singularly authored works, it is hard not to wonder about the coincidence of these references with the timeline of Deleuze's collaborations with Félix Guattari who was more explicitly concerned with ecology and ethology. The first work published out of this decades-long collaboration was *Anti-Oedipus* in 1972, a work which was surely in its embryonic stages as Deleuze completed the first edition of *Spinoza: Practical Philosophy* (1970), where ethology and Uexküll are employed to describe Spinoza's philosophy.[3] Still, if we were to obsess over the extent to which Deleuze was likely aware of Uexküll's work, we would miss an important point; even if Uexküll and ethology played a minor role in, or were absent from, Deleuze's early work, this insight regarding the structural reciprocity of subjective reflection and its object, as well as the virtual worlds produced in virtue of this reciprocity, is clearly at work at the heart of each thinker's philosophy. Even if Deleuze has not been significantly influenced by ethology or the life sciences more generally, there are certainly cases where it seems that the two could be brought into dialogue in productive ways. For instance, in *Cinema 1: The Movement-Image*, Deleuze critiques the idea of a grand, dialectical holism present in early twentieth-century Soviet cinema, and his critique would no doubt speak to the version of organicism pervasive in Soviet biology of the same era. Or, in a more modern context, it is not hard to imagine that an ontological theme that I will discuss in *Deleuze and Ethology* – that virtual relational networks subsist in actual lives – would speak fruitfully to the contemporary problematic of holobionts and hologenomes in evolutionary biology – the idea that consortia consisting of organisms, and the microbial ecosystems that they host, constitute a single individual, and that their entanglements constitute a singular, individual genome. And so, by laying out this particular problem through the work of Jakob von Uexküll, I want to suggest that there is a structurally similar problem at work in Deleuze's philosophy. Moreover, because of the persistence of this problem regarding the way individuals are affectively entangled thanks to the meaning and significance they have for each other, and because of the light this casts on Deleuze's project, I want to suggest that we would best understand this as an *ethological* project.

Deleuze's version of Uexküll's problem extends from a foundational element of his philosophy: his criticisms of Hegel. Deleuze's critical rejection of Hegel comes by the way of Jean Hyppolite, the translator and philosopher who introduced a novel reading of Hegel to post-war France.[4] As opposed to Alexandre Kojève's humanist reading of Hegel, which had previously been the standard interpretation of Hegel in France, Hyppolite argued that Hegel's project was fundamentally concerned with the ontological relation between the world and its sense. In other words, the famous 'Absolute Spirit' whose unfolding is expressed in the Hegelian dialectic is nothing other than the sense of the world. While Deleuze favours Hyppolite's interpretation of Hegel, he argues that this project will only succeed through the renewal of our understanding of difference. This is a complex issue that I will explore in detail in Chapter 1; however, the ultimate consequence of this view is a relational view of individuals whose genesis and transformation hinge on the sense and significance they have for each other. These relations are grounded in an affective continuity between beings and are animated by the sense in which individuals constitute problems for each other.

Deleuze is famous for his adoption of the Nietzschean project of overturning Platonism – that is, of inverting the traditional subordination of difference to identity. Of course, Deleuze's project is a philosophical one, and philosophical scholarship is a sufficient reason for this interest in upending Platonism. After all, as A. N. Whitehead famously put it, '[T]he European philosophical tradition is [just] ... a series of footnotes to Plato.'[5] However, Deleuze's obsession with difference speaks to an ecological problem that cuts to the heart of his ethology. Insofar as Deleuze is concerned with providing an account of living beings that speaks not only to their intrinsic properties and powers – their 'internal milieu' – but also to their extrinsic, ecological conditions, the problem of difference is what facilitates this renewed, relational conception of the genesis and transformation of living beings. Indeed, I will argue in *Deleuze and Ethology* that Deleuze's ethology is thus fundamentally opposed to ontological individualism, at least where it concerns the actual lives of existing beings. Difference is thus a significant problem because it is here that Deleuze finds the ontological scaffolding for a fully relational account of being and life. In other words, the foundation of a relational account of being and life is necessarily difference, or, rather, *differential relations*. This is a well-known claim, and it drives the interest in the differential calculus that constitutes the bulk of Chapter 4 of *Difference and Repetition*. My interest here, however, concerns the role that difference plays in an interpretation of Spinoza – interpreting the differentiation of the attributes as constitutive of the absolute, that is – and its centrality in the evolution of Deleuze's thought regarding the reciprocity between environments and the individuals that populate them. A positive conception of difference is, then, the engine of Deleuze's ethology precisely because it animates a robust, relational account of individuals and the transformation of the worlds they inhabit. In this sense, an individual for Deleuze is neither self-contained nor isolated; she is never really distinct from her environment. On the contrary, she is embedded in a milieu that is implied in everything she does, in every facet of her mode of life. When Deleuze argues that an individual's milieu is implied in her life, it is because her actions are determined by the affects through which her relationships with the world are enfolded into her individuality. Moreover, because these affects determine her actions, the relationships she has with her milieu subsist in her every action. Of course, her environment also contains other subjects undergoing the same types of affective transformations and determinations, and so her embeddedness constitutes a complex dynamic of reciprocal entanglement.

Thus, for Deleuze, to emphasize the importance of ecological conditions in the definition of a being is to emphasize the affective entanglements of the myriad lives that interact in the ongoing transformation of an impersonal life. A focus on relations as primary, on life as an interaction of forces and relations, entails both anti-essentialism and anti-humanism, because, when Deleuze engages with the human condition, he reduces consciousness to being a symptom of the interplay of affective forces at work in and on bodies. What fascinates Deleuze about bodies, about our necessary embodiment, is that they can never really be domesticated to the whims and desires of human lives. Consequently, in this book, I will treat bodies as the sites of the interplay of ecological forces, which is to say that bodies are not enclosed structures interacting with an environment. A body is, rather, a *'relatively closed system'*[6] that expresses a set of affective relations under a particular set of conditions. This does not just describe human bodies, but *all* bodies insofar as they are expressions of ecological processes and relations. I argue that Deleuze does not conceive of bodies as mere extended objects; instead, they are the correlation of an idea and an expression of that idea in an empirical occurrence. It is not the body as a particular state or being that interests Deleuze, it is the *process* through which a set of relations is expressed in something actual, something *sensible*. In this sense, Deleuze is more interested in embodiment as an affective process, than he is in bodies as objects.

I want to emphasize here how rapidly Deleuze's concern with life's ecological conditions comes to challenge what counts as a life. As Levi Bryant writes of the anti-humanism suggested by Deleuze's ecological concerns, '[T]he human and its relation to the world can no longer be treated as a privileged starting point for philosophical investigation. Humans are among beings, rather than a privileged point around which being is organized.'[7] Deleuze's ontological project, insofar as it responds to the problem of ecological conditions, does not begin from the point of view of human beings who are thrown into the world; it begins, rather, from the point of view of the relations that constitute humans as one being among many. This does not entail rejecting questions about the value and richness of human life. In his *Onto-Ethologies*, Brett Buchanan considers the extent to which such a rejection of humanism leads to reformulating these questions about human life:

> While we emerge from the critiques of our humanist tradition, an increasing focus is being paid to how and where we find ourselves within nature and the world at large. 'What does it mean to be human?' becomes a question of life and the living being. Attention to the status of human beings need not disappear, of course, but it does become framed by a broader emphasis on nature and life. What are the relations within nature? And how do we assess these ontological relations?[8]

So, with respect to the question of the relationships between living beings and their environment, we cannot begin from the privileged point of view of a human life and then move out into its environment in order to ask how it makes sense of the world to which it relates. Instead, the question becomes an ontological one: How is an individual a function of its environment? An appraisal of the nature of the individual and its relations with others in its environment goes beyond ontology in its traditional sense, insofar as it also concerns the individual's ways of being and relating. As such, it approaches ethical questions about the ways that the conditions of individuals' lives are immanent to individuals' modes of life – how they actually live and relate to each other.

Even though Deleuze's project still asks traditionally ontological questions (*What is being? What is an individual? How does an individual relate to being as such? How does an individual thus relate to the conditions of its individuality?*), his move towards the primacy of affect and affective continuity, and its concretization of the Nietzschean emphasis of becoming over being, means that ontology is not adequate for capturing the nuance of this dynamism. Indeed, further stressing the shortcomings of ontology with regard to expressing the primacy of affect, this prioritization of becoming, and affective continuity as its concrete mode, emphasizes the centrality of ethics as an important element in Deleuze's project.[9] So, while, of course, each element of Deleuze's project has histories, genealogies and movements to which it connects, and so belongs to its own series, we risk betraying Deleuze's project as a developing series if we reduce it to isolated elements. Consequently, if we are to try and describe the series running through Deleuze's project, and how these elements converge and formulate a more specific problem, I suggest that we might name this project ethology. For Deleuze, an ethological project is not only concerned with the ontological question of the sense in which the individual is a function of its environment. It also engages the inevitable correlation of these ontological questions with traditional ethical questions about the conditions and consequences of the individual's mode of life:

> When one speaks of an ethology in connection with animals, or in connection with man, what is it a matter of? Ethology in the most rudimentary sense is a practical science, of what? A practical science of the manners of being. The manner of being is precisely the state of beings, of what exists, from the point of view of a pure ontology.[10]

Deleuze's conception of ethology is thus an outgrowth from the entanglement of ethics and ontology. Ethology is not simply the sum of ethics and ontology; it is the product of ethical problems, the modes of life of living beings, seen 'from the point of view of a pure ontology' such that these ethical problems are transformed into ethological problems: the modes of life of living beings in the sense that they constitute 'manners of being'. A Deleuzian shift from the ecological conditions of the genesis of living beings to an ethology about the modes of life *qua* manners of being makes a new series of problems accessible insofar as ethology deploys ontology to ask practical questions about the manner and comportment of individual lives or modes of existence. It is this intersection of ontology and ethics in Deleuze's practical philosophy that this book will explore.

While it does not seem prima facie problematic to suggest that an individual has some capacity for comprehending or understanding her place in a particular milieu, the nature and effects of an individual's production of sense and meaning is a complicated issue. Indeed, this is where we encounter the significance of Deleuze's anti-essentialism; for Deleuze, being is a question of meaning, of sense rather than essence, and so he sees the production of meaning as the fundamental ontological question.[11] Even so, the production of meaning is by no means straightforward. In Deleuze's project, the production of meaning ceases to be an epistemological problem and it becomes an ontological one. Or, more accurately, true to the anti-dualism he finds in his primary influences – Spinoza, Nietzsche and Bergson – Deleuze resists the qualitative dualism between the real and the ideal so that ontology and epistemology can no longer be neatly distinguished. Deleuze does this by conceiving the production of sense as the primary motor of his ontology. This sense 'does not qualify [as] a being; it is an extra-being [because it] designates a quality, a mixture of things'.[12] When I look at the tree outside my window and say that its leaves are green, greenness is said of the leaves and thus it is part of the sense of the leaves. But this sense is not a quality that is reducible to the leaf; its greenness designates a mixture of light, chemistry, structure and so on. The sense of the tree's leaves is always attributed to them, but it is not reducible to them precisely because it says something about how it is constituted as a member of our shared world. In *Difference and Repetition*, Deleuze is quite clear about what his anti-essentialism entails; we can retain the concept of an essence, but only on the condition that essence is transformed into the event or sense that expresses what actually happens.[13] And so, sense comes to stand in place of essence; indeed, in his interpretation of Spinoza, Deleuze argues that the expression of sense constitutes the substantive content of its object. In short, while the expression of greenness does not cause the actual existence of the tree's leaves, it does constitute them as objects with a certain meaning and significance in a more or less densely populated world.

Deleuze pits ontology against anthropology in order to derive genuinely philosophical problems. Where anthropology is concerned with what it means to be human, ontology is concerned with what it means to *be*. Deleuze's philosophy thus criticizes the anthropological bias that he contends motivates the work of many philosophers before him. Deleuze is concerned, rather, with the ethological problem of what it is to be a living being constituted as an expression of a host of ecological relations. It is precisely for this reason that I am interested in his *Cinema* books. It is in these volumes more than anywhere else that he hones this discussion by focusing our attention on the constitution of our bodies as expressions of affective relations within particular environments. By the time of the *Cinema* books' emphasis on affect and the affective continuity of actual beings, the dual senses of sense – of meaning and the bodily organs of perception – have become synonymous with the affective entanglement of bodies, and the simultaneous expression of the significance of these entanglements as the determination of the direction these entanglements will take.

This emphasis in Deleuze is not at all restricted to his own project. A problem attracting increasing attention among philosophers concerns the aforementioned collapse of the humanist conceit that humans are a species apart from the rest of nature. Once humans are themselves immanent to the same nature as all other entities, ethical problems shift away from an all-too-easy identification with moral questions such as what rights do other organisms have, what duties do we owe them, and how ought we treat them towards ethical problems of the sort that Deleuze finds in Spinoza such as what is a body – the locus of a set of relations – capable of, how and under what conditions are these capacities transformed, how does this knowledge affect our relations with other beings, how do we affect them, and how are we affected by them. This question of how our capacities are transformed by how we understand other organisms is getting increased attention from both academic philosophers and writers aiming to bring ecological issues to popular audiences.[14]

In an excellent intervention into this transformation of ethics, Miguel de Beistegui compares the conception of desire that appears in *Anti-Oedipus* with Deleuze's interpretation of Spinoza's concept of conatus:

> [T]he problem of ethics, and of life, ... focuses on desire as the distinctly human (and over-human) *conatus*, as the concept that designates the question of what we are capable of, how far we can go, and how we can overcome the human, all too human condition. ... Since the *conatus* is the tendency to persevere in one's essence, that is, the tendency to be what one *can* be, desire is a power of expression (of the substance, or nature), and not, as classically conceived, the sign of a human deficiency oriented towards the possession of an object that is lacking, or, worse still, of a transcendent Law. Desire, in short, is not the expression of an originary, structural lack, but of plenitude, and an ontological potential (*puissance*) that seeks its own expression.[15]

If *Deleuze and Ethology* skews in a metaphysical direction, it is always with an eye towards these broader questions. Disciplines within contemporary humanities, disciplines like posthumanism and animal studies, provide rich responses to these ethical problems (indeed, they often do so by invoking Deleuze's emphasis on affect); however, that humanist conceit about the exceptionalism of humans lurks in the shadows, haunting such work as a foil that must be invoked and critiqued over and over. *Deleuze and Ethology* focuses so intently on Deleuze's metaphysics not just because it gives us the conceptual vocabulary for meaningfully posing these questions but also because it refuses any and all positions from which one might posit such exceptionalism. The account *Deleuze and Ethology* will offer is, at first blush, then, an ontological one, insofar as it will try to demonstrate that the production of meaning is an ontological process that is reciprocal with the determination and transformation of the conditions of life. However, because this work argues that Deleuze's project, insofar as it is ontological, is simultaneously and inexorably concerned with the manners of life of actual organisms, Deleuze's philosophy is not exhausted by ontology. This is because of the two moves that receive their most sustained development in the *Cinema* books. The first is the need to think from an individual's point of view while simultaneously undermining the transcendence of a subjective point of view by describing its immanence to a field of relations. Second, because of the emphasis on affect as the motor for the reciprocity of particular individuals and the whole of which they are a part, we cannot discuss Deleuze's relational ontology without being confronted by changes in the modes of life of its population. This is why I suggest that Deleuze's project is an ethological one; rather than just synthesizing ethics and ontology – both of which would be more or less classically conceived – and assigning it a portmanteau name, to call Deleuze's project ethology is to recognize the transformation each of these problems undergoes in his philosophy. Ontology moves away from essentialism, from questions of what beings are, and instead moves towards questions of how the production of meaning constitutes the conditions of a being as this or that actual, living being. Deleuze redefines ethics in his reading of Spinoza so that it is no longer concerned with normative claims about what is good or right, but is a problem of power:

> If Spinoza is the highest expression of philosophy, or the 'prince of philosophers', it is because he realised that the greatness of thought, and the human conatus, consisted not in its ability to distinguish and abstract itself from the plane of nature, and posit its own being on the basis of a being (whether itself, or God) in excess of nature, but to express nature in its infinity.[16]

That is, how one actually lives, and how one thinks about her own life, is always reciprocal with the transforming conditions of life. Consequently, this book is interested in the ways that an individual expresses evolving ideas of – that is, *makes sense of* – its relationality, and how these ideas interact with the transformation of its capacity to participate in its environment. What this means is that the ethical register of Deleuze's ethology is concerned with ontology's problematics, but it is concerned with them from a particular point of view. Chapters 1 and 2 will examine questions of how the constitution and expression of the sense of relations are ontological problems; however, that we know that Deleuze will eventually pose these questions from the points of view of living beings forces us to bear always in mind that these ontological problematics are important in roads to the transformation of ethics.

Given that this book does not devote much space to discussing specific films, filmmakers or cinematic genres, the approach taken here may seem to some to be a counterintuitive treatment of a two-volume project called *Cinema*. *Deleuze and Ethology*'s approach is not intended to undermine the importance of Deleuze's volumes for a consideration of the cinema, nor to underplay the insights that his own analyses of specific films provide in these volumes. Nor does it wish to suggest that those studies that have engaged with these volumes at face value, as books that help us to better understand the cinema, have somehow missed the point; this is especially the case given that a number of scholars working on Deleuze's aesthetics have informed my own, alternative understanding of Deleuze's *Cinema* books, as well as their relation to his philosophy more generally – key titles include Anne Sauvagnargues's *Deleuze and Art* (2013), Gregory Flaxman's *Gilles Deleuze and the Fabulation of Philosophy* (2011), John Mullarkey's *Refractions of Reality: Philosophy and the Moving Image* (2008) and Ronald Bogue's classic *Deleuze on Cinema* (2003). However, I do want to suggest that the significance of the *Cinema* books cannot be exhausted by discussions of film and cinema because, at the same time as being a clear philosophical expression of a love for the cinema, they are also connected to other problems. And these other problems, I contend, have not received the attention they deserve.

In this case, I want to try and formulate what I would suggest is central to these problems by emphasizing how Deleuze adopts a concept from Henri Bergson to name and concretely formulate the logic of how the affective continuity of the world is differentiated into particular beings: *the sensory-motor schema*. This concept names the genetic conditions of actual individuals and their ongoing movement and transformation. Once it is named, Deleuze deploys this concept to do something that he had not successfully done in any previous work – offer a concrete way to think about the individual as a function of its environment *from the individual's point of view*. That is, by the time of the *Cinema* books, Deleuze's philosophy had reached a point where properly conceptualizing the genesis of the plane of immanence required taking into account an individual's point of view as a crucial element of this genesis. In this way, *Deleuze and Ethology* argues that the *Cinema* books constitute two important achievements that are necessary for the success of Deleuze's philosophy of pure immanence by responding to two very specific problems. First is the need for sensible experience to act as a ground for the transcendental field. That is, experience must determine the intensive transformations that constitute the conditions for actual change. The second problem is the breakdown of the continuity of experience that leads to these transformations. In response to these problems, Deleuze blends his reading of images in Bergson's *Matter and Memory* (1896) with his reading of Spinoza in order to emphasize the double role of affect.

Cinema's sensory-motor schema is an immanent logic that determines action to the extent that it is an empty, formal schema that derives its content from the affective entanglement of living beings. Indeed, as I argue in Chapter 4, it is only through experience that this schema is able to determine actions. The sensory-motor schema does not merely receive a name in these books; *Cinema* is philosophically novel in that the sensory-motor schema developed therein is, according to Deleuze, a specifically cinematic concept, even though it has its origins in Henri Bergson, a philosopher notoriously critical of cinema. In his *Creative Evolution* (1907), Bergson criticizes cinema for reproducing the illusion of movement as a series of poses – static positions, or *frames* – that are juxtaposed in a particular sequence. Deleuze responds by adapting *Matter and Memory*'s philosophy of continuous images to argue that, in fact, what is actual is divided up into such poses; however, the distinctions between these poses are only 'artificial'.[17] Reality, Deleuze argues, cannot be reduced to what is merely actual; implicit in the actual figures that are artificially distinct from each other is a profound continuity such that the determination of their actual existence is grounded in a series of relations.

Appropriately, then, in the last decade or so, the *Cinema* books have made increasingly frequent appearances in discussions of Deleuze's metaphysical project. Unfortunately, however, they are too often considered a mere recapitulation of his ontology, and consequently the philosophical novelty of Deleuze's encounter with cinema is passed over. I argue that, far from merely rehearsing earlier work, Deleuze's *Cinema* volumes rework key elements of his metaphysical project. This, of course, does not mean that the *Cinema* books are all entirely novel or always representative of the sophistication of Deleuze's earlier work. In his book *Gilles Deleuze's Philosophy of Time: A Critical Introduction and Guide*, James Williams criticizes the *Cinema* books for their 'conflation of the philosophical use of the [concept of the] image … with the cinematic image'.[18] Indeed, because the books depend on a simplified distillation of Deleuze's philosophy of time, Williams suggests that 'the film works add little and in fact might take away from his philosophy of time in its most consistent and extensive form'.[19] For Williams, this is 'why many of the best commentators on Deleuze's work on cinema reconstruct the underlying philosophy on the basis of other more purely philosophical works'.[20] Rather than reconstructing Deleuze's ontology and using it to interpret the *Cinema* books, the present work attempts to intervene in these debates by taking at face value a comment Deleuze makes about the necessity of understanding a philosopher's oeuvre as a developing project. In a lecture on Spinoza, Deleuze comments on what it means to engage critically with a philosopher's work: 'You never say that a philosopher contradicts himself; you will ask such-and-such page, in what sequence to put it, at what level of the sequence?'[21] Deleuze suggests that if we want to evaluate the concepts a philosopher develops, we can do so only by asking after the sequence in which the concept appears. In other words, any critical interrogation of a philosopher must be sensitive to the place of her concepts within a developing project. This means that if we want to grapple with Deleuze's concepts, we will only achieve some measure of success if we uncover the problems motivating the work and consider these concepts relative to the development of certain responses to those problems. Thus, I put the *Cinema* books in the context of Deleuze's developing project to illuminate the power of these books relative to a problem that persists throughout Deleuze's broader project. In order to shine a light on the importance of these books to this persistent problem, *Deleuze and Ethology* follows roughly the chronology of the development of Deleuze's philosophy. I do not claim to offer an exhaustive account of Deleuze's philosophy or oeuvre – such a project would, for obvious reasons, be doomed to fail. What I offer in *Deleuze and Ethology* is a sketch of how Deleuze's philosophy develops in response to this problem through a number of key texts.

For this reason I have chosen to focus on the main points in the development of a response to this problem, and so, in Chapter 1, I provide a brief account of Uexküll's functional circle, Deleuze's concern with an ontology of sense and the semiotics at the heart of each in order to develop an initial formulation of the philosophically robust ethological problem that persists in Deleuze's philosophy into the 1980s and the publication of his two-volume *Cinema* project. Regarding sense and its production, this work does not aim to provide a comprehensive portrait of Deleuze's manifold discussions of sense. Instead, this chapter will reflect on how Deleuze's process philosophy requires this emphasis on sense insofar as the problem of sense defines a metaphysical project that is concerned with a conception of the substantive content of reality being identical with change and becoming. For Deleuze, reality operates in two simultaneous senses: actual and virtual. Actual beings are processual in the sense that the reality of their existence is the continuity of the relations connecting beings with each other. The virtual, which I will explore briefly in Chapter 1 and in more detail in Chapter 3, is the reality of these relations; it is the reality that subsists in, but cannot be reduced to, actual beings and is processual in the sense that it is the reality of the systematicity immanent to actual beings. The relevance of Deleuze's *Cinema* books is, as I argue in Chapters 4 and 5, that the motor of these processes, and the reciprocity of the virtual and the actual, is affect and affective continuity.

Insofar as this book aims to tease out the logic of a peculiar, process-oriented holism at work in Deleuze's oeuvre, Chapter 1's discussions of sense are an attempt to anticipate the need to describe the mode of actual beings' interactions with each other as simultaneous with the constitution and transformation of the whole of which they are parts. *Deleuze and Ethology* thus begins with an elaboration of Uexküll's insights about the entanglements of life, and how these entanglements traverse species distinctions, in order to sketch a route through Deleuze's project in order to attempt a reconstruction of the metaphysical logics at work behind such deceptively simple statements as 'the primacy of reciprocity' and 'affects and affective continuity are the genetic conditions of life'. The contribution this book makes to such concrete ethological questions is thus a portrait of Deleuze as a metaphysician, a 'pure metaphysician',[22] who develops a conceptual vocabulary that both grounds and necessitates such questions about the interrelationship between ontological grounds and conditions, and the actual lives lived by the beings so conditioned. Uexküll's famous example of a tick is not merely an assertion that affect is primary. It offers a logic by which affective reciprocity constitutes empirical bodies (the tick and the passing mammal) as subjects and objects by virtue of their significance for each other. In this way, Uexküll gives us a structure to approach the problem of immanence in Deleuze's metaphysics. Moreover, a discipline that was heavily influenced by Uexküll's concern with the ways that living beings interact in virtue of their meaning for each other, *biosemiotics*, brings us into direct contact with the conceptual engine of Deleuze's metaphysical project. From this point of view, we can best understand a problem that Deleuze takes from Hyppolite's reading of Hegel: the internal differentiation of sense. With this problem in mind, Chapter 1 develops a term of art, 'making sense', in order to develop a provisional form of the ethological problem that will drive *Deleuze and Ethology*'s reading of Deleuze.

I begin this reading in Chapter 2 by exploring how Deleuze's engagement with Spinoza enables him to argue that the conditions of change occur holistically and reciprocally with the actual world. Deleuze's encounter with Spinoza is a pivotal moment for the development of his holistic ontology. In 1956, Deleuze published an essay about Bergson, 'Bergson's Conception of Difference' and suggested that being would be disclosed through a concept of difference in itself.[23] Twelve years later, in *Expressionism in Philosophy: Spinoza*, Deleuze published a significant interpretation of Spinoza that develops a relational ontology of univocal being that is crucial to his overall project. Spinoza is well known for his thesis of substance monism, a thesis in which the modification of a single substance is expressed or conceived according to an infinity of attributes. On Deleuze's reading, the attributes actually constitute substance as a qualitatively heterogeneous but numerically single whole. This constitution follows from an attributive expression of the sense of substance and is simultaneously a production of infinite modal expressions of the constitution of the whole. This production is the production of the plurality of actual lives that fill out the world. The reciprocity of substance and modes outlined in this reading of Spinoza is the crucial first step towards Deleuze's development of a holistic ontology. However, in *Difference and Repetition*, Deleuze criticizes Spinoza's metaphysics and sets about developing the tools that will allow him to retain this ontology while outmanoeuvring the problem he has with Spinoza. In his Spinozism, the logic of reciprocity between substance and modes means that the identity of substance is not determined by the modes even though their production follows from the constitution of substance. In light of this criticism, Chapter 3 elaborates how the more familiar elements of Deleuze's philosophy – the three syntheses of time, multiplicity and the distinction between the virtual and the actual – are elements of Deleuze's effort to salvage a holistic ontology that replaces the identity of substance with the differentiation of degrees of power expressed by the modes.

In Chapter 4 I turn to *Cinema 1* to show how, in his engagement with cinema, Deleuze returns to Bergson to argue that the reciprocity of the actual world and the whole is grounded in the formalization of sensibility in experience. In other words, the determination of the conditions of experience is reciprocal with experience itself. This argument takes the conceptual tools outlined in Chapter 3 and uses them to develop the logic of a part/whole reciprocity with affect as the double-sided process which simultaneously expresses the relationships between beings and constitutes the whole as the continuity of the relations which subsist in actual beings. The discussion in Chapter 4 concentrates on how Deleuze adapts two arguments made by Henri Bergson – the critique of concepts of movement in *Creative Evolution* and the concept of the image in *Matter and Memory* – to conceptualize actual beings as points within an affective continuum that are only artificially distinguishable.

In Chapter 5 I explore *Cinema 2* in order to return to the ethological themes of Chapter 1 and how they refract broader ethical questions. My reading of *Cinema 2* foregrounds a concept Deleuze adopts from Kant: experiences of the sublime. In this respect, I am not the only Deleuzian who sees his project as more Kantian than is often acknowledged and considers that his project is more sensible when read in these terms.[24] Just as in Kant's *Critique of Judgement*, for Deleuze, experiences of the sublime derail the synthetic, apprehensive function of one faculty – the imagination – and force the intervention of the faculty of reason that necessarily produces a novel idea of the object of the imagination.

In short, the sublime is significant because it is the sort of experience in which the sense-making processes that determine action are taken to a limit at which they break down. This breakdown confronts the subject of experience with a new idea of the whole and thus forces it to think differently. This new idea and the possibility of making sense differently is, Deleuze argues, the condition for forging new connections, as well as novel modes of participating in our constitutive relations. That is, experiences that rupture the logic by which action is traditionally formulated are also the condition for the transformations with which Deleuze's ethology is concerned.

Let us emphasize a concrete hypothesis which is served by all the arguments that appear throughout the following five chapters, and which can be provisionally formulated now in anticipation of a more sophisticated articulation in the overall conclusion. Experiences that follow from disruptions to, and breakdowns in, the logic by which beings make sense of the world – experiences of the sublime, experiences Deleuze characterizes as 'too big for me'[25] – interact with the determination of their capacities in such a way as to transform and enhance the degree of power by which they participate in particular relationships. From an ontological point of view, this hypothesis emphasizes that the ongoing successes and failures of beings to sensibly navigate their world are reciprocal with the transforming conditions of their continuing efforts to sustain their relationships. There is an important caveat here. This does not imply that Deleuze's ontology is materialist; at least, it is not materialist in the traditional sense that reality reduces to what exists materially. I will discuss this in detail in Chapter 3 in the context of an explication of the reciprocal determination of the virtual and the actual; however, we must emphasize from the outset that living beings do not supervene on these transforming conditions. Insofar as the former are all that actually exists, the latter is a subsistent sense of the former, but it still has a reality proper to it. It is the reciprocity of these fully real senses of living beings that is at stake in Deleuze's ontology. From an ethical point of view, this hypothesis about the reciprocity of the transformation of beings' capacities and the disruptions to how they make sense of their worlds asks why these particular experiences of the sublime are so vital to the transformation of our modes of life. That is, the ethical dimension of Deleuze's ethological project is concerned with the way that the power which characterizes the life lived by an actual being is transformed and enhanced by experiences that rupture the conditions by which a being makes sense of its world. Developing this as a problem, and articulating Deleuze's insights for generating a solution requires a dual approach that blends the transformations that both ethics and ontology undergo in his work. On the one hand, we must start by setting out the importance of the ethical question; on the other hand, we must consider how a discussion of ontology lends itself to a particular answer. At the end of these discussions, we can articulate a more sophisticated version of our hypothesis by thinking through how and why Deleuze's project lends itself to such a reading, as well as consider what it might mean in terms of a transformation of our modes of life for such a hypothesis to be true.

1

The problem

An ethology of sense

Introduction

Deleuze's clearest articulation of what constitutes ethology comes in the context of his 1980 lectures on Spinoza:

> Ethology in the most rudimentary sense is a practical science, of what? A practical science of the manners of being. The manner of being is precisely the state of beings, of what exists, from the point of view of a pure ontology. ... We are trying to compose a kind of landscape which would be the landscape of ontology. We are manners of Being in Being, that is the object of an ethics, i.e. an ethology.[1]

We need not concern ourselves at the moment with the Spinozist context of this comment – Deleuze's Spinozism is the theme of Chapter 2 – the main point here is that Deleuze approaches ethology as an ontological problem. Ethology is typically a science concerned with animal behaviour and, more precisely, how that behaviour enables the animal in question to succeed in its environment; however, when ethology becomes a philosophical problem, contends Deleuze, it becomes a problem of how particular beings – their capacities and actions, the state of their being beings – relate to, or express, Being. This is why Deleuze equates ethology with ethics; ethology is not concerned with morality and its obsession with laws governing how beings *ought* to behave. It is concerned with how beings actually do behave, with the capacities – the 'degrees of power', to use a Spinozist formulation – that inhere in and are expressed by those behaviours, and how those behaviours and powers constitute an expression of Being. In other words, ethics for Deleuze is concerned with an individual's power, what those powers express and the conditions under which that power transforms.

This chapter is concerned with posing the ethological problem that persists throughout Deleuze's philosophy, and so I will flesh out Deleuze's description of ethics as an ontological problem of the manners of being. I will not engage with the growing literature on the place of ethics in Deleuze's oeuvre; I will instead focus on the extent to which this is best characterized as an ethological problem grounded in Deleuze's transformation of ontology. I will argue here that sense is the fundamental ontological question to the extent that sense concerns the unfolding of meaning within being such as it is expressed through the relations of actually existing beings.

Ethology

In terms of its empirical interest in animal behaviour, ethology has existed since at least the nineteenth century when Darwin took up a concern with the phylogenetic similarities between humans and animals and, with the former as a special case of the latter, explored the possibility that behavioural analogies between species might point towards shared affective and cognitive states.[2] But ethology as a specific discipline is often considered to have its beginning in the 1930s in the work of two biologists: Nikolaas Tinbergen and Konrad Lorenz. Where Tinbergen published the discipline's classic text, *The Study of Instinct*, in 1951, Lorenz spent much of the 1930s, 1940s and 1950s defending ethology as a legitimate inductive science that attempted to infer and articulate the laws governing innate patterns of behaviour on the basis of verified and reproducible observations.[3] While Lorenz's attempts to describe a historical narrative for the birth of ethology on the basis of how he believed a science ought to be inductive certainly had an undeniable degree of enthusiastic naivety, one aspect of his work is particularly important for understanding why ethology would matter to Deleuze's philosophy: Lorenz's conception of ethology emerged partly from his frustration with the debate between the mechanistic and vitalist factions in biology in the early twentieth century.

The mechanists and the vitalists constituted schools of thought that attempted to account for living organisms by, respectively, either reducing them to physical or material processes or differentiating between living and non-living things by attributing to the former some non-physical principle that animated them. Lorenz's fascination with animals began when, at the age of six, he was given a baby duckling that began to relate to him as though he were its mother. This 'imprinting', as he famously called it, the behaviour whereby ducks and geese follow and become attached to the first moving object they encounter after hatching, is a classic example of what Lorenz later argued was an empirical fact of innate behaviour that called for scientific enquiry without becoming bogged down in the 'antagonistic exaggerations'[4] of mechanists and vitalists. By *innate*, Lorenz wanted to describe forms of behaviour that were neither entirely self-caused nor wholly learned, and thus could not be reduced to mechanists' inclination towards crude behaviourism, the thesis that all behaviour reduces to either immediate reflexes or learned responses to external stimuli. In short, innate behaviour on Lorenz's account is behaviour that is actualized in response to some environmental condition, but only in as much as it is the determinate expression of some pre-existing capacity.

The study of animals' behaviour is thus couched in terms of an animal's capacities relative to its environment. And this brings us to the historical figure who is crucial to the ethological register of Deleuze's project: Jakob von Uexküll. Outside of biology, Uexküll is most famous for his concept of *umwelt*, commonly taken to mean 'environment' or 'surroundings', but used by Uexküll to refer more precisely to the intensive world particular to any organism that is constituted by the collection of sensible investments that the organism has in its surroundings. Initially, we might suspect that Deleuze would be ambivalent towards Uexküll, given the latter's avowed Kantianism. As Uexküll sees it, 'The task of biology consists in expanding in two directions the results of Kant's investigations: – (1) by considering the part played by our body, and especially by our sense-organs and central nervous system, and (2) by studying the relations of other subjects (animals) to objects.'[5] Indeed, the *umwelt*, which he famously describes using the image of a soap bubble surrounding a particular organism, is described in exactly this way: 'The soap-bubble of the extended constitutes for the animal the limit of what for it is finite, and therewith the limit of its world; what lies behind that is hidden in infinity.'[6] This definition appears in the context of a discussion of space where Uexküll is concerned to describe space in terms of its constitution as the perceptual field of a particular organism, and his emphasis on a distinction between absolute, physical space and finite, intuitive space – the organism's *umwelt* – certainly evokes Kant's dualism.

In spite of his Kantianism, however, there are two key aspects of Uexküll's interpretation of biology's task that make him relevant to Deleuze: first, his distinction between physical and intuitive spaces is much less robust than Kant's and ultimately has more in common with Bergson and Deleuze's theory of multiplicities and, second, Uexküll inspired a discipline that is strikingly consonant with Deleuze's empiricism: biosemiotics – a science in which perception and the subsequent determination of action are semiotic functions that express the transformation of the perceiver's surrounding world. In the first instance, it is hard not to wonder if there might be an historical explanation for Uexküll's Kantianism. This is not to downplay the influence of Kant on Uexküll's theoretical biology; however, his *Theoretical Biology*, originally published in German in 1920 (with a second edition in 1928), and in English in 1926, reads like a biologist trying to incorporate the insights of phenomenology into his own discipline. And so, while Kant is undoubtedly valuable to Uexküll's enterprise, there are enough implications of Bergson's project in *Theoretical Biology* that one wonders what might have happened had Uexküll turned to *Matter and Memory* instead of *The Critique of Pure Reason*. If we turn to a description of umwelt theory by Uexküll's eldest son, Thure, we can see exactly why this cries out for a connection to Deleuze:

> [W]e would say that the [semiotic structure of the umwelt] describes the structure of systems and that it is therefore valid within a system, but also valid between systems, once these have been joined together in a suprasystem.[7]

Theoretical Biology's first chapter, 'Space', begins with a quote from Kant to emphasize a theme that will define the chapter, that space is not a container through which we move but is a subjective principle by which we organize sense perceptions and thereby constitute them as signs of a meaningful object. However, as we will see in this chapter's discussions of Uexküll's functional circle, and semiotics, this theme also speaks clearly to an idea that Deleuze adapts from Bergson, that space is the immanent principle that determines the form of the relationship between organisms. Indeed, this question of space, and Thure von Uexküll's idea of a suprasystem in which various sets of relationships are joined, anticipates the development of a Deleuzian theme that we will follow throughout *Deleuze and Ethology*; not only is space the immanent principle in the organization of a relationship, these relations simultaneously express the constitution and transformation of a whole.

For now, though, we will turn to Uexküll's conceptualization of the reciprocity characteristic of the structure of these relations. In *Theoretical Biology*, Uexküll describes the frustration awaiting adherents of dualism if they seek in physiology the intermediary of the relationship between bodies and ideas, between 'the world of the flesh and the world of the spirit'. For Uexküll, affective states are not the properties of some substantially distinct mental phenomena. Rather, they are a function of bodies and the determination of other bodies as problematic, as embodying relevant meaning: 'We might at least expect that the very marked centralisation which is expressed in the apperceptive process of our ego, should be discoverable in the central apparatus of the body.'[8]

Uexküll and the functional circle

Uexküll is an important touchstone for Deleuze's ethology because his famous account of a tick and its relationship to its environment stresses the affective content of the tick's world. The intensity of the tick's world is defined by its affective entanglement in its world: '[A] body affects other bodies or is affected by other bodies; it is this capacity for affecting and being affected that also defines a body in its individuality.'[9] Deleuze argues that an individual, understood in terms of its affects, is inseparable from its relationships as well as the degrees of power that it expresses in those relationships:

> You will not define a body (or a mind) by its form, nor by its organs or functions, and neither will you define it as a substance or a subject. ... You will define an animal, or a human being, not by its form, its organs, and its functions, and not as a subject either; you will define it by the affects of which it is capable.[10]

When Deleuze takes up Uexküll's example, it is because this tick is defined in terms of its three primary affects: its receptivity to light, smell and temperature.[11] As Brett Buchanan suggests, 'At issue, therefore, is how the tick relates to its surroundings, where the emphasis is neither on the tick ... nor on the environment ... but on the "affective" relation itself.'[12] From the point of view of Deleuze's metaphysics, it is trivial to say that, for example, the tick has the property of being blind such that its possession of this property is prior to its deployment in an encounter. Of course, ticks are blind, but this is beside the point. The ethological issue concerns how the photosensitivity of the tick's skin, in lieu of eyes, constitutes a capacity through which the tick's world is transformed within an actual, lived encounter.

This reference to Uexküll is not merely a coincidental emphasis on affect; there is also a particular similarity between Uexküll's conception of perception and action, and the taxonomy of images that Deleuze undertakes in the *Cinema* project. Even though *Cinema 1* was published a decade and a half after the major portion of Deleuze's engagement with Spinoza, it appeared only three years after *A Thousand Plateaus*, where, in addition to the appearance of the most explicitly ethological reading of Spinoza attached to Deleuze's name, Uexküll's theory of coding is a powerful, if only implicit, influence on the text's theory of de-, trans- and over-coding.[13] Moreover, even less time had passed since the 1980–1 course he taught on Spinoza at the University of Vincennes, the lecture course in which the above-mentioned comment about ethology appeared, and so, given the remarkable common ground between how Uexküll describes the practical relations between an animal and its world, and Deleuze's interpretation of Bergson's conception of images, it does not seem a particularly long bow to draw to suggest that Deleuze's familiarity with Uexküll, as well as the latter's influence, extends beyond scattered references. As such, in this section I will offer a brief summary of Uexküll's argument in anticipation of later chapters in which the *Cinema* books are explored in detail. This is to provide a context for redescribing Deleuze's project. As I have already suggested, describing Deleuze's philosophy as ontology, ethics or a philosophy of x (of *biology*, of *mathematics*, of *art*, of *literature*, of *politics*, etc.) is inadequate for appreciating the whole of Deleuze's philosophy as a philosophy of life. This is not to say that his philosophy is none of these things; it is, and a lot more besides. However, there is a significant thread that develops through these moments, and it is this thread that I want to try and say something about in this book, and taking up Uexküll's theory of organisms as functional circles (*Funktionskreis*) will set out a broad sketch of the reciprocal relationship between an individual and its environment that will anticipate a number of key ethological themes in Deleuze's philosophy.

When Uexküll explores the issue of the constitution and transformation of an individual organism's world, he does so in terms of the significance with which that surrounding world – its *umwelt* – is imbued. At the same time, he describes the organism in question as a functional circle through which actions are determined relative to that significance. In *A Foray into the Worlds of Animals and Humans*, Uexküll outlines the workings of his version of biosemiotics, a theory and discipline which Uexküll helped pioneer, and which has become a complex field of study concerned with the role of the interpretation of codes and signs in the life sciences, or, more specifically, in the life sciences' objects of study. Uexküll's contribution came from the effort to rethink animals' behaviour, not as a composite of mechanistic reactions to external stimuli, but as organic responses that spring from attributing meaning and significance to the world. Of course, the pressure point for such a theory is going to be how we interpret signs. In anticipation of our later analyses of Deleuze's encounter with cinema, we should not consider signs in their linguistic sense; that is, as phonemes or graphemes which refer to some object beyond them. Rather, signs must be understood in an empirical sense, as the fundamental objects of an encounter. For both Uexküll and Deleuze, any and every being inhabits a world imbued with meaning – a world that is intensive and specific to the particular being in question – and, as such, beings never react immediately to objects they come up against, but respond to them mediately, and in terms of the objects' particular significance. Elaborating the content of that adverb, *mediately*, is the ultimate task of this book; however, we will be best served by grounding this goal in an understanding of how the material conditions of this call and response – what Deleuze will call 'signaletic material' (*matière signalétique*) and Uexküll calls 'marks'[14] – are experienced, and the apparent object of the encounter (the signs' supposed referent) is only constituted as this or that object with substantive content as a consequence of the encounter with the sign. To get a sense of how this works, we must turn to a diagram from early in *Foray*: the functional circle that for Uexküll 'shows how subject and object are interconnected with each other and form an orderly whole' (Figure 1).[15]

In his account of the development of the theory of the *umwelt*, Carlo Brentari describes in detail an issue that Uexküll himself only glosses in *Foray*'s discussion: the functional circle is a repudiation of, and response to, the idea that animals react reflexively to external stimuli. Uexküll rejects this view by invoking a holistic, almost teleological, view of nature where the stimulus to which an organism responds is never a first cause because the stimulus must always be understood in its context in an ordered whole that is determined in large part by the receptive structure(s) of the organism. Of course, there are two terms here that might appear problematic, *holistic* and *teleological*; however, both of these issues receive longer treatments elsewhere in this book that we need

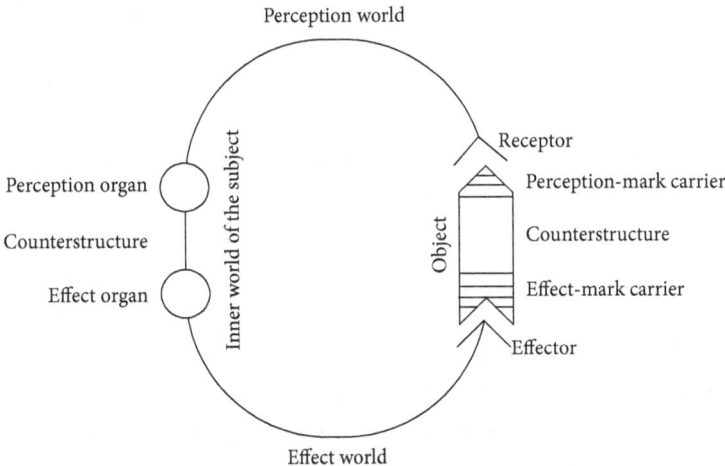

Figure 1 Jakob von Uexküll's functional cycle. Uexküll, *Foray*, 49.

only anticipate here. In the first case, holism, Deleuze's theory of multiplicities, as well as the theory of an open whole that is developed in the *Cinema* books, contains a peculiar form of holism where the whole itself does not supervene on the individuals that constitute its parts, but is instead determined reciprocally with them, as a transforming, immanent whole constituted as an expressive assemblage of the sense and significance of individuals' own worlds. In the latter case, teleology, Deleuze's interpretation of Bergson's critique of the verb *realize*, the ensuing conception of the reciprocity of the virtual and the actual as a dialectic of problems and solutions, and the philosophy of differen*t*/*c*iation ensures that what is perceived, insofar as it constitutes a problem given to a particular body, is qualitatively distinct from the body that perceives it. In other words, the conditions that determine future actions, and the future actions themselves, do not resemble one another, and so the future actions which follow from a perception do not resemble that perception insofar as it constitutes a problem. Future actions, therefore, are indeterminate relative to the present situation which interpolates them. The salient point is that, as Brentari notes, 'behavioural modalities triggered by the recognition of stimulus combinations or ... object shapes and contours [necessarily gesture towards] a cognitive phenomenon that implies the presence ... of *schemata* capable of ordering stimuli into constructions endowed with meaning'.[16] Modes of behaviour, or, as Deleuze calls them, 'manners of being', imply the existence of structures within the subject for whom the external object, as a collection of signs specific to their encounter, takes on particular meaning to which the subject responds.

But, not only does Uexküll share with Deleuze this approach to subjects as making sense of their objects, they both describe the relationship of sense-making in semiotic terms. That is, while the first point of continuity between Uexküll's and Deleuze's respective ethological philosophies is their grounding in a theory of perception as subtractive, they each understand empirical relations as grounded in the transmission of signs and the cultivation of meaning, or specific significance. Each rejects the traditional idea of perception as a more or less accurate representation of some object; instead, perception is a palimpsest of signs or marks subtracted from the object and presented as a problem to which a subject can meaningfully respond. Uexküll's conception of the functional circle begins with the subject's place within a perception world – 'a particular world composed with the features the animal itself perceives of the outside world'[17] – or, rather, a particular object that has caught the subject's attention.

The subject engages with this perception world through the expression of perception signs (*Merkzeichen*) and the cultivation of perception marks

(*Merkmal*). For Uexküll, any organ of perception, say, the tick's photosensitive skin, is a composite of cells, each of which is a machine operator and corresponds to a particular sign presented by the particular object. In this brief discussion in the introduction to *Foray*, Uexküll describes an event that happens between the subject and the object, an event that excites the subject and induces a response. On the one hand, he describes the object as posing a problem to which the composite of perception cells will respond. That is, the object is constituted as a group of stimuli to which the composite of perception cells corresponds, and it presents itself to the animal subject 'in the form of questions'.[18] On the other hand, Uexküll refers to perception marks as 'imparted' onto the object as a consequence of how the various perception cells coalesce and organize the object's signs.[19] Taken together, they suggest a problem that is generated between the subject and object. It is expressed by the subject, or, more correctly, the composite of cells that constitutes the subject's perception organs. This expression *is* the perception marks imparted to the object. But the problem is always expressed *of* the object insofar as signs, taken as a whole, constitute the object as an object of sensation; this is how abstract predicates become the qualities, the intensities, specific to this particular encounter. As Uexküll describes it, it is through the expression of this problem as the problematic sense of the object that the 'sensation "green" becomes the "greenness" of the lawn. ... We recognize ... the lawn by the feature "green".[20] In other words, it is only in the affective encounter that the abstract predicate green becomes an intensity – it becomes a predicate *of* something – to which we can respond. An organism does not respond to green, it responds to the lawn insofar as *it* is green.

With regard to the expression of actions, impulses, movements and so on – what Uexküll calls 'effects' – Uexküll sees a similar coupling between the subject and the object. Following from the expression of these perception marks, there is a modification within the remaining cells in the subject such that it expresses an ensemble of effect marks (*Wirkmal*) that correspond to effect signs (*Wirkzeichen*) in the object. These effect signs in the object necessarily correspond to the effect marks expressed by the subject because, if they did not, the subject's effects would fail as responses to the questions posed by the perception marks. From this point of view, this is primarily a question of a transformation in the subject's world; the object's role, according to Uexküll, is limited to its dual role as the carrier of perception and effect signs. Because it is a relatively simple case, it has only three functional circles, Uexküll returns to his example of a tick to think through this issue in concrete terms. In the first case, the butyric acid emitted from the sweat glands of a passing mammal, there are three factors at work: the mammal's sweat glands constitute the feature carrier – the object – in the tick's world; the butyric acid is the perception sign; and, from the point of view of the tick's perception organ, the butyric acid constitutes an olfactory feature that is translated as a perception mark. In other words, the butyric acid functions for the tick as a material encounter that transforms a feature of the tick's world into a problem that demands a response. Insofar as it constitutes a problem, the butyric acid elicits a response in the form of an assemblage of effect marks expressed *by* the tick, but expressed *of* the feature carrier to the extent that the object becomes a carrier for effect signs imparted onto it by the subject. Not only is this transformative for the subject, but 'the effect mark', as Uexküll puts it, 'extinguishes the perception mark'.[21] That is, the object, insofar as it is a feature of the subject's intensive world, ceases to constitute a particular problem to the extent that the effect mark is sufficient to transform the former's significance; in the tick's case, this means that the mammal has ceased to be the carrier of butyric acid and becomes instead a surface with a particular topography and temperature.

What is so compelling about *Foray*, Uexküll's most popular work, is that the bulk of it is devoted to imagining the multitude of ways that different organisms inhabit their own worlds and constitute functional circles with their own signs, marks, rhythms, spaces and durations. However, if our description of Uexküll's theoretical biology stopped here, it would evince a problem that would put it at odds with Deleuze's philosophy; insofar as the object exists for the subject, Uexküll's view contains a version of transcendence that Deleuze will criticize in phenomenology. That is, if Uexküll's portrait of subject/object relations is taken up by a version of phenomenology that fills the gap between the subject's perception organs and effect organs with consciousness, then the conscious subject transcends the object with which it relates in as much as the former's imparting marks, determines the latter's form and content. But this problem persists only as long as we view the subject abstracted from its plane of immanence. That is, once we take ethology's next step and view an organism in the context of its natural environment, we find that the object's being for the subject is the form of its participation in a milieu that constitutes the genetic conditions of the subject's appearance. And, ironically, this insertion of the organism into its *milieux* gestures towards the possibility that, even though in *Theoretical Biology* his conception of the subject closely resembles the Kantian transcendental unity of apperception, Uexküll's theoretical biology might be less Kantian than he realizes.

In a rightly famous passage, Uexküll provides a beautiful image of a meadow as being populated by all manner of ostensibly banal creatures – beetles, butterflies, gnats, dragonflies and others – that are each enclosed in their own intensive worlds. In this discussion, Uexküll emphasizes that each animal is inseparable from the intensive world it inhabits: '[A]ll remain permanently enclosed in the bubble that encloses their space.'[22] But the objects in an animal's world are not reducible to the perceptive world in which they constitute problems. Throughout *Foray*, Uexküll reflects on the theme of an object appearing in many worlds. For instance, the tree in my front garden is an object, that is, a feature carrier, in my world, but it is also an object in the worlds of possums, bats, stray cats, myriad lizards, at least half a dozen species of birds, and many other animals that elude my attention. It is always the same tree, but insofar as it is a specific feature carrier in a specific perceptual world, there are manifold senses in which this tree is an object. In order to posit an object that exists for myriad subjects, Uexküll distinguishes between the perceptual world wherein the object is given to the subject as constituting a problem and an operative world into which a particular perceptual world can be embedded alongside other perceptual worlds. This idea of a broader world into which many perceptual worlds can be embedded is necessary in order for Uexküll to claim that different subjects can experience the same object; even though the particular experiences might only have few, if any, elements in common, Uexküll's view of perception is a subtractive one, and as such, it presupposes an object that is more than these perceptions. This operative object is always more than any particular perception and is, perhaps, more than the addition of all actual perceptions. Given Uexküll's avowed fondness for Kant, it might be tempting to read this move as an adaptation of Kant's dualism between noumenal and phenomenal worlds; there is a noumenal world that contains a particular object – a thing-in-itself – and a phenomenal world in which the ideal qualities imparted to the object by the subject constitute the former as an object of perception. And, because these qualities are all we are able to access, the object of our perception constitutes the terminus of our perception meaning that, while we can deduce a necessary correlation between the thing-in-itself and the object of perception, the content and qualities of the former is permanently concealed behind the latter.

But such an interpretation would miss Uexküll's more fundamental point that the worlds with which we interact are not exhausted by those properties of which we are consciously aware.[23] This distinction is inseparable from Uexküll's subtractive conception of perception, because, if the animal's perception organs have a selective function and discriminate between what is immediately relevant to it, and what is not, then there will always be elements of the object that pass the animal unattended. If I say that the koel in the tree outside my window has a conscious or cognitive awareness of the bright red berries it is eating, this term *cognitive* does not imply a psychological theory in which the bird's behaviour implies a type of purposive, goal-oriented awareness that is analogous to humans. Rather, insofar as these berries are feature carriers in the subject's world, any description of these objects is inexorably bound to the functional circle in which they are referred to the subject who constitutes them as such. In other words, there are elements of the koel's world that are expressed, as Deleuze would put it, *virtually*; there are elements of the koel's world that, as problems and, through an ineluctable reference to a particular relationship, elicit a response.

To say that the koel is conscious of these berries is only to emphasize that the particular qualities of the berries that constitute perception signs are defined as such because of the bird's attention to them. Yet, there are elements of the bird's world which, while they receive no direct attention from this koel, are still crucial to what Uexküll calls the bird's locomotive functions. The clearest example he provides is the medium in which birds live: air. For instance, because the koel is feeding on the fruit in a flowering palm tree, it moves between 5 and 6 metres from the ground, depending on the wind's effects on the tree. As such, there is clearly a host of environmental factors at work more or less directly in this bird's attempt to remain stable as it feeds. Unfortunately, there is a looming danger of a vicious circularity in trying to define which of these elements are in the bird's perceptual world – that is, signs of which it is conscious – and which remain in its operative world, because categorizing the elements in this way would require a precise definition of the distinction between the bird's worlds, and yet this distinction is the very issue at stake.

In the final section of *Foray*, Uexküll tentatively explores a further consequence of his thinking, that a subject in one world can be an object in another; or, as he puts it, 'We still do not know how much of the subject's own body carries over into its environment.'[24] His exploration is tentative in the sense that this is a difficult question to pose, and his example struggles to break free from reiterating how the same object can, in different registers and through different tones, become myriad objects, in myriad worlds. But there is one relationship in his example that is telling. He describes an old oak tree and the way it constitutes a home, feeding ground and a nursery for a bark beetle. On the one hand, the tree's bark protects the beetle from would-be predators, and its hidden soft wood provides food for both the beetle and its larvae. However, the hard bark is not a perfect protection for the larvae for, as they burrow through the soft wood, the ovipositor of an ichneumon wasp makes light work of the bark as it searches for larva to parasitize with its eggs. The point here is not simply that the oak tree constitutes different worlds for the different insects, but that these are each beings who, in their own worlds, constitute subjects, but in the others' constitute objects. For the larvae, the wasp, or at least its ovipositor, is a threatening object, and for the wasp, the beetle larva is an object necessary for its reproductive cycle. In both cases, subjectivity and objectivity subsist in each but is only actualized in, expressed of, specific relations, and, consequently, neither subjectivity nor objectivity can be attributed to either being as actual properties independently of a relationship in which it would be expressed.

Hegel, Hyppolite and Deleuze: Difference and sense

While Deleuze famously considered Hegel an enemy, the reality of his relationship to Hegel's Idealism is much more fraught. This does not mean that Deleuze has any sympathies for Hegel's system; what makes Deleuze's relationship with Hegel fraught is that the latter's phenomenology of absolute spirit, and the negative dialectic at its heart, was an early counterpoint against which Deleuze formulated the key ontological problems that he would carry with him through all subsequent projects. Indeed, Hyppolite's development of an ontological reading of Hegel that rejected the humanist interpretation offered by Alexandre Kojève was a seminal influence on the anti-humanism of Deleuze's own philosophy. Of course, calling Deleuze's project anti-humanist does not mean that he is anti-human; his anti-humanism entails a vision of a post-Hegelian ontology that is, paradoxically, opposed to Hegel while being unthinkable without Hegel's dialectical conception of the relationship between consciousness and its objects.

Following Hyppolite, Deleuze rejects the tradition that considers Hegel's description of the tensions between finite consciousness and its struggle for an absolute that it can never attain as a quintessentially human struggle. Instead, for Deleuze, humans are one of many expressions of a becoming that is not human, even though human being is entirely immanent to these expressions. That is, while humans are the concrete site of the dialectical relations between things and their meaning (their *sense*), neither the meaning attributed to objects nor the logic by which this attribution proceeds is produced by a human consciousness, even though that consciousness is the site of its expression. This theme is ethologically significant because it suggests that, while humans are a unique case (in that they are a particular species), they are a unique case among myriad other unique cases, and what they are a unique case of is decidedly inhuman.

One of Deleuze's earliest publications was a review of Hyppolite's *Logic and Existence* where he affirms Hyppolite's argument that essentialism must be replaced with an ontology of sense: '*Philosophy must be ontology, it cannot be anything else; but there is no ontology of essence, there is only an ontology of sense*'.[25] Central to Deleuze's understanding of Hyppolite's interpretation of Hegel is the distinction between philosophy and anthropology; anthropology would be an empirical discourse of human beings and their modes of being in the world. Importantly, anthropology would thus necessarily preserve a 'naïve error'[26] where thought and the thing thought would remain distinct from each other. Indeed, this error is preserved in Kant's transcendental idealism insofar as, as Deleuze puts it, the thing is identical to the thought that takes the thing as its object; however, they are only identical to the extent that the thing is determined relative to thought. Thus thought never gets beyond faith and will fail to think the thing-in-itself – the thing as being, that is.[27] This does not entail a criticism of anthropology per se; if nothing else, if 'anthropology' were used as a pejorative with which to beat empiricism, this would amount to a rejection of Hume, a profound, if under-acknowledged, influence on Deleuze's project. Philosophy, however, must get beyond this error and recover the identity of the thing and the thought in which it is reflected.

For Hyppolite, Hegel's philosophy of speculative contradiction goes beyond this error insofar as thought is immanent to its object. How he does this anticipates a theme that will be crucial to our understanding of Deleuze's reading of Spinoza; the thing and its reflection in thought are not only expressions of being, they are expressions *of* being, *to* being. That is, being or the Absolute reflects on itself in the dialectical relationship between thought and its object. From the point of view of being or the Absolute, thought is not an external reflection on an object, but an expression of an objective part of itself, *in* thought, *to* itself. Hyppolite formulates it thus: 'Speculative contradiction is the contradiction of the Absolute itself that negates itself by positing itself; but this meaning of negation, which is not only subjective but also inherent to being, is the decisive point of the Hegelian dialectic, the characteristic of speculative thought in relation to empirical thought.'[28]

While the absolute is neither separate nor separable from the dialectical relation between thought and its object, it is not reducible to them either. The absolute is a whole constituted as the transforming sense expressed *in* thought, but expressed *of* its object. Thus, thought is nothing more than the idea of its object, expressed for itself. But this poses a decisive question for an ontology of immanence: For whom is sense expressed? That is, we know that sense is expressed in thought, and of an object, but who or what is sense expressed to? To say that sense is expressed to some being external to the actual world would reinstate transcendence, and so we are left with a paradox: How can we posit knowledge that is more than the actual world, thus more than empirical knowledge, while denying that there is anything other than the actual world? This paradox is the origin of Deleuze's description of his project as *transcendental empiricism*. This transcendental empiricism means that Deleuze follows Hyppolite in saying that being is sense. It is an empirical project precisely because being's being sense means that it is not essence – it does not refer to something outside of the world – but the sense of this world, expressed for itself. It is transcendental in the sense that the actuality of the world does not exhaust its reality, and so philosophy is obliged to engage with the reality of the conditions of the actual and articulate their ontology.

For all he follows Hyppolite, Deleuze still criticizes a subtle point; for Hegel and Hyppolite, the dialectical relationship between thought and its object is predicated on a negative conception of difference. This negative conception of difference is the 'contradiction of the Absolute' that will be key to understanding why Deleuze marshals Spinoza against Hegel. The absolute expresses itself in the particular, but this does not mean that the particular is to be understood as external to the absolute: 'The infinite is not beyond the finite, because then it itself would be finite; it would have the finite outside of itself as its limit. ... This unity results from the very reflection of which it is the movement, the mediation.'[29] To be sure, the infinite is expressed by the finite, the absolute by the particular, but the infinite has no existence external to the finite because it is expressed in the latter, as its becoming and openness. To the extent that this expression constitutes an immanent expression of the sense of the finite *in* the finite, the infinite constitutes a self-reflection of the finite.[30]

Herein lies the sense of negative difference critiqued by Deleuze's generation. As long as difference remains the relationship of mediation between the thing and its reflection in thought – its sense, that is – then it will remain a purely negative relation between two identities. As Hegel writes, '[Self-consciousness'] essence and absolute object is "I"; and in this immediacy ... of its being-for-self, it is an *individual*. What is "other" for it is an unessential negatively characterized object. But the "other" is also a self-consciousness; one individual is confronted by another individual.'[31] For Deleuze, the question that will rehabilitate the ontology of sense is deceptively simple: How can we construct a concept of difference such that identity is produced through the expression of difference? As with Hegel, the finite, for Deleuze, is the expression of the infinite under a determinate relation. Unlike Hegel, for whom this relation is contradiction, or negative difference, for Deleuze this relation must be positive difference: '[C]an we not construct an ontology of difference which would not have to go up to contradiction, because contradiction would be less than difference and not more?'[32] Simply put, if we are to develop a robust conception of difference as the expression of sense, then difference must be more than contradiction. Indeed, as if to affirm this point, Deleuze published an article just two years later in 1956, 'Bergson's Conception of Difference', where he argues that it will be through a renewed conception of difference – difference as more than contradiction – that we will be able to posit a coherent conception of being.

We will turn in Chapter 2 to Deleuze's reading of Spinoza in order to consider how the Absolute (or *Deus, sive natura*, to use Spinoza's famous phrase) is constituted through the operation of a positive formulation of difference. For the remainder of this chapter, however, I will be concerned with fleshing out a meaningful formulation of this deceptively simple question as an ethological question. In the next section I will develop a working definition of semiotics, a problem that interests both Deleuze and Uexküll. This way, in the final section of this chapter, I will be able to return to the relationship between individuals and the absolute and so formulate a properly ethological problem that will guide the remainder of *Deleuze and Ethology* by elucidating and anticipating the significance of this discussion of Hegel. This theme centres on how the dialectic of problems and solutions constitutes the genetic condition for the emergence of actual individuals: 'Individuation emerges like the act of solving such a problem, or – what amounts to the same thing – like the actualisation of a potential and the establishing of communication between disparates.'[33] Importantly, we must understand how the dual topics of sense and semiosis lead to a convergence between Deleuze and Uexküll on the question of how individual lives constitute the expression of solutions to problems. In order to explicate this issue, however, we will need to look provisionally at what is, perhaps, the concept most commonly associated with Deleuze: the virtual. We will explore this properly in Chapter 3, where we will see that it exists as a response to a very specific problem arising from Deleuze's effort to read Spinoza against Hegel – to preserve an ontology of sense where identity is constituted as the contingent expression of difference, that is. However, it is important to understand tentatively that, for Deleuze, while actual objects present as problematic for subjects, the reality of the problems, considered structurally and for themselves, is not reducible to objects themselves. And, since organisms respond to problems, and not directly to objects themselves, the genesis and transformation of actual beings and their actions happen relative to structures that are not themselves actual: 'It is sufficient to understand that the genesis [of actual forms] takes place in time not between one actual term, however small, and another actual term, but between the virtual and its actualisation – in other words, it goes ... from the conditions of a problem to the cases of solution.'[34]

Semiotics

Uexküll's functional circle solves a specific problem faced by his theoretical biology. If animals are subjects and not merely automatons blindly acting and reacting, then biology will require a framework that enables it to think structurally about the relationships between individual organisms. Uexküll employs musical metaphors (tones, harmonies, etc.) to describe the complex way that organisms' life-worlds are interwoven in virtue of their meaning for each other. Because of this, Uexküll is an important forerunner of biosemiotics, a discipline that, from the point of view of the life sciences, uses semiotics in an attempt to engage with the production, attribution and evolution of meaning between and within individuals.[35] Uexküll, for his part, never discusses semiotics, or at least never in any depth. However, he does pay considerable attention to the problem of meaning and argues that it is a mistake to suggest that animals enter into relationships with objects. The objects of experience in animal worlds are always meaning-carriers. All objects are, in fact, manifold, and Uexküll provides as an example the stem of a flower which, as a meaning-carrier, has changing features depending on the life-world in which it appears: in an ant's world it has certain features insofar as it constitutes a topological problem; different features in the world of a cicada larva which taps into the stem's vascular structure to access the liquid it needs for its house; its features are primarily visual and olfactory for the girl who picks it as a decoration for her top; and, it has different features again for a cow who is concerned only with eating it.[36] There are what Uexküll calls 'neutral objects', but these are abstractions where researchers are able to predict and manipulate an organism's response to meaning-carriers in order to study an organism's behaviour. One could, of course, read an object against this process and argue that the neutral object is never truly neutral, as it still constitutes a particular meaning-carrier for the ethologist who is currently using it in her research. This point will be important for the development of Deleuze's particular semiology insofar as the meaning-carrier is always a set of features subtracted from the reality of the object in view of the needs and capacities of my body. For now, however, we will consider the tripartite structure Uexküll gives to the relational schema in which animals count as subjects. Instructive in this regard is Uexküll's son Thure, who was concerned with the place of semiotics in medicine. Thure von Uexküll suggests that a concern with meaning is a concern with signs, as signs just are the meaning-carrier overlaid with meaning, where meaning in this case is the quality of the meaning-carrier's being referred to the needs and capacities of the subject.[37]

This issue of meaning is central because, as Brett Buchanan notes, for all that Uexküll describes an individual organism as belonging to a singular world, the umwelt theory comes into its own by locating individual organisms in ecological relations that constitute them as such.[38] Uexküll poses the umwelt in Kantian terms; the object of the organism's experience is always mediated by the organism's needs and capacities, and the meaning thereby attributed to the object. In this sense the organism never experiences a neutral object – an object in-itself, as it were. Importantly, however, the meaning expressed by the organism is always expressed of the object. So, even though it is expressed in terms of the organism's needs and capacities, this would be an empty formalism, 'meaning' would be devoid of content, without its reference to a specific object. As a consequence of this, the fundamental element of the organism's genesis is the 'duet' it enters into with another organism.[39] In other words, the genesis, development and transformation of the organism, as an actual entity, is inseparable from its relations with another organism. The crucial point here is if we consider the tick and its relation with a passing mammal, we are mistaken if we assume that the relation is between the tick and the mammal – between two organisms, *as* organisms, that is.[40] The tick never perceives the mammal as a whole organism. The tick – or, to be more precise, its olfactory sense organ – perceives the butyric acid as a sign, a 'perception mark', that constitutes an element in the problem formulated by the tick.

While Uexküll does not use the term *biosemiotics*, and was most likely unaware of the work of semioticians such as Saussure or Peirce, the discipline has moved in that direction because 'terms such as system, structure, unit, code, etc.' elucidate the umwelt theory in a more precise way 'than do the illustrations drawn from music, which Uexküll favoured'.[41] One of the primary touchstones for biosemiotics is the work of Charles Saunders Peirce,[42] whose sign theory is an important influence on how Deleuze deploys the logic of expression to work out an interpretation of Bergson's own philosophy of images at work in his ethology. What puts this encounter with Peirce at the heart of his ethology is that, as for Uexküll's ethology, Deleuze's ethology emphasizes the expression and transformation of meaning – that is, the sense and significance of objects. And, while cinema, and the philosophy of images developed through it, can never be reduced to linguistics, the features and logic of expressionism will be found at work in the cinema: 'There is ... no reason to look for features in cinema that only belong to a language system [; however,] language features which necessarily apply to utterances will be found in the cinema, as rules of use, in the language system and outside of it.'[43] Insofar as they are the objects of immediate experience and thus the constitutive elements of problems, signs are not exclusively linguistic phenomena, and so, because, it elucidates the workings of the relations between propositions and sense, linguistics offers us the best model for understanding the structural relations that compose and express problems.

Ronald Bogue has observed that Peirce's influence on Deleuze's *Cinema* books is general, as opposed to the specificity of Bergson's influence. However, there are specific elements of Peirce's project that allow us to anticipate the significance of semiotics for Deleuze's relational ontology. Peirce's theory of signs comes in the context of his version of phenomenology, what Peirce calls 'phaneroscopy' where the *phaneron* is Peirce's name, more or less, for what Deleuze will call the image – what is given in experience without reference to an external object. What is telling is that the phaneron is not quantitatively divisible; the phaneron is composed of parts – 'indecomposable elements' – but these are not parts that admit of countable divisibility. While he makes it through reference to Mendeleev's periodic table, and the valency of its chemical elements, Peirce's point is not too dissimilar to Deleuze's description of the elements of a problem. The parts of the phaneron are not the parts that constitute the classical Sorites problem; they are elements that allow for orientation and adjustment in certain relational contexts. Thus, we see how semiotics is not primarily about language, but about the relational structure of what is given in experience.

Accordingly, we will not understand Peirce's semiotics – and, ultimately, Deleuze's differentiation of the image – if we mistake its tripartite structure for referring to actually distinct parts. The three elements of Peirce's semiotics – firstness, secondness and thirdness – are more like facets or intensive degrees which make it possible for the object to be given in experience, to constitute a problem and to induce an action, that is, to 'draw a response'. Firstness concerns the sense in which a thing or an idea is this or that thing.[44] That is, firstness concerns the degree to which an element of experience is given as an element that is singular and particular, and that it refers to nothing else. Firstness is not so much the object as an object, for that implies reference to the subject of experience, as it is the 'as it is given' of what is given in experience – the redness of the berries or the sharpness of the butyric acid.

Where firstness is the phaneron insofar as it refers to nothing other than itself, secondness is the phaneron referred to something. Peirce describes it as resistance and struggle, but we can think of it as the sense in which the phaneron is not present to us except insofar as it demands action and effort from us. As Peirce puts it, the vividness of the object of experience – the vividness of firstness – 'is a sense of commotion, an action and reaction, between our soul and the stimulus'.[45] Secondness is thus not entirely dissimilar to the moment of negative reflection in Hegel: 'We become aware of ourself in becoming aware of the not-self. ... The idea of other, of *not*, becomes a very pivot of thought. To this element I give the name of Secondness.'[46] As the example of chemical valency was intended to show, secondness is not a discrete part of the object, but a differentiable element that marks firstness as having some significance for us.[47] If firstness was the givenness of the object, secondness is the fact that we cannot let this object pass by unattended, and that we are compelled to respond.

In this context, thirdness is not a third element so much as an element which brings the first and the second into this relationship: 'By the third, I mean the medium or connecting bond between the absolute first and last. The beginning is first, the end second, the middle third. The end is second, the means third.'[48] Using the example of baking, Peirce describes thirdness as the logic or law which determines secondness – action – relative to firstness – quality.[49] This is crucial for understanding the significance of the sign: the flash which refers a thing to an idea which it produces or modifies.[50] In baking an apple pie, Peirce contends, I do not want this or that particular pie, even though that is all I can act upon. My desire is for the pleasure that the pie will bring about. That is, the desire that leads to baking the pie is a desire for a quality, an intensity of affect. Thirdness, the degree to which the object, the pie or its constituent parts, constitutes a sign, is precisely the sense in which the pie refers to an idea of quality or intensity.

What we find in Peirce is thus a theory of the sign as an element of the object – and it is important to emphasize that the sign is an element that inheres in the object of experience – that brings the qualitative 'thisness' of the object into a relation with the object's inducing my action. In other words, it is through the sign that the object – as this or that particular object – refers to an idea of quality or intensity. We could put this in Hegelian terms; it is the sign through which the object – as a thing experienced sensorially – refers to or invokes an idea – sense as meaning or significance – in its being given to a subject who reflects on it. This is the significance of the sign for Deleuze, although we must add one crucial point. In the *Cinema* books, he argues that Peirce's schema implies a zeroness, a 'degree zero',[51] that constitutes the ontological condition of first-, second- and thirdness. This implication comes about through a criticism that Deleuze makes of Peirce; Peirce assumes the existence of a subject for whom the first-, second- and thirdness are given. As a consequence, the schema reduces to a psychological phenomenon whereby the object as fact (secondness) is referred to an idea (firstness) through some form of abductive inference. In this way, Peirce treats first-, second- and thirdness as given facts, rather than deducing their existence. Deleuze's move here is why Bogue is right to consider Deleuze more Bergsonian than Peircean; for Deleuze, the deduction of first-, second- and thirdness should proceed through an analysis of perception.[52]

This criticism of Peirce passes silently over the fact that Peirce has his own theory of perception, and signals the *Cinema* books' turn to a Bergsonian theory of images. This theory of images is rich and will be explored in detail in Chapter 4; for now, however, we will only require one facet of this discussion before moving on to an attempt to pull these threads together in order to formulate a properly ethological problem in Deleuzean terms. Within the theory of perception that Deleuze adapts from Bergson's *Matter and Memory*, individuals – the subjects assumed in Peirce's phaneroscopy – are constituted as functions of a transforming relational plane. In the *Cinema* books, Deleuze describes the universe as an assemblage of movement-images; that is, following Bergson, the universe is composed as the continuity of sensible experience. This continuity is decomposed or differentiated into three avatars that correspond to Peirce's tripartite semiotics: affection, action and relation. Perception is implied by this differentiation because '[t]he movement-image is the object; the thing itself caught in movement as continuous function. The movement-image is the modulation of the object itself.'[53] Once movement is liberated from the moving body, the object and its representation become indistinguishable. This argument is lifted directly from the first chapter of *Matter and Memory*. The distinction between object and image – between secondness and firstness – implies the immobilization of movement. The crucial question here anticipates Deleuze's criticism of phenomenology. Phenomenology reinstates transcendence by taking as given a subject – either Cartesian or Kantian – to whom movement is referred. So, since movement cannot be referred to a subject, how, and in what sense, is movement immobilized?

In the *Cinema* books, Deleuze answers this by describing perception as bipolar and arguing that the movement-image is referred alternately to a centre of indetermination, an opaque screen or, simply, a body. This is a complex argument and we will return to it in due course. What is important at this juncture is a provisional description of how the immobilization of movement is dual; it is simultaneously the expression of the absolute in an actually existing being, as well as function of the absolute's constitution and transformation. This requires a fundamentally dynamic conception of individuation. Once we introduce time to this discussion, once we take seriously the rejection of transcendence and locate the production of subjectivity within the becoming of the world, we see a profound collapse of the boundaries that ought to define individuals. Not only is the outside open to the inside, but interiority becomes exteriority reflected at a certain intensity.[54] The subject against whom the movement-image is immobilized is thus changeable and transformed through this immobilization. Even though this subject's perception is the subtraction of 'relevant' elements from movement – a continuous universe – this relevance is determined by needs and capacities which are themselves referred to the subject's orientation on a plane of becoming.

In Chapter 2, we will consider how Deleuze fleshes out the logic of this dynamism through his reading of Spinoza, and how this logic turns around the conception of internal difference that is required by an ontology of sense. For the final section of this chapter, I want to turn briefly to a discussion that Deleuze elaborates in the third chapter of *Difference and Repetition*: How does the question of sense guide our understanding of the formulation of problems? What I would like to set out here is *making sense*, and variations where necessary (*sense is made*, *makes sense of*, etc.), as a term of art that captures the complex ethological significance of the formulation of problems as the formulation of the conditions of beings' relationships with each other. In *Deleuze and Ethology*, I want to use this phrase to describe the ontological operation by which the expression of some object's meaning resonates with the expressor's experience of that object, and the reciprocity of meaning and experience functions as the interface between a being and its world.

Making sense: The simultaneity of a virtual whole and its actual parts

The French *sens* and the German *sinn* have a third meaning that is absent from the contemporary meaning of the English *sense*, but which is an important element of how 'making sense' fits with the Deleuzian understanding of problem formulation. This is *sense* as direction. In the *Cinema* books, Deleuze employs the word *plan* to describe shots; however, the French *plan* is also used to describe planes such as the famous plane of immanence. So, by virtue of his choice of terminology, Deleuze formulates the planes on which life is lived as shots in the cinematic sense of an image with a specific composition. But there is a third sense of *plan*, a local map. *Carte* (as in cartography) is used to describe a large-scale map; *plan*, meanwhile, describes a local map, as in *plan de Paris*. In this sense, sense is quite literally the construction of a route through space. As we will see later, Deleuze's appropriation of the idea of multiplicities liberates beings from a space that would be indifferent to them. A multiplicity is a space determined reciprocally with the events that occur within it. Thus, the dialectical relationship between things and their expression as ideas thus plots a direction through a space that is defined by, and constructed simultaneously with, the events that occur across it. Problems then are not problems in the pejorative sense of situations or things which require repair; a problem is, rather, an element of an organism's environment understood in some relevant sense as significant and requiring a response. And, insofar as it draws a response, the problematic sense of this object, in conjunction with the sense made of it, determines the intensive space of their encounter.

Admittedly, this neologism 'making sense' has none of the flair for which Deleuze and Guattari's vocabulary is famous, but my hope is that using a verb phrase rather than a noun captures an important, tripartite process; we need to think of *sense* as simultaneously describing the constitution of a world (the sense in which *sense* refers to meaning or significance), determining the transformation of that world (the sense in which *sense* refers to a sensible or affective relationship), and constituting a path taken through a world in virtue of the transforming powers of the being who makes (produces) sense (the sense in which *sens* refers to direction taken). We must be careful with our phrasing; language wants us to formulate this proposition in the active voice: 'x makes sense of y.' However, it is crucial to remember that it is more correctly phrased passively: '[S]ense is made of y by x.' The tenor of Deleuze's review of *Logic and Existence* emphasizes that the absolute, the sense of being for whom and to whom sense is expressed, cannot be understood in human terms. This means that, while actual beings and their interactions are the site of the phenomenal expression of sense, it is always expressed to something, and for something, other than themselves. Even though I say 'the koel outside my window expresses the sense of the tree's berries,' I mean 'the sense of the berries expressed by the koel's action is neither expressed to the koel, nor for the koel'. In Hegelian terms, this means that the sense expressed by the koel is really the self-reflection of the absolute, for whom and to whom sense is expressed. What we will see, however, is that Deleuze takes this Hegelian formulation as his starting point and channels it through, first, Spinoza, and then Bergson, in order to transform this problem into an ontological picture where the affective entanglements of actual beings express the constitution and transformation of the worlds that beings inhabit and share.

To understand the sense of passivity that informs this philosophy of affective entanglement, we need a provisional definition of the virtual. When formulating this definition, we must be careful not to make the error that A. N. Whitehead called 'the fallacy of misplaced concreteness'. The mistake, that is, whereby we confuse abstractions for concrete things.[55] Of course, Deleuze is emphatic that the virtual is not abstract, but Whitehead's point still stands. For all that it is not abstract, the virtual *is* opposed to the actual. Steven Shaviro describes it neatly when he calls the virtual the 'transcendental condition of all experience'.[56] That is, 'virtual' is the name given to the ontological status of the reality of the sense and significance of empirical facts – a reality that is not itself reducible to actual entities themselves. Following Deleuze's reading of Hegel, we know that it would be a mistake to posit 'the' virtual as something that exists independently of actual objects and entities. The empirical world is all that actually exists. And yet, because philosophy cannot be reduced to anthropology, we know that the reality of the empirical world cannot be reduced to its actuality. The paradox that confronted Deleuze, like Hyppolite before him, is how to articulate the thought of something that is more than the empirical world, while simultaneously denying that there is anything more than the empirical world. We see this paradox front and centre of Deleuze's philosophy of the virtual. The virtual does not refer to anything outside of the empirical world; rather, it articulates the reality of the transcendental conditions of the empirical insofar as they subsist in the actual beings that populate the empirical world. The virtual is thus a consubstantial expression of the sense of the empirical world.

The problem of problems, if we can put it that way, is the problem of how the duality of sense circumscribes some object of experience as a significant component of a life-world and thus constitutes a problem to which an organism will respond. As in Uexküll's functional circle, an object is not problematic in the sense of an antagonistic situation that must be overcome; it is problematic in the sense that it is the determination of some environmental stimulus as something that, in virtue of its significance, induces some response from us: 'Is it not the peculiarity of questions to "draw" a response?'[57] It is this problem that I hope to describe with the phrase 'making sense'. The koel outside my window does not make sense of a berry through some cognitive project that would describe the coherence, or lack thereof, in some proposition about the said berry. Rather, it makes sense insofar as it is engaged in a productive, dialectical relationship whereby the fruiting palm tree in which it hangs induces this or that behaviour on the part of the koel.

Since Chapter 2's exploration of Deleuze's reading of Spinoza will show how Deleuze converts the expression of sense into an ontological operation, I will close this chapter with a brief look at the discussion of the relationship between propositions and sense as it is expressed in *Difference and Repetition* and *The Logic of Sense*. It is in this discussion that we see that Deleuze shares a common sentiment with Giorgio Agamben's analysis of Uexküll's work: this project of making sense occurs before propositions can be evaluated for their truth or falsity. That is, sense is a condition of truth, and truth is a description of the degree to which a proposition makes sense.[58]

Deleuze begins his analysis by noting two dimensions of a given proposition: what it expresses and what it designates. In the former case, the proposition says or expresses some idea, and in the latter, it refers to some object to which the idea applies. This leaves a strange situation whereby the sense of a proposition – the idea it expresses – remains indifferent to the truth of the proposition, which is always a measure of the adequacy of the proposition's reference to an object. Deleuze's response is to highlight that this situation is a product of treating this scenario – the distinction between the idea and the object, the expressive and the descriptive dimensions of the proposition – as a description of the transcendental conditions of possible experience, rather than the genetic conditions of real experience. Essentially, this is the problem of confusing anthropology and philosophy. The solution is to understand the relations between expression and designation as internal to sense: 'The relation between a proposition and what it designates must be established within sense itself: the nature of ideal sense is to point beyond itself towards the object designated.'[59] This is what it means to say that '[s]ense is the genesis or the production of the true, and truth is only the empirical result of sense';[60] the relationship between the object and the proposition it designates is not one of the adequacy of an idea to an external object, but of the internal differentiation of sense. So, the real question is, if '[s]ense is what is expressed by a proposition, ... what is this *expressed*?'[61]

This discussion of the expressed – the expressed as idea as distinct from a concept – takes us impatiently into Chapter 2. For now, we will consider a chapter of *The Logic of Sense* – 'The Third Series of the Proposition' – where Deleuze clarifies the sense in which sense is a dimension of the proposition, or, more correctly, that the proposition only exists because of its interiority to sense. This is because this clarification offers a provisional sense of what it means to describe the relationship between the proposition and the object as the internal differentiation of sense. These dimensions are not distinct elements which together constitute the proposition. They are, like the elements of Peirce's phaneron, 'distinct relations' internal to the proposition.[62] According to Deleuze's analysis, the proposition has three dimensions: denotation, or its reference to an object; manifestation, or its relation to one who speaks; and, signification, the relationship between the proposition and the universal or general concepts which would measure its adequacy to the designated object.[63] It would be a mistake to reduce this to a philosophy of language. *The Logic of Sense* is a sophisticated and subtle treatment of meaning and its relationship with the structures of language. But if we consider this in terms of the problem that Deleuze inherits from Hyppolite (and, not incidentally, 'logic of sense' is a phrase from Hyppolite's *Logic and Existence*) – the relationship between being and thought – the structure of the proposition concerns the self that reflects (manifestation), the object on which it reflects (denotation), and the universal or general concepts that make it possible for the self to meaningfully infer or deduce the properties of a particular object (signification). This is why the logic of language is so crucial to Deleuze. When we are concerned with speech, a domain that concerns God and the world, we see that, à la Kant, manifestation is the necessary condition for the correspondence of denotation and signification. But when we treat language per se as a domain concerned with the logic of relations, a 'proposition is able to appear only as a premise or a conclusion, signifying concepts before manifesting a subject, or even before denoting a state of affairs. It is from this point of view that signified concepts, such as God or the world, are always primary in relation to the self as manifested person and to things as designated objects.'[64]

In either case, however, we find ourselves in the circle of the proposition. If signification and denotation are primary to manifestation, then we remain trapped in a vicious circle where signification implies denotation, and vice versa, to infinity. If we suppose that manifestation is primary to signification and denotation, we presuppose an I, and end up confusing anthropology for philosophy – the very problem that Deleuze wanted to escape. Consequently, we need to consider the fourth dimension of the proposition: sense. Sense cannot be posited a posteriori, as an ad hoc solution to the circle of the proposition. Sense must function *a priori*; it must be at work as a necessary part of the logic of the proposition. Sense is thus the fourth dimension of the proposition:

'[T]he expressed of the proposition ... an incorporeal, complex, and irreducible entity, at the surface of things, a pure event which inheres or subsists in the proposition.'[65] So, to rephrase the question from *Difference and Repetition*:

> The question is as follows: is there something, *aliquid*, which merges neither with the proposition, nor with the object or state of affairs which the proposition denotes, neither with the 'lived', or representation or the mental activity of the person who expresses herself in the proposition, nor with concepts, or even signified essences? If there is, sense, or that which is expressed by the proposition, would be irreducible to individual states of affairs, particular images, personal beliefs, and universal or general concepts.[66]

Sense has a complex status, and characterizing the ontological aspect of this complexity is the task of Chapter 2, where Deleuze's reading of Spinoza will raise this question to the heart of processes that will constitute the essence of God, or nature. For now, we can affirm that sense does not exist outside the proposition, even though it does not merge with the proposition. Thus, sense inheres or subsists in the proposition. But the three dimensions of the proposition – denotation, manifestation and signification – do not exhaust sense. Signification, as an ideal quality, or predicate, is always an attribute expressed of the object denoted by the proposition, but expressed as in the infinitive form – the yet-to-be-red of underripe berries. Sense thus exists in the proposition, not the object, and, yet, because it is always predicated of the object, sense does not disappear into the concept. Thus the concept and the object are internal to the differentiation of sense.

Conclusion: Sense and the formulation of problems

We have covered considerable ground in this chapter, but our goal was a simple one: to formulate an ethological question which would be appropriate to Deleuze's philosophy. This problem is spiritually very close to the problem that motivated Uexküll's biology. As Agamben puts it, Uexküll's gift is the insight that our epistemic endeavours, including science and its occasional conceit to describe the world *as it actually is*, are in fact the construction and transformation of the terms and parameters of our own life-world. This is not an anti-intellectual, or anti-science, claim. Agamben's point, rather, is that a world is always primarily a world for some observing, experiencing being: '[T]here exists a forest-for-the-park-ranger, a forest-for-the-hunter, a forest-for-the-botanist, a forest-for-the-wayfarer, a forest-for-the-nature-lover, a forest-for the-carpenter, and finally a fable forest in which Little Red Riding Hood loses her way.'[67] In other words, Uexküll's biology is built on the insight that a world, before it is referred to questions about truth or falsity, is a world inhabited by a being who participates in the construction and transformation of that world in terms of its needs and capacities. This does not detract from the degree to which a given proposition is true. It draws our attention to the fact that that degree always refers back to an ensemble of relations in which it makes sense: a proposition does not make sense because it is true – *it is true because it makes sense*.

A significant portion of Uexküll's career was devoted to defending this insight against the mechanistic interpretations of non-human animals that were prevalent in the life sciences when Uexküll was alive. The primary goal of this chapter has been to articulate Deleuze's take on this insight and how he extends it. What Deleuze eventually does with Uexküll's insight is argue that these life-worlds are constituted as the sense or significance that subsists in actual beings, and is grounded in an affective continuity that binds them. However, before we can understand that, we must understand how Deleuze understands the dialectical relationship of ideas and their objects. He does not broach this subject directly – he never actually wrote explicitly on Hegel – but his interpretation of Spinoza is telling in this regard. The primary lesson that Deleuze learns from Spinoza is that all actual occurrences are dual. Where we are used to thinking in Cartesian terms, where a body has access to, and communicates with, ideas, Spinoza's insight is that all that actually occurs occurs in parallel with an ideal expression or formulation of that occurrence. This does not mean that what actually occurs corresponds to an ideal representation of that occurrence; rather, what actually occurs occurs in parallel to an expression of the sense and significance of that occurrence for a particular being, in a particular milieu. These parallel occurrences proceed via an internal differentiation that constitutes Spinoza's famous single substance as the sense of the reciprocity between ideas and actual occurrences. In this sense, Deleuze is interested in the immanence of thought to life. Insofar as ideas are problematic, the expression of ideas constitutes the determination of the objects of experience as problems to which action is a response. The expression of sense is thus the determination of a route traced across a relational plane. What we will see in Deleuze's Spinozism is that the internal differentiation of sense qualifies actual beings as modes of life, but what we will see as his Spinozism is transformed is that modes, or the movement from which they are indistinguishable, and their relationships occur reciprocally with the internal differentiation of sense.

This alone is not sufficient for solving the paradox of an ontology of sense. What it does achieve, however, is the formulation of a logic according to which ideas and things are expressed as the internal differentiation of sense. The whole which contains them is constituted through this differential expression. That is, just as in the logic of the proposition, sense, Spinoza's *Deus, sive natura*, is constituted as a heterogeneous system that has no existence outside of its expression in ideas and objects. An interesting change occurs between Deleuze's two books on Spinoza, 1968's *Expression in Philosophy: Spinoza* and 1970's *Spinoza: Practical Philosophy*; substance becomes pluralized and the whole which is expressed through ideas and objects becomes multiple. This is why the Bergsonian phrase Deleuze ultimately uses for the absolute – *le tout* – describes beings in their particularity at the same time as it describes their unity. Rather than describing a unity which would supervene on the particularity of individuals, the absolute refers simultaneously to each individual being in her particularity, as well as to the immanent systematicity of each.[68] The logic of this change is something we will explore in Chapter 3. Chapter 2, however, is concerned with the first incarnation of Deleuze's reading of Spinoza and how a logic of internal difference constitutes a whole of sense that contains its parallel expression in ideas and objects.

2

On Deleuze's Spinozism

Expression and sense-making in the logic of holism

Deleuze's 1968 reading of Spinoza, the focus of this chapter, constitutes his first major attempt at a systematic response to the problems that appeared as early as his 1954 review of *Logic and Existence*. If we understand substance in Spinoza as directed at the same problem as the absolute in Hegel, this will make substance the sense of what actually exists. The ethological significance of reading Spinoza's substance in the same sense as Hegel's absolute cannot be overstated. Substance ceases to be a type of thing and is instead the substantial content of this or that being from the point of view of its relations. Deleuze reads Spinoza as unseating substance from being an abstraction to which the actual world is compared (a theme famously criticized by Hume), and converts it into the sense of the relations that subsist in actual beings without being reducible to them. In this sense, we can read Deleuze's reading of Spinoza's triumvirate (substance, attributes and modes) in terms of sense, the qualities according to which it is differentiated and the expressions of degrees of that differentiation. It is important that we recall the differentiation of Peirce's phaneroscopy; his theme of differentiation that does not admit of countable parts is crucial to Deleuze's understanding of the internal differentiation of sense. The internal differentiation of substance/sense never constitutes it as more than one. And *constitutes* is meant in its strongest sense here; substance does not exist outside the expressive differentiations of its attributes. Spinoza's modes are, then, the actual entities whose sense substance *is*. Insofar as they are also expressions of sense, these modes express quantitatively the ratio of the attributes' constitution and transformation of substance.

Consequently, this chapter will demonstrate that Deleuze's reading of Spinoza defends two themes that are crucial to the ethology that he develops throughout his career. First, he constructs a system in which the whole and the individuals who are its parts are generated simultaneously. In the terms of Spinoza's *Ethics*, the expressive event in which substance is constituted as quantitatively unique and absolutely infinite is the same event through which the modes are produced as correlates of degrees of power. The second theme Deleuze develops in his interpretation of Spinoza follows from the logic of this simultaneity: the process which guarantees that the modes are produced in the same event as substance is constituted requires that substance be constituted through expressions that *make sense*. That is, substance and modes relate through complex dynamics wherein sense is differentiated, expressed and apprehended. Substance is produced through the expression of sense. And, by the same token, a modal universe is produced on condition that these sensible expressions are expressed to a mind which comprehends them.[1]

In short, the initial formulation of Deleuze's ontology that we find in his reading of Spinoza anticipates persistent ethological themes: individuals and the whole to which they belong are produced simultaneously and reciprocally but only insofar as the relationship between the two turns on the production and expression of sense. As we track the development of Deleuze's ethology in later chapters, we will come to see how he transforms the logic he finds in Spinoza. For now, however, we can understand Deleuze's 1968 reading of Spinoza as the first full-fledged attempt he makes to develop a holistic understanding of beings that is predicated on a positive conception of difference as the internal, constitutive determination of Being. From this point of view, beings, Spinoza's modes, are understood in terms of their participation in the transforming dynamic expression of the ecological significance that characterizes them. To work through these themes, we must begin, therefore, with two terms that are present in Deleuze's earliest publications – *univocity* and *immanence* – and are key to tracking the logic of how an actual world coincides with the internal differentiation of sense.

Univocity

While it is initially a scholastic term for describing the relations between God and his creations, *univocity* is crucial for grasping how Deleuze understands the relations between sense and its objects. For the scholastic philosophers, there were generally three conceptions of how the relations between God and the world could work. These relations describe the predicative relationship between Being and beings. Or, in Spinoza's case, substance and its modes, for, as we will see, it is through the identification of substance and the absolute that Deleuze treats discussions of God and his creations as synonymous with discussions of sense, its expression and its modifications. And so, this problem of predication concerns the sense in which we say that a thing lives its being a thing; that is, how we understand a being insofar as it is a being: univocally, equivocally and analogously. In the case of univocity, the sense in which Being is predicated of a being is the same for all beings. This is wholly amenable to Spinoza's conception of a God who causes the world immanently given that, as Daniel Smith points out, 'God [will thus be] cause of all things in the same sense that he is cause of himself'.[2] At EIP11, Spinoza employs a form of the ontological argument for the existence of God to argue that God's existence follows necessarily from his essence, and then, at EIP16, Spinoza argues that infinitely many modes are produced actually and necessarily in accordance with the essence of God. That is, the existence of both God and the infinite diversity of beings that populate the actual world follow necessarily from the essence of God. In this case, univocity is the name for the fact that God and beings follow from the essence of God *in the same sense*.

Deleuze argues that, running through Duns Scotus, Spinoza, Nietzsche and Bergson, among others, there is a tradition implicitly concerned with the problem of univocity, and in this tradition, he finds a desire to 'conceive of several formally distinct senses [of modes of being] which none the less refer to [B]eing as if to a single designated entity, ontologically one'.[3] Deleuze argues that

> [B]eing, ... insofar as it expresses itself, is said in turn in a single and same sense of all [beings]. In the ontological proposition, not only is that which is designated ontologically the same for qualitatively distinct senses, but also the sense is ontologically the same for individuating modes, for numerically distinct designators or expressors: [univocity] involves a circulation of this kind.[4]

Deleuze retains the concept of an essence since it is a key concept for Spinoza; however, he redefines it so that an essence is no longer the defining quality of Being, where Being would have a single and same sense, but is instead the sense in which a being, an individuating difference or intrinsic modality, is said to relate to Being. That is, all the modalities which express Being are different to each other but they express Being, Being is said *of* them, in the same way. This is why Deleuze argues that the 'essence of univocal [B]eing is to include individuating differences, while these differences do not have the same essence and do not change the essence of [B]eing'.[5] Deleuze establishes univocity as the ground to work through an ontology of difference in itself rather than an ontology of difference as merely the differentiation of the similar. The driving concern of

Deleuze's ontology is, therefore, to articulate the process of individuation or the production of individuals as events which express differentiation within univocal being.

This claim, that actual individuals express differentiations *within* univocal Being, is offered quite literally when Deleuze argues that individual modes are the actual side of 'intrinsic modalities of [B]eing, passing from one "individual" to another, circulating and communicating underneath matters and forms'.[6] These intrinsic modalities are not actual modes, but they are substantive events that occur within the attributes which characterize actual, finite modes. We must note that *Being* here does not refer to *a* being, *a* one, who would contain all beings and whose unity would transcend the plurality of modes. Rather, in anticipation of arguments later in this chapter, we might describe Being as an existential plane; the univocity of this plane consists in the fact that all beings, even the most diverse, populate or belong to it. In this sense, Deleuze argues that there is a single 'voice' of Being which includes all its modes, including the most diverse, the most varied, the most differenciated. Being is said in a single and same sense of everything of which it is said, but that of which it is said differs: it is said of difference itself.[7]

For Deleuze, this is why 'univocal Being belongs only to difference'.[8] The equality or *univocity* of Being resides in difference as a transcendental principle which inhabits individuating factors and is actualized in hierarchically organized modes which express this Being: '[The] words "everything is equal" … resound joyfully, on condition that they are said *of* that which is not equal in this equal, univocal Being.'[9] What this means is that even though the doctrine of univocity denotes a strict equality of Being at the level of its being an infinitive – that is, the verbal form *to be* is the same for all beings – the degrees of power which characterize actual beings are themselves *unequal*. Insofar as finite modes are identical to a *potestas* – that is, what a body is actually capable of[10] – which follows necessarily from the essence of God, finite modes, actual beings, are characterized by a degree of power. These degrees of power are quantitative, and thus univocal Being still admits of a certain hierarchy and method of distribution.[11] This hierarchy makes it possible to 'conceive [of] a reconciliation between analogy and univocity';[12] the analogous in Being concerns the intrinsic modes or individuating factors. The modalities intrinsic to univocal Being are, of course, different; they 'have nothing "really" in common'.[13] In other words, the modes characterized by degrees of power contained within the attributes are distinct; by definition they are the differentiation of power. However, these distinct modes still interact with each other, and so the sense of analogy that

Deleuze claims is reconciled with univocal being is precisely the relationality of intrinsic modalities insofar as they are quantitatively diverse. Thus, Deleuze claims, even where Being is called equal, or univocal, in relation to itself it is 'unequal in relation to the modalities which reside within it'.[14] On the face of it, then, it would seem that, even though difference is a generative principle for Being (that is, Being can only be expressed univocally if it is said of that which differs), the modalities of Being, as intrinsically different, can only relate by virtue of being analogous to one another. However, in order to avoid 'distorting the two theses',[15] univocity and analogy, and confusing *generic* difference with *specific* difference, Deleuze insists we understand how ontological difference is 'presupposed by the forms, matters and extensive parts'[16] of Being in its empirical expressions: 'We must show not only how individuating difference differs in kind from specific difference, but primarily and above all how individuation precedes matter and form, species and parts, and every other element of the constituted individual.'[17]

And so, the problem of the intrinsic modalities of Being engages with different kinds of difference: on the one hand, it deals with *generic* or *individuating difference* which precedes matter and form and constitutes individual modes; on the other hand, it deals with *specific difference* which differentiates the modes. Confronting this problem is one of Deleuze's primary tasks in his reading of Spinoza. Consequently, it is to the differential relations between the attributes and the constitution of substance through differentiation that we must soon turn.[18]

Immanence

The problem of immanence is a central concern for Deleuze; it runs throughout his early work on Hume, Nietzsche and Bergson, and he repeatedly hints at how a plane of immanence will work. However, it is in *Expressionism in Philosophy: Spinoza* that Deleuze constructs an operating plane of immanence for the first time. Right up until his last book, *What Is Philosophy?*, a collaboration with Félix Guattari, Deleuze describes immanence as a generative operation that refers to no preceding identity. This operation generates individuals as 'intensive features' of this field.[19] *What Is Philosophy?* was published in 1991, nearly four decades after Deleuze first articulated the problem of immanence in his book on Hume, *Empiricism and Subjectivity*, so, of course, its arguments cannot simply be read backwards into an interpretation of this problem. However, Deleuze's reading of Spinoza is a crucial moment in the passage between the two; as he says in *What Is Philosophy?*, 'Spinoza was the philosopher who knew full well that immanence was only immanent to itself and therefore that it was a plane traversed by movements of the infinite.'[20]

There are four features of Deleuze's Spinozism that are fundamental to his conception of immanence: substance is defined as a heterogeneous field whose constitution must itself be explained; individual beings are described as 'intrinsic modalities' of being;[21] attribution is a dual process which constitutes the plane of immanence and simultaneously expresses the modalities of being which are actualized in individual beings; and, finally, finite beings are expressions of the infinite under determinate relations.

Deleuze's reading of Spinoza owes a great deal to scholasticism insofar as he reads Spinoza as intervening in a long-running theological debate concerning the nature of God as a causal agent. As with univocity, the scholastics offered three conceptions of how God's being a cause could take place: through immanent, emanative and transitive causation. Emanative and transitive causes are not entirely dissimilar insofar as both entail understanding the causal agent as external to its effects. Transitive or efficient causation is a strictly mechanistic view of causation in which the powers proper to a cause are transferred to its effects, even if only partially, in order that the effect be realized. In the case of emanative causation, however, the agent remains within itself; that is, its powers remain in itself such that the agent's effects *emanate* from their cause as an overflowing of its abundance. Crucial to the distinction between emanative and transitive causes is the origin of laws by which God's creation proceeds. In a discussion of the place of concepts of causation in Spinoza, Pierre Macherey argues that a transitive cause produces 'an effect externally in accordance with an extrinsic law'.[22] This claim, however, implies limitations on God insofar as God becomes subject to laws which are not his own, or do not follow from his nature. While this may seem a peculiar claim to make about the theistic god, it is precisely the claim made by Christian theologians who, attached to a scriptural account of creation, needed to posit the world as produced by, but *external* to, a god that functions as an agent exploiting the means or agency of other elements in order to fabricate artefacts which are themselves only the constituent parts of a larger chain of effects and 'are thus removed to an infinite degree from that which constitutes their proper nature'.[23]

With respect to immanence, Deleuze's fundamental claim is that the expressions of the powers of a causal agent cannot be conceived distinctly from the agent's possession of those powers.[24] Deleuze finds an account of this in

Spinoza's ontology insofar as Spinoza identifies the cause of the world with the world caused. That is, for Spinoza, the being of God, or the being of the cause, is said in the same sense as the being of the caused. This complicates emanative causation precisely because the cause is no longer separate from and unaffected by the beings it causes. Rather, determined beings are in their cause or their cause is in them, such that the causal process is complicated by the beings that are its effects. It is in this sense that Deleuze describes a relationship of reciprocal determination between actual beings and their power. The immanent cause's causing things to exist follows from its nature and in producing effects it expresses its own power. The particularity of immanent causation is that an effect remains in its cause. Macherey argues that Spinoza's demonstration of EIP18, the proposition that God is the immanent cause of all things, operates in terms of these descriptions of emanative, transitive and immanent causes.[25] Thus, on Deleuze's reading, when Spinoza describes his conception of a God in whom all things exist and, consequently, must be conceived, he describes a universe where each thing explicates God yet, simultaneously, God 'complicates' all things, that is, 'comprehends them in itself'.[26] Thus, God, encompassing all things and operating only in order to express or perfect its own nature, is the cause of all things. However, because all things are in God both conceptually and actually, that is, as possibilities and as effects, God is an immanent cause. With these two concepts, immanence and univocity, we can turn to how Deleuze understands the qualitative differentiation of the attributes as occurring within substance, even though substance has no existence outside of the differentiation of its attributes.

Attribution, distinction and the constitution of substance

Deleuze argues that the differentiation of the attributes constitutes substance and that the expressive operations by which substance is constituted by the attributes form one half of a reciprocally determining relationship between an individual and its environment. This argument that the attributes constitute substance is fundamental to Deleuze's reading of Spinoza because it enables Deleuze to describe substance as constituted by degrees of differentiation. In this section, I will consider the way that qualitative distinctions among the attributes account for the constitution of substance. Following this, I will set out to demonstrate how, for Deleuze, a modification of substance is, *in fact*, an actualization of the degree to which substance is constituted.

In his final essay, 'Immanence: A Life', Deleuze argues that, for Spinoza, 'immanence is not immanence *to* substance; rather, substance and modes are in immanence'.[27] His point is that nothing, neither substance nor mode, transcends the plane of immanence in which all beings express powers of becoming. Twenty-seven years earlier, in *Expression in Philosophy: Spinoza*, Deleuze argues that '[i]mmanence is revealed as expressive, and expression as immanent, in a system of logical relations within which the two notions are correlative'.[28] This correlation between expression and immanence raises a problem for Deleuze's reading of Spinoza: How is a system of expressions constitutive of a plane of immanence? Deleuze's response is that the differentiation of the attributes constitutes substance and that the degrees to which the attributes are differentiated are themselves expressible as degrees of power which correspond to and characterize modal existences. The essence – the degree of power – of an actually existing being is the expression of a degree of an attribute's participation in the constitution of a whole. Substance and modes are *in* immanence insofar as each is determined wholly by the operations of the attributes. For Deleuze, the attributes are 'verbs rather than adjectives'.[29] That is, the attributive operations that determine substance and modes can only be characterized by what they constitute, not what they are: '[I]*t is not the attribute* that exists through itself, but that to which the essence of each attribute relates, in such a way that existence necessarily follows from the essence thus constituted.'[30] The essence constituted by an attribution is the essence of substance and the essence contained in an attribute is the determination of an actual mode, and, in this sense, the attributes *are* the operations of immanence.

Robin Durie argues that Deleuze's reading of Spinoza turns on an interpretation of substance 'as a complex whole, or aggregate' which is constituted by really distinct parts.[31] Spinoza appears to deny this when he argues that 'no substance ... insofar as it is a substance, is divisible';[32] indeed, Spinoza states that to think of substance as divisible would require that substance be finite. This, of course, is an obvious contradiction of the very definition of a substance.[33] However, this only seems contradictory because of the irreconcilability of a concept of a One which has no parts and a concept of a One with parts. In this case, the problem of the One and the many appears intractably contradictory precisely because it takes two essentially different things – a concept of the One in its heterogeneous sense and a concept of the One in its homogeneous sense – and obsesses over the irreconcilability of the two. In other words, the problem of the one and the many begins from static concepts and asks after their relationship as though they are already established. As Durie argues, the problem arises from assuming 'the principle of the identity of substance' and then trying to derivatively understand the diversity of this very identity. Instead, Durie urges, the reader must begin from the logic of this diversity and then understand how the identity and unity of substance is generated.[34] This is why Deleuze claims that Spinoza sets out from infinity; Spinoza, Deleuze argues, does not begin with a concept of God which he is obliged to explicate in terms of its relationship to the many. Rather, he sets out from an 'innocent' concept of an absolute infinity; that is, '[A] novel conceptual frame [which will] bring out the power and the actuality of positive infinity.'[35] This absolute infinity is the conception of God that Spinoza articulates at EID6, 'By God, I understand a being absolutely infinite, that is, a substance consisting of an infinity of attributes, of which each expresses an eternal and infinite essence.'

Spinoza's argument for the existence of God rests on defending the coherence of predicating an infinity of attributes of a single substance. Indeed, his argument against the absurdity of inferring a substance for each distinct attribute is prefaced by EIP4: 'Two or more distinct things are distinguished from one another, either by a difference in the attributes of the substances or by a difference in their affections'. The method of distinguishing two or more things we conceive to be distinct can, Spinoza claims, operate either by a difference in the attributes of substance or by a difference in the affections of substance.[36] In other words, distinction must operate in one of two ways; it can either be carried out through an attempt to distinguish substances or it can be a distinction between the modes of that substance.[37] For Spinoza it is simply absurd to posit a distinction between substances because to do so would be to ask after two or more absolutely infinite beings. The former method – distinction between substances – must, by EID3, EID4 and EID6, concern itself with the distinction between attributes as well as the understanding of how such a distinction expresses 'an eternal and infinite essence' of substance. Conversely, distinction between modes, the latter method, must concern itself with the sense in which an attribute constitutes a modification of substance.

Deleuze's interest in Spinoza's argument for the necessity of distinguishing substances through their attributes revives the discussion of immanent causation – that Deleuze revives this discussion is of the utmost importance to the broader discussion of his ethology and the reciprocity between finite beings and the whole of which they are a part. Because immanent causation is a process whereby a cause remains in itself even as it is expressed in its constitution and its effects remain internal to it, it is through the theory of distinctions that Deleuze interprets and appropriates Spinoza's claim that substance 'is the immanent, not the transitive, cause of all things'.[38] Deleuze argues that it is in the scholium to EIP8 that Spinoza develops a positive demonstration of the argument for distinguishing substances by their attributes through highlighting the absurdity of the inverse proposition that substances could be accounted for through transitive or 'external' causality.[39] This demonstration consists of three parts which establish that because it is a contradiction of the very concept of substance to suppose that an absolutely infinite being is subject to causal processes which refer to finite things and that because '[n]umerical distinction requires an external cause to which it may be referred,'[40] *then numerical distinction cannot operate on or within a substance.* In other words, given the nature of numerical distinction, it is inapplicable to substance precisely because of substance's infinity; consequently, numerical distinction is applicable only to finite modes that involve the same attribute.[41] We will recall that, for Spinoza, a mode is precisely that finite being which is in and conceived through another;[42] therefore, the modes distinguished numerically *must* involve the same attribute, because the modes are, by their nature, numerical or quantitative. As Deleuze puts it, '[N]umerical distinction can … only [ever distinguish] modes that involve the same attribute. For number expresses in its own way the character of existing modes: the composite nature of their parts, their limitation by other things of the same nature, their determination from outside themselves.'[43]

For Deleuze, Spinoza's argument must be understood in the context of seventeenth-century metaphysics, particularly against René Descartes, of whose argument that modes and attributes are identical[44] Spinoza is especially critical. However, Deleuze retains what Durie calls a 'Cartesian clue' insofar as he imports into his Spinozism a Cartesian notion of attributes as qualities: 'Any given attribute is a quality, in that it qualifies a substance as this or that, but also a mode in that it diversifies it.'[45] This means that Deleuze is able to distinguish the attributes qualitatively, even as what they constitute remains numerically indistinct.[46] From this, Deleuze sets about interpreting Spinoza in terms of an expressionistic logic which allows the introduction of qualitative, *real* distinction into God while maintaining that substance is indeed numerically one.

This problem of attributive distinction emerges from EIP9 and EIP10 where Spinoza argues that substance has an infinity of attributes. The qualitative distinctions between the attributes are, Deleuze claims, real and yet they exclude any numerical division from the concept of substance.[47] The distinction between the attributes concerns the *nature* of the attributes such that together they constitute a substance that is qualitatively heterogeneous even though the constituted substance is quantitatively unique. Deleuze thus posits the attributes as expressions of qualitative degrees of substance – or essences – thus introducing real distinction into substance while retaining a rigorous sense of substance's unary nature. From this point of view, Durie argues, 'we can begin to see the significance of Deleuze's claim that attributes are the *dynamic* or *genetic* elements of substance'.[48] Deleuze argues that the existence of the essence of substance follows from the attributes insofar as it is expression in the attributes that gives existence to the essences. At EIP11, Spinoza adapts the classical ontological argument for God's existence to argue that the existence of substance follows necessarily from its essence.[49] Thus, to the extent that attribution expresses essence and essence has no existence outside of its expressions,[50] the dynamism here flows from the attributes to essence. And, to the extent that the existence of substance follows necessarily from its essence, the dynamism then flows from essence to substance.[51] This is how Deleuze justifies the argument that Spinoza introduces real distinction into substance; as long as the attributes are really distinct then the constitutive elements of the essence of substance which they express will also be distinct. However, distinct though they are, the essences are never expressed *of* the attributes; the essences are always expressed as essences *of* substance.[52] In other words, the existence the essences have in their expression in the attributes is never enough to give substantial content – in its general sense – to the essences. This content fills the essences only because they are said *of* substance – in its specific sense – and its nature *as* multiplicity.[53] Thus 'the relationship from attribute *to* essence *to* substance' consists of a recursive dynamism that generates its own terms.[54]

In this context, we can see a crucial element of how Deleuze interprets Spinoza's argument that there is only one substance. Substance, the object of the sense expressed by the attributes, consists of parts – that is, it is *heterogeneous* – from the point of view of the attributes. However, from the point of view of the constituted substance, we cannot speak meaningfully of parts. This is because the distinctions among the attributes are *qualitative* distinctions and qualitative distinctions are never numerical.[55] Consequently, substance cannot be considered to consist of enumerable parts and is, in the most precise sense, singular. In other words, substance as multiplicity – substance *qua* substance – is distinct from its essence only insofar as there are qualitative distinctions among the essence of substance – as that 'which is expressed'[56] – that are absent in substance. At the same time, substance quite literally has no existence external to its expression *through* the essences. It is the attributes that constitute this difference between essence and substance precisely through their rendering the essences as real, existing qualities. And, because substance achieves existence through the expressive differentiation of its essence, it is through differentiation that substance exists and thus exists as cause of itself – as an immanent cause – because it is rendered as difference in itself.[57] So, Deleuze claims that it is through the qualitative differentiation of essences – the expression of distinct essences relative to each other – under the formally determinate relation of expression that substance is constituted as existing. From here he must demonstrate how this determinate differential relation also generates modes.

Attribution and the production of the modes

When he fleshes out his interpretation of why the constitution of substance is simultaneously the production of the modal universe, Deleuze sets out an argument that will be crucial to his entire ethological project. The existence of the actual universe follows from the expression of the constitution of substance as a series of sensible propositions. That is, to the extent that substance is constituted through the expression of propositions – the attribution of essence to substance – the modal universe is the consequence of these propositions *making sense*. For Deleuze, even when they are predicated of different beings, 'infinite beings and finite beings, substance and modes, God and creatures', the attributes retain their essential nature.[58] As such, a central element of his reading of Spinoza is the latter's argument that God causes the modal world at the same time and in the same sense as he is the cause of himself. At EIP25, Spinoza argues that, because the modes are the affections or modifications of substance, 'God must be called the cause of all things in the same sense in which he is called the cause of himself.'[59] In other words, 'Particular things are nothing but affections of God's attributes *or* modes by which God's attributes are expressed in a certain and determinate way.'[60] This is an argument that Deleuze reads as describing a relationship of equivalence between God's self-causation and God's production of the modal universe.[61] For Deleuze, the activity of the attributes – attribute as *attribution* – is crucial to the simultaneity of God's self-causation and immanent causation of modes.

To unpack the reasoning behind Deleuze's interpretation of this relationship between God's self-causation and the production of a modal universe, we need to understand what it means for an essence, in its expression, to be referred *to* substance. That is, we must turn to why the method of the attribution *of* essence *to* substance determines the production of modes. When Deleuze describes expression and outlines the relationship between substance, attributes and essences, he presents the beginnings of the linguistic sense of expression that he will foreground for thinking through the production of modes. In the articulation of this linguistic sense, Deleuze makes the following, pivotal, claim:

> One distinguishes in an expression ... what it expresses and what it designates. What is expressed is, so to speak, a sense that has no existence outside the expression; it must thus be referred to an understanding that grasps it objectively, that is, ideally. But it is predicated of the thing and not of the expression itself; understanding relates it to the object designated, as the essence of that object.[62]

By emphasizing the correspondence between an essence and the sense of an expression, this argument reiterates Deleuze's claim that the essence of a substance has no existence outside of the attribute which expresses it. At the same time, as Durie puts it, 'for an expression to "function," that is, for it to have sense',[63] its referral of essence to substance must be disclosed to an understanding that comprehends the expression. Employing the conclusion of the ontological argument – that whatever is in God's power necessarily exists – and drawing on EIP16 – that 'from the necessity of the divine nature there must follow infinitely many things in infinitely many modes, (i.e. everything which can fall under an infinite intellect)' – Spinoza argues that '[i]n God there is necessarily an idea, both of his essence and of everything which necessarily follows from his essence'.[64] Deleuze takes this to mean that '[i]nfinite understanding is ... the form of the idea that God necessarily has of himself or of his own essence'.[65] In other words, there is necessarily within God a power for the deduction of the properties of his essence and it is this that we call understanding. This is why, when essence is expressed as the essence of substance, it is expressed *to* substance. Spinoza defends this proposition by recourse to two earlier propositions: the aforementioned EIP16 and EIIP1, 'Thought is an attribute of God, *or* God is a thinking thing.' So, in the scholium to EIIP3, Spinoza argues that God's production of the world corresponds necessarily with his self-understanding: 'God acts with the same necessity by which he understands himself, that is, just as it follows from the necessity of the divine nature ... that God understands himself, with the same necessity it also follows that God does infinitely many things in infinitely many modes.' This means that, as God's power is expressed through an infinity of attributes, God's power is expressed as an extended thing and as a thinking thing. As a result, because the attributes are infinite in their own kind, God's power of extension is infinite, as is his power of thinking.[66]

This is to say that the production of the modal universe follows from the expression of essence as a sensible proposition. This is why Deleuze says that if the sense of the expression is to function, it can do so only by being referred to an understanding which apprehends it as essence. It follows that the dynamic of substance, attribute and essence is double; on the one hand, attributes express essences but express them as essences of substance and in so doing attribute to substance the heterogeneous essence which constitutes its existence. On the other hand, this process of the attribution of essence can only function by virtue of an understanding which grasps the essence as referred to its object: *substance*. The question, then, is how does this double expressivity not merely account for the expression of essence but also the production of a modal universe? At this point Deleuze makes, as Durie puts it, 'the most audacious wager in his attempt to secure an immanent ontology of univocity from Spinoza's text'[67] insofar as he reads expression in linguistic terms:

> Attributes are univocal or common forms, predicated, in the same form, of creatures and creator, products and producer, formally constituting the essence of one, formally containing the essence of the others. The principle of necessary production thus reflects a double univocity. A univocity of cause: God is cause of all things *in the same sense* as he is cause of himself. A univocity of attributes: God produces through and in the same attributes that constitute his essence.[68]

For Deleuze, the univocity of the attributes means that there is a doubleness implicit in attribution. Deleuze claims that Spinoza is 'too careful a grammarian to allow us to miss the linguistic origins of "expression",'[69] and it is precisely this linguistic element of expression which Deleuze employs to support his argument that attribution is double. The use Deleuze makes of linguistics here is elaborated in an early, crucial series from *The Logic of Sense*, 'Third Series of the Proposition':

> On the one hand, [sense] does not exist outside of the proposition which expresses it; what is expressed does not exist outside its expression. This is why we cannot say that sense exists, but rather that it inheres or subsists. On the other hand, it does not merge at all with the proposition, for it has an objectity [*objectité*] which is quite distinct. What is expressed has no resemblance whatsoever to the expression. Sense is indeed attributed, but it is not at all the attribute of the proposition, it is rather the attribute of the thing or state of affairs.[70]

Deleuze is concerned with the relationship between an attribute (the proposition or expression), essence (sense) and substance (the state of affairs, or, the object of the proposition). His argument is that a proposition expresses a particular sense without the latter ever collapsing into the former. In other words, the proposition expresses a sense even though the sense never simply collapses into its expression and even though the sense does not exist outside of this expression. This is what Deleuze means when he says that sense 'subsists' in its expression. At the same time, by referring to a particular object, the sense that is expressed by the proposition is always said *of* an object that is not the proposition. And, while sense never collapses into its expression, it never collapses into its object either. Thus sense is expressed *by* one thing (the proposition) and expressed *of* another (the object) yet it is never reducible to either.

What is striking about this dynamic is the fact that *the proposition cannot state its own sense*. That is, the proposition can express the sense of the object but it cannot simultaneously state its own sense, the sense in which it is an expression of the sense of a designated object. However, as Durie observes, this further sense – the sense of the expression which expresses the sense of the object – can itself become a further object for a subsequent proposition.[71] In other words, the initial proposition, being unable to express the sense of the object at the same time as expressing the sense of expressing this sense *as the sense of the object*, engenders a new proposition which takes the sense expressed of the object as the object of *its* expression. What is crucial here is that, even though it is expressed as a new object with its own sense, this object is in fact the initial sense expressed of the initial object. What is occurring here is a relationship between a proposition and its object where the former expresses the sense of the latter. The generation of the second proposition is in fact a repetition of the first whereby the sense of the initial proposition is now the designated object. Of course, this process can be infinitely repeated by making the sense of the expression of the second proposition an object in its own right and so on.[72]

The logic of this linguistic relation informs the expressionistic logic of Deleuze's ontology. To refer this process to the triad of substance, attribute and essence, we would say that the initial proposition is the attribute which expresses the sense, or *essence*, of a designated object: *substance*. The proposition expresses a sense which has no existence outside of its expression but it expresses this sense as the sense of an object. The generation of the second proposition is, in fact, the generation of modes as the re-expression of the proposition with a new object: the sense of the attributive expression. In both expressions the sense is ontologically *the same sense*. In the former expression, the sense subsists in the attribute and is expressed as the essence of substance. In this expression the subsisting sense is said to *constitute* the essence of substance precisely because the expression gives it existence. In the latter expression the sense is expressed as the essence *contained in* the attribute as the affection of substance. According to this logic, the second level of expression reproduces the first as the latter's modification. Deleuze writes,

> Substance expressed itself in attributes, each attribute was an expression, the essence of substance was expressed. Now each attribute expresses itself, the dependent modes are expressions and a modification is expressed. It will be recalled that the essence they expressed had no existence outside the attributes, but was expressed as the absolute essence of substance, the same for all attributes. The same applies here: a modification has no existence outside the mode that expresses it in each attribute, but it is expressed as a modification of substance, the same for all modes differing in attribute.[73]

Deleuze's point is that each mode is generated as a modification of substance as it is contained in an attribute; therefore, the essence contained in the attribute, the modal essence, will differ across each and every mode. This operates as the second level of expression, where the first level – which is, in fact, the other side of the attributive expression that constitutes substance – presents each different attribute as that which expresses a qualitative or intensive aspect of a substance which remains the same for all attributes. Neither object of attribution, substance or mode, can be conceived as existing independently of the relationship of attribution; however, as the attributes are either the constitutive expressions which attribute essence to substance or the modifying expression which contains the modal essence, neither substantial nor modal essence can be conceived as reducible to an attribute which exists in their absence. Furthermore, because each attribute refers to a single substance, even as it differs according to the substantial essence it constitutes and the modal essence it contains, Deleuze is able to claim 'that we can conceive of several formally distinct senses which none the less refer to [B]eing as if to a single designated entity, ontologically one'.[74] Thus a phrase which has been repeated continuously in this chapter – *in the same sense* – now has a more precise and more robust meaning. We can now see the extent of Deleuze's use of univocity; insofar as we can say that through the constitutive expression of a single and same – though qualitatively heterogeneous – essence, attribution simultaneously generates numerically distinct modes. This is how Deleuze interprets Spinoza's argument that God produces the world at the same time as he produces himself, or as Deleuze puts it: 'Things remain inherent in God who complicates them, and God remains implicated in things which explicate him.'[75]

The expressive operation of attribution is double. On the one hand, it constitutes the essence of substance as a heterogeneous multiplicity. On the other hand, because substance is constituted heterogeneously, there is always a quantitative sense of these expressions – that is, the ratio of attributes subsistent in substance. These quantitative senses are the objects of a series of expressions which produce actual, finite modes as expressions of the absolute infinity of substance under a determinate relation: the differentiation of the attributions. Insofar as these attributions express the constitutive ratio of God's qualities, they express modifications of God's power. Thus Deleuze argues that, for Spinoza, modes are characterized by the degree of power that is expressed by their existence. It is to this issue that we now turn.

Modification as the expression of power

Deleuze argues that Spinoza's identification of modal essences with degrees of power situates Spinoza's account within long-running theological debates concerning the identity of power and action. Spinoza intervenes in this debate by setting out a correlation between power and actual capacity:

> [In place of] the distinction of power and act, potentiality and actuality, was substituted the correlation of a power of acting and a power of being acted on or suffering action, both actual. The two currents meet in Spinoza, one relating to the essence of substance, the other to the essence of modes. For in Spinozism all power bears with it a corresponding and inseparable capacity to be affected. And this capacity to be affected is always, necessarily, exercised. To *potentia* there corresponds an *aptitudo* or *potestas*; but there is no aptitude or capacity that remains ineffective, and so no power that is not actual.[76]

At the beginning of this passage, Deleuze is referring to the power of the whole: the unlimited potential – *potentia* 'as force or capacity'[77] – through which God exists necessarily. This power is identical with God's essence; as Spinoza says, 'God's power is his essence itself.'[78] Thus God possesses an infinite power of existing insofar as 'being able to exist is power'.[79] Of course, even though this claim comes as part of his adaptation of the ontological argument, Spinoza is not suggesting that existence is a power of the things which exist. Rather, Spinoza's point, claims Deleuze, is that 'the capacity to exist (that is, the possible existence involved in the essence of a finite thing) is a power'.[80] In other words, substance contains a power to exist insofar as a corollary of the power by which it is constituted is a capacity – *potestas* or 'that which an individual body can do'[81] – expressed in the production of actual beings. This brings us to the other side of the distinction in this passage; corresponding to the absolute power of God is a capacity that is expressed as the modal essences which characterize existent or individual beings as parts of the whole. In this sense, the power expressed by actual beings is an expression of the degree to which they are a function of the whole of nature. This is what Spinoza means when he says that '[m]an's power, therefore, insofar as it is explained through his actual essence, is part of God *or* Nature's infinite power, that is, of its essence'.[82] This does not efface the importance of actual modes or individuals; rather, it denies that individuals have a substantial life independent of the whole insofar as an actual mode is dependent on its interrelationship with the other modes that fill out its environment. The power of a finite mode is determined by its belonging to the whole of nature. Deleuze's claim is that, for Spinoza, a being that does not exist of itself, that is, 'has no power of its own except insofar as it is part of a whole, that is, part of the power of a being that does exist through itself'.[83]

To see how modification – the expression of a modification of substance in an actual mode – can be understood as an expression of power, we must continue with this linguistic reading of Spinoza.[84] Deleuze begins by arguing that

> [a]ttributes ... have an essentially dynamic role. Not that they are themselves powers. But, taken collectively, they are the conditions for the attribution to absolute substance of an absolutely infinite power of existing and acting, identical with its formal essence. Taken distributively they are conditions for the attribution to finite beings of a power identical with their formal essence, insofar as that essence is contained in this or that attribute.[85]

A modal essence, then, is not a substance which is cause of itself. Rather, an essence is a power contained in an attribute and characteristic of a finite being, *an essence is a degree of power in virtue of which the being exists*. This is why Spinoza adopts the ontological argument and says that the object of this attribution – substance – necessarily exists. That is, when understood in their collective sense, the attributes are what attribute to substance the very power of existing which constitutes it as a single and same designated. However, if they are understood distributively, the attributes are the conditions under which a modification or variation of substantial power is taken as identical with the essence of the finite beings (*potestas*) which modify that substantial power (*potentia*). In this case, modes are the expression of the sense of the attributes' expression of the essence of God.

From what has been described so far, we know that the existence and nature of substance is constituted through the attributive expression of the essence of substance. We also know that actually existing things, modes, are in fact the expression of the quantitative degree of the first level of expression, hence Deleuze's claim that the modes express 'a certain degree, a certain quantity, of a quality'.[86] That is, where attributes constitute substance through their expression of substantial essence, the modal essences contained in the attributes express the intensity or degree to which a specific attribute expresses an essence at this moment or that. It is in this sense that Deleuze argues that '[m]odal essences are ... distinguished from their attributes as different degrees of intensity'.[87] This description does not mean that modes are constituted by attributes the same way the attributes constitute the essence of God. Deleuze is emphatic on this point: 'Attributes constitute the essence of substance, but in no sense constitute the essence of modes or of creatures. *Yet they are forms common to both*, since creatures imply them both in their own essence and in their existence.'[88] The existence of a mode is distinct from its essence, that is, the existence of a mode does not follow from its essence; however, both the existence and the essence of a mode imply an attribute. On the one hand, the existence of a mode implies an attribute insofar as each being is a mode of Being because it involves an attribute; for example, a body implies the attribute of extension insofar as it is a modified expression of a power of being extended. On the other hand, the essence of a mode implies an attribute insofar as it expresses the degree to which a body is a modification of a power of being extended. As such, the attributes are called containers of modal essences in the most literal sense since the modes are expressions of the degree to which an attribute constitutes a degree of essence within the configuration of substantial essence which all attributes, understood collectively, constitute. Summarizing this dynamic doubleness of the attributes, Deleuze says that

> [i]t is as though to each attribute there belonged two quantities, each in itself infinite, but each in its own way divisible in certain conditions: an intensive quality, which divides into intensive parts, or degrees, and an extensive quantity, which divides into extensive parts.[89]

In the first case, Deleuze is describing the constitutive relationship between substance and attributes; the attributes are infinite in their kind insofar as they can be divided into intensive parts only. In the second case, extensive division and extensive parts, he is referring to Spinoza's conception of modal essences – the sense of the attribute's expression – as those things which are infinite by virtue of their cause but when conceived abstractly are able to be viewed as finite and divisible.[90] This dynamic raises a very specific issue, though: Under what conditions, according to what logic, does one infinite relate to the other? That is, how do the intensive parts of a qualitative infinity relate to the extensive parts of a quantitative infinity?

Deleuze addresses this problem through his reading of modal essences. Modal essences exist independently of the mode's existence precisely because they are contained in their respective attribute as the sense of the attribute's expression of the substantial essence; thus Deleuze describes modal essence as 'a pure physical reality'[91] distinct from the mode to which it corresponds. It is in this sense that Deleuze reads Spinoza's argument that modal essences constitute neither their own existence insofar as they are essences[92] nor the existence of the mode to which they correspond.[93] Therefore, whenever we encounter an essence of this kind, the necessity of its existence comes from God and not from its own nature. In other words, the existence of the essence of a mode is caused not by its own nature but as the consequence of the necessary existence of the essence of substance. The nature of the cause of these essences produces them as intensive degrees within a total, *actually infinite*, system. Thus any distinction between modal essences operates only abstractly insofar as we conceive one essence independently of the system of intensities implied by this one, apparently, distinct degree.

Playing on the tension between the two quantities he suggests belong to the attributes, Deleuze interprets modal essences as 'intrinsic modes or intensive quantities'.[94] In this case, an attribute is simultaneously qualitative and quantitative; in the former case its role is the predication of a quality or essence to substance. In the latter case it is this predication which designates the attribute as quantitative or *modal* precisely because it always poses the question of the degree to which the quality is expressed. Consequently, modal essences characterize the contingent existence of things or beings while remaining ontologically distinct from them. This is why Deleuze argues that

> [o]nly a quantitative distinction of beings is consistent with the qualitative identity of the absolute. And this quantitative distinction is no mere appearance, but an internal difference, a difference of intensity. So that each finite being must be said to *express the absolute*, according to the intensive degree that constitutes its essence, according, that is, to the degree of its power.[95]

Modal essences are thus distinct from their corresponding attribute precisely because they are constituted quantitatively as the degree to which the attribute expresses the essence it constitutes. Returning to EIID7, it is clear that, for Deleuze, when Spinoza describes individuals 'concurring' in one action to the extent that their cooperation constitutes a mode which is itself singular, he is describing a process that is intensive, that is 'quantitative and intrinsic'.[96] There is a *quantitative* distinction of modal essences insofar as they are distinct from each other as well as from the attribute that contains them. However, the modal essence is *intrinsic* precisely because it is always contained within an attribute and thus cannot be considered extrinsic. Modal essences are thus constituted as infinite series corresponding to the intensive quantities of the attribute which contains them. In this vein, Spinoza argues that '[e]very mode which exists necessarily and is infinite has necessarily had to follow either from the absolute nature of some attribute of God, or from some attribute, modified by a modification which exists necessarily and is infinite'.[97] Even though each modal essence is characterized as an infinite series, it is only infinite because of the status of another thing, namely the intensive quantity characterizing the attribute which contains it. For Deleuze, this is also the sense in which modal essences are divisible. As essences they are not divisible into extensive or extrinsic parts; however, each essence can, if conceived as an intrinsic modality, be conceived as distinct, singular and particular. What is more, even though the essences form part of a concrete system where each is involved in the production of every other, 'each essence is', as Deleuze puts it, 'produced as an irreducible degree, necessarily apprehended as a singular unity'.[98]

In brief, we have established here that, on the one hand, modal essences are expressions of the degree to which an attribute expresses or constitutes the essence necessary to the existence of substance. In other words, *a modal essence is always constituted as a degree of power intrinsic to univocal being*. On the other hand, modal essences also express the qualitative distinction within substantial essence, that is, the distinction carried out by the process of attribution, as a quantitative distinction. That is, insofar as '[e]ach substantial quality has intensive modal quantity',[99] we can say that, in producing himself, God produces the things in the world as quantitatively distinct expressions of his own power.

Conclusion

On its face, Deleuze's reading of Spinoza is a profound, if perverse, exercise in doing the history of philosophy. And, to be fair, it certainly is such an exercise and it had a profound impact on French philosophy's turn to Spinoza in the 1970s. However, it is also crucial to unpacking the metaphysical logic at work in Deleuze's ethology. If we replace the vocabulary of God and his creatures with Hegel's absolute and the finite beings that live therein, or with Hyppolite's actual world and the reciprocity it has with its transforming sense, we see that Deleuze finds in Spinoza a robust logic where the internal differentiation of sense simultaneously constitutes its existence and substantively characterizes finite beings who express that constitution. As such, there are two key themes in this discussion that are crucial to the account of Deleuze's ethology that I want to develop. First is the simultaneity of substance and modes. The modal universe is produced at the same time substance is produced. Of course, substance does not produce the modes. The attributes, insofar as they are expressions through which essence is attributed to substance, constitute substance. Because the modes follow necessarily from the essence of substance so constituted, what actually exists is produced simultaneously as another level of the event through which substance is constituted. The second theme involves the phrase that has been repeated throughout this chapter: *in the same sense*. Deleuze argues that for the attributes to successfully express essence to substance, these expressions must be apprehended as such. Thus, Deleuze invokes Spinoza's claim that God possesses an infinite power of understanding. The sense in which the attributes express the essence of substance is apprehended by this infinite power of understanding as the idea of an essence. The idea of God is the '*objective formal distinction*' that correlates necessarily with the real formal distinction that occurs in the constitution of the essence of God.[100] The understanding of the idea of God is thus not a viewpoint on the idea but the formal being of the idea of God.[101] But it is precisely the successful apprehension of the idea of God that determines the quantitative degrees that characterize actual modes. These essences do not cause the existence of the modes to which they correspond, however; they only determine an assemblage of material parts as a particular mode if they express the essence of substance as a sensible proposition.

From this follows the only substantive criticism Deleuze makes of Spinoza. In Spinoza, the modes are produced through differential relations and characterized by degrees of power that express these relations. However, insofar as the production of the modes follows necessarily from the constitution of substance they 'are dependent on substance, but as though on something other than themselves'.[102] In other words, while the modes are produced differentially, their differentiation follows from the constitution of the *identity* of substance. In Chapter 3 I will explore how working through this problem is a crucial step in the transformation of Deleuze's ethology. Chapter 3, indeed, elaborates some of the tools Deleuze develops to enable him to present identity as a consequence of differentiation and the constitution of substance as reciprocal with the differentiation of the modes. In turning to consider these developments, I raise a number of questions that remain underdeveloped or implicit in this discussion: What is the ontological status of a subsistent relation? How can we characterize concretely the relationship between the degrees of power and the actual, existing modes which express them? How does Deleuze flesh out his conception of 'reciprocal determination' between actual beings and the powers they express without violating Spinoza's argument that the relationship between an existing mode and its essence is not causal? And, finally, how does Deleuze treat duration, what Spinoza calls 'an indefinite continuation of existing'?[103]

3

On Deleuze's Bergson

The transformation of the whole

In this chapter I argue that, in response to the apparent independence of the identity of substance, Deleuze reconceives Spinoza's substance-attribute-mode dynamic in terms of living beings and the ontological conditions and status of their power. In order to achieve this, Deleuze must do two things. First, he must show how a mode and its essence are properly immanent to each other. Second, he must demonstrate how the existing being and the degree of power it expresses exist without reference to anything other than the structure of their reciprocity. This chapter outlines Deleuze's transformation of the holistic ontology he finds in Spinoza into an ontology in which the whole – the univocal sense of Being – is conceived as generated by the degree of power expressed in an existing entity. I also explore a key claim that Deleuze makes with respect to the relationship between a mode's essence and its existence, namely, that a 'mode is just its own essence insofar as the essence actually possesses an infinity of extensive parts'.[1] Reflecting on the ontology of *Expressionism* in *Difference and Repetition*, Deleuze set himself a challenge: 'All that Spinozism needed to do for the univocal to become an object of pure affirmation was to make substance turn around the modes – *in other words, to realise univocity in the form of repetition in the eternal return*'.[2]

When Deleuze returns to Bergson and Nietzsche to develop his ontology beyond *Expressionism*, he renames substance and modes – the whole and actual lives, respectively – but he retains the challenge of making the differentiation of the modes the motor of the constitution of substance. This challenge can only be faced with a renewed conception of time – *eternal return* – in which the expression of a degree of power in an actual, finite being is entirely a product of a differential relation – *repetition*. This chapter will explore the way that the more familiar elements of Deleuze's philosophy are part of his response to this challenge. We will see that the pairing of the virtual and the actual is how Deleuze, following Bergson, reconfigures the ontological status of a being and its power; that finite beings are not produced as expressions of the constitution of 'something other than themselves' but as moments in the dialectical reciprocity of individuals and the whole; that the whole is a multiplicity constituted by the association of the many as such; and that 'repetition in the eternal return' is a complex series of simultaneous syntheses – the famous 'three syntheses of time'. Where Chapter 2 showed how Deleuze's reading of Spinoza produced a form of holism where finite beings are expressions of the constitution of a heterogeneous whole, and Chapter 4 will argue that the Bergsonism of the *Cinema* books has at its heart a holism where the heterogeneous whole is constituted through the differentiation of actual lives in the course of affective encounters, this chapter systematically examines the crucial concepts that enable Deleuze to make this transition. In order to understand these concepts, we must begin with a reflection on the criticism Deleuze makes of Spinoza – the criticism that leads to the aforementioned challenge.

Deleuze's Nietzschean critique of Spinoza

In the course of his discussion of Nietzsche in *Difference and Repetition*, Deleuze develops the only substantive criticism he makes of Spinoza. Although this criticism receives a mere two pages of explicit attention in *Difference and Repetition*, I argue that it is central to understanding Deleuze's subsequent arguments for the reciprocity of the virtual and the actual. Deleuze's criticism of Spinoza concerns the determination of the identity and essence of the finite modes; although substance is constituted heterogeneously and through differential relations, the determination of the degrees of power which characterize modes proceeds through the expression of the constitution of an identity which is not of the modes. That is, he objects to a monism that prioritizes the identity of the one over the differentiation of the multiple; as such, Deleuze seems to be arguing for a strict reciprocity between the virtual and the actual. The determination of the virtual whole must be reciprocal, in the strongest sense, with the differentiation of actual beings. It is, thus, impossible to overstate the importance of Deleuze's objection to a monism that privileges the identity of an ideal unity over an actual plurality. The criticism he offers in no way constitutes a rejection of Spinoza; it does, however, represent an acknowledgement that the demands of a philosophy of difference go beyond the resources that Spinoza's monism alone can provide. Deleuze's claim is that Spinoza allows substance to retain an independence from the modes insofar as the modes only have existence through their reference to substance while substance exists solely through the expression of its own essence. Deleuze turned to Spinoza in search of an ontology that would drive his Bergsonian project; an ontology, that is, that would make it possible to think difference as a generative principle. In doing so, Deleuze was able to thoroughly describe modes as expressions of degrees of power that participate univocally in the constitution of an active, common sense of Being. Being is active and common precisely because everything that the modes express is expressed of substance's univocal attributes. Unfortunately, however, this prize is won at the cost of a metaphysical system in which the modes are dependent on a prior identity that remains ontologically distinct from them. Deleuze criticizes Spinoza because substance – that *of which* the modes are said – remains independent. In Deleuze's own words, as expressions of substance, 'the modes are dependent on substance, but as though on something other than themselves'.[3]

Making substance turn around the modes will, Deleuze contends, require 'a more general categorical reversal according to which being is said of becoming, identity of that which is different, the one of the multiple, etc.'.[4] This categorical reversal confronts the asymmetry of substance and modes by foregrounding a relationship of reciprocal determination between a mode and the degree of power it expresses. Insofar as it is the expression of a relational degree, a mode can only be considered the transitory description of a set of relations which constitutes its ground. That is, as a being, a mode can only be said of that which becomes. *Difference and Repetition*'s invocation of the Nietzschean concept of the eternal return represents the introduction of a new way of thinking about time that turns on the repeated expressions of degrees of power. Deleuze's complaint about Spinoza is that modes – as expressions of that which differs (degrees of power) – are always said of an identity that remains consistent through all its changes. In other words, we could always say that the degrees of power are degrees *of God's power*. Within the Nietzschean categorical reversal, Deleuze wants the very identity said of the modes to be said only of the differences in power expressed by the modes; this reversal is the beginning of the form of time Deleuze calls *repetition*: '[A]n identity, produced by difference, is determined as "repetition"'.[5] In order to explicate the workings of this form of time, the remainder of this chapter will focus on Deleuze's reading of Bergson, beginning with a discussion of how future events relate to the conditions of their actualization.

Bergson's critique of the possible and the real and the genesis of novelty

Deleuze develops the categorical reversal of difference and identity through a return to Bergson and the retrieval of a conceptual coupling that will allow him to redefine the ontological status of powers and modes: the *virtual* and the *actual*. As well as emphasizing a qualitative difference between powers and modes, the use of the concepts of the virtual and the actual also allows Deleuze to affirm that powers and beings are fully real:

> The virtual is opposed not to the real but to the actual. *The virtual is fully real insofar as it is virtual.* ... Indeed, the virtual must be defined as strictly part of the real object – as though the object had one part of itself in the virtual into which it plunged as though into an objective dimension. ... The reality of the virtual consists of the differential elements and the relations along with the singular points which correspond to them. The reality of the virtual is structure. We must avoid giving the elements and relations which form a structure an actuality which they do not have, and withdrawing from them a reality which they have.[6]

Deleuze affirms this coupling of virtual and actual against the more common coupling of the possible and the real on the grounds that thinking in terms of the realization of possibilities denies the reality of the possible and then attempts to describe the passing into reality of possibilities through a subtractive process. This subtraction occurs because the possible is supposed to be ideally infinite – that is, it contains everything whose idea does not contain logical contradiction – and the process of realization is one whereby 'some possibles are supposed to be repulsed or thwarted, while others "pass" into the real'.[7] In this scenario, what actually occurs is a diminished realization of what is possible insofar as the real contains *less* than the possible. Against this, Deleuze argues that because of the difference between the actual and the virtual, the virtual has a reality of its own that is neither diminished nor represented in the actual:

> [T]he virtual cannot proceed by elimination or limitation, but must *create* its own lines of actualization in positive acts ... [because] the actual does *not* resemble the virtuality it embodies. It is difference that is primary in the process of actualization – the difference between the virtual from which we begin and the actual at which we arrive, and also the difference between the complementary lines according to which actualization takes place.[8]

In setting out the opposition of these two conceptual pairs (virtual and actual, possible and real), Deleuze glosses an early article by Bergson on the problems of thinking in terms of possibility and reality. In 'The Possible and the Real', Bergson affirms that 'reality is created as something unforeseeable and new'[9] and argues that the processes by which possibilities are realized are, by virtue of being 'subtractive', unable to account for this novelty. Bergson's first point is that the possible has only ever been conceptualized in terms of a retrospective representation of the real such that, when we describe what might be possible in the future, we trade on an error in how we conceive the past. Bergson's claim is that when we conceive the past as a representation of the present, we construct a series of images of what must have been possible given what is currently real:

> As reality is created as something unforeseeable and new, its image is reflected behind it into the indefinite past; thus it finds that it has from all time been possible, but it is at this precise moment that it begins to have been always possible, and that is why ... its possibility, which does not precede its reality, will have preceded it once the reality has appeared.[10]

For Deleuze this is the first of two rules to which the process of realization is subject: *the rule of resemblance*.[11] Where Bergson contends that a concept of the possible as something that resembles the real cannot account for the novelty of life, Deleuze is even more emphatic and suggests that this rule violates a robust conception of difference and consequently renders actual existence the arbitrary occurrence of an idea in space and time. Deleuze asks, 'What difference can there be between the existent and the non-existent if the non-existent is already possible, already included in the concept and having all the characteristics that the concept confers upon it as a possibility?'[12] Insofar as the possible refers to 'the form of the identity in the concept'[13] since, 'from the point of view of the concept, there is no difference between the possible and the real',[14] Deleuze suggests that 'it is difficult to understand what existence adds to the concept when all it does is double like with like'.[15] Deleuze echoes Bergson when he says that the possible is 'retroactively fabricated in the image of what resembles it'.[16] By contrast, the relationship between the virtual and the actual is the expression of difference; insofar as it is the actualization of a power, *actuality must differ from the virtual*. That is, actualization must proceed by differenciation. The second rule that follows from the first is *the rule of limitation*. When we ask after the future as though its potential events were aligned with possibilities subsisting in the present, we project our mistake about the past and the possible into our conception of the future. If, as Bergson suggests, the possible is generated through the retrospective reflection of reality, the possible must, accordingly, be generated as more than the real. There is a common illusion regarding possibilities and realization, Bergson contends, and it consists in the assumption that the real adds something – namely existence – to the possible. Contrary to this illusion, Bergson contends that realization is, in fact, a subtractive process. The conception of possibility criticized by Bergson and Deleuze construes the passage from possibility to reality as subtractive insofar as it requires the real in order to generate an idea of what is possible. Thus possibility necessarily consists of more than the existence that realizes it.[17]

In his *Philosophy and the Adventure of the Virtual*, Keith Ansell-Pearson takes up this issue in the context of a broader reading of the history of ideas regarding biology, evolution and natural selection. Ansell-Pearson notes that this conception of possibility leads to the belief that there is a reservoir of sorts – a store of possibilities – that supplies the particular possibility that passes into reality as that present becomes past and is supplanted by a new present. Accordingly, the current present is assumed to consist in a similar store of possibilities and the future to consist of one of these possibilities, which is selected and realized. This conception of duration as the repeated selection of images of past realities according to a mechanistic selection process – a process that is wholly given and indifferent to the images upon which it operates – is, Ansell-Pearson claims, precisely the target of Bergson's critique.[18] This process of selection is also Deleuze's target when he describes the rule of limitation at work on realization: '[R]ealization involves a limitation by which some possibles are supposed to be repulsed or thwarted, while others "pass" into the real.'[19] Overturning such an illusion is precisely what Deleuze wants to achieve through the virtual and the actual. In addition to being actualized through a differenciation, processes of actualization must involve genuine creation. If actualization is the expression of difference, then it will render existence genuinely new and not the merely arbitrary realization of a possibility: 'Actual terms never resemble the singularities they incarnate. In this sense, *actualisation ... is always a genuine creation*.'[20]

Rather than describing the movement from past to present to future as a straight line whereby each implies a storehouse of ideal possibilities from which an idea is selected and brought into existence, Deleuze conceives the relationship between the virtual and the actual dialectically. Virtual and actual respond to, and are determined by, each other. The virtual, on his account, is a set of conditions which subsist in the actual world and constitute a problem to which an instance of actualization is a response or solution. That is, the actual is a plane composed of events of actualization which do not add existence to an idea but which 'solve' a virtual problem. This dialectic is the heart of Deleuze's ontology, and it is to this discussion that we now turn.

The dialectic of problems: The virtual and actualization

When he develops his conception of the virtual and the actual, Deleuze calls it a *dialectic of problems*; however, he is careful to distinguish his use of the word *dialectic* from Kantian or Hegelian senses of the concept when he notes that 'we do not mean any kind of circulation of opposing representations which would make them coincide in the identity of a concept'.[21] The dialectic in this case is inspired by the work of Albert Lautman, an early twentieth-century philosopher of mathematics. Lautman's conception of dialectic concerns the relationship between problems and solutions, which remain distinct. As Deleuze explains in *Difference and Repetition*,

> [A] problem has three aspects: its difference in kind from solutions; its transcendence in relation to the solutions that it engenders on the basis of its own determinant conditions; and its immanence in the solutions which cover it, the problem *being* the better resolved the more *it is* determined.[22]

The use of the term *transcendence*, while requiring explanation, does not present a problem for Deleuze's ontology of immanence. In a study on Lautman's influence on Deleuze, Simon Duffy notes that transcendence is used in a common sense way to describe the fact that the problems themselves are 'posed ... relative to the connections that are [only] likely to be supported by certain dialectical concepts'.[23] In other words, within a dialectic of problems and solutions, the problem is transcendent because it is given to the solution which must respond to it. It must be emphasized, however, that this transcendence of the problem does not imply an anteriority of the problem relative to its solution. As with the case of an attributive expression of sense which subsists in its expression without being reducible to either the attribute that expresses it or the substance of which it is said, the problem subsists in a solution that explicates it. That is, a problem cannot be reduced to its determination in a corresponding solution precisely because it is the conditions of the problem which engender a solution. However, it is not until a solution is actualized that the reality of the problem is made explicit. At the same time, the problem is immanent in the solution because the extent to which it is able to be resolved hinges upon the terms of the solution's actualization. Since the problem *as such* only has reality insofar as it is explicated by a solution, it is said to be immanent in the solution, even though it is given to the solution that explicates it and is determined by conditions that go beyond the particular solution – that is, it is *transcendent*. For Deleuze, it is this dialectic of problems which governs the appearance of everything which makes up the world.

Deleuze takes on Bergson's rejection of the traditional conception of the realization of possibilities as a way of describing the relationship between a being and what that being can become. By appropriating Bergson's critique of the possible and the real, Deleuze argues against the concept of asymmetry between possibility and reality. He affirms an equality between beings and what they can become insofar as the actual state of an existing being and the subsistent conditions of its becoming are equally real. The difference between a being and the conditions of its becoming – between the actual and the virtual – is a difference in kind. Together their interaction accounts for the genesis and becoming of the world:

> It is sufficient to understand that the genesis takes place in time not between one actual term, however small, and another actual term, but between the virtual and its actualisation – in other words, it goes from the structure to its incarnation, from the conditions of a problem to the cases of solution, from the differential elements and their ideal connections to actual terms and diverse real relations which constitute at each moment the actuality of time. This is a genesis without dynamism, evolving necessarily in the element of a supra-historicity, a *static genesis* which may be understood as the correlate of the notion of *passive synthesis*, and which in turn illuminates that notion.[24]

Deleuze argues against the assumption that actual events follow each other sequentially. Actual events follow each other but their relationship is one of association, not causation.[25] The association of actual events proceeds dialectically and progresses through a virtual problem. This is an important argument to the extent that it reinforces Deleuze's claim that repetition produces novelty.[26] As this chapter progresses, we will see that the progression from one actual event to another proceeds via a complex process that Deleuze calls different/ciation: the determination of a virtual problem proceeds through differentiation and the actualization of a solution proceeds through differenciation. Because the dialectic of problems has these differential expressions driving it, and because the virtual and the actual are defined by their qualitative difference, neither the concept of the present nor the conditions it determines as the ground of the future are sufficient to provide the idea of a future, actual event. Indeed, even when actual events resemble each other, this resemblance is always grounded in difference. Thus 'new' events are generated as ontologically novel. However, in order to confront these complex issues, we must first understand what Deleuze means by *multiplicity*, given that it is the structure of the problem and the way that Deleuze is able to describe the logic of the association of sets as immanent.

Multiplicities

In reading Spinoza, Deleuze persistently characterizes substance as an intensive multiplicity; it is always a heterogeneously generated system which remains numerically one. As outlined earlier, however, even though Spinoza's metaphysics delivers a conception of substance as multiplicitous, it contains a pitfall insofar as the identity of the multiplicity remains independent of the very modes which give it its existence. To avoid this pitfall, Deleuze suggests that 'instead of using the one and the multiple as adjectives, one substitutes the substantive multiplicities in the [genesis of] form: there is nothing that is one, there is nothing that is multiple, everything is multiplicities'.[27] As with Lautman and the dialectic of problems, Deleuze foregrounds a figure in the history of mathematics, Bernhard Riemann, in order to rethink the concept of multiplicity.[28] Riemann's geometry takes up the issue of the constitution of space as such. As Arkady Plotnitsky describes it, a manifold is a conglomerate of local spaces which can be mapped infinitesimally through a Cartesian or Euclidean map – that is, by a single, consistent co-ordinate map – while the map itself cannot be accounted for by Cartesian or Euclidean space.[29] In other words, every point in a space has a local neighbourhood that can be treated as Euclidean; however, because the sites of the syntheses of these local spaces are themselves mappable spaces, the overall manifold cannot be treated as Euclidean. The significance of Riemann's work is clearly stated in *A Thousand Plateaus*: 'It was a decisive event when the mathematician Riemann uprooted the multiple from its predicate state and made it into a noun, "multiplicity".'[30] Deleuze and Guattari write that 'Riemannian space at its most general thus presents itself as an amorphous of pieces that are juxtaposed but not attached to each other.'[31] 'Multiplicity' does not denote a given system that would unify the one and the many, it describes the generation of a system from the organization of the many as such.

In his reading of Bergson, Deleuze foregrounds a particular conception of multiplicity: continuous multiplicities. A continuous multiplicity is a space that finds the principle of its metric in the phenomena that occur across its surface.

This idea of a space determined by the events that occur across its surface is of particular interest to Bergson; however, where Bergson diverges significantly from Riemann is, as Miguel de Beistegui points out, in the insistence that continuous multiplicities belong primarily to the order of duration and not space in virtue of the fact that the terms by which one would map an ongoing duration are continually encroaching on and dissolving into one another in a way that resists the kind of quantification and division possible with an elapsed duration.[32] The question of time and duration is an issue we will defer until later in this chapter; however, it is important to emphasize that Deleuze's and Bergson's respective interests converge on this idea of multiplicities which cannot be quantified and submitted to an abstractly generated metrical principle. As Deleuze stresses, it is crucial to conceptualize the system of the multiple in such a way that it is the multiple *as such* which generates its own principle. Indeed, the final clause of this passage from A *Thousand Plateaus* could be read as a direct response to *Expressionism* insofar as Deleuze's reading of Spinoza allows an external term – God or nature – to determine the unity of the modes. The project for Deleuze now is to generate that term from the relationship of the modes understood as a multiplicity.

The concept of multiplicity enables Deleuze to address this problem by making it possible to move from the dialectic of problems to the conception of time as the repetition of actualizations. This is because lived time for Deleuze is constituted precisely by repetitions in the actual world, and yet these actualizations do not occur from one actual term to another but through the movement from the generation of a problem or Idea as a response to a set of actual terms, to the generation of a new set of actual terms as a response to the problem. Multiplicity is an important concept precisely because it is the structure of the problem: a 'structure or an Idea is a "complex theme", an internal multiplicity – in other words, a system of multiple, non-localisable connections between differential elements which is incarnated in real relations and actual terms'.[33] This concept is crucial to the conception of time that drives so much of his work, and so Deleuze is careful to establish the conditions under which ideas or multiplicities are generated.[34] Of course, multiplicities have no modal existence. In describing the generation of a multiplicity, one is in fact describing the conditions under which actual terms determine the formulation of a problem to which a later actualization is a response.

Deleuze tells us that for a multiplicity to emerge three conditions must be met; first, the multiplicity's constitutive elements must retain no assignable function. That is, as the virtual side of the actually existing term, these elements must be stripped of sensible form or signification and must lose all similarity to the actuality to which they correspond. Indeed, it is this first condition that leads to what Deleuze, in the *Cinema* books, calls a *centre of indetermination* precisely because, bearing no similarity to the actual term, the virtual term as such does not presuppose a prior identity which defines its form. The second condition concerns the reciprocal determination of the elements of the multiplicity and the relations in which it participates. This is the aforementioned importance of the continuous multiplicity; the relations between the elements of a multiplicity which, 'whether they characterise the multiplicity globally or proceed by the juxtaposition of neighbouring regions', generate the metric of the multiplicity.[35] Yet, at the same time, the elements of the multiplicity must be defined intrinsically. That is, the elements of the multiplicity are only relevant to the multiplicity by virtue of their participation in the determination of the multiplicity. Deleuze insists upon this exhaustive reciprocity so as to resist any independence either on the part of the multiplicity or its elements. Finally, the third condition for the emergence of a multiplicity is the event of the actualization of a differential relation. These, then, are the three conditions that must be met in order for an Idea – a *problem* – to be defined structurally. We see in all three conditions the interaction of the actual term and the problem to which it responds – first through their difference and then through their reciprocal determination – and, indeed, the final condition is precisely the grounding issue for the final section of this chapter. The multiplicity is not prior to the existence of actual objects; rather, the pair virtual problem/actual solution is simultaneous. For all that their respective reality is formally distinct, the virtual and actual are existentially indistinguishable. In other words, the multiplicity does not exist in the absence of the terms that actualize it, nor can an actual term exist in the absence of the 'differential elements' and 'ideal connections' that condition and constitute it. Deleuze's summary of the issue drives at precisely this interactive simultaneity:

> For a potential or virtual object, to be actualised is to create divergent lines which correspond to – without resembling – a virtual multiplicity. The virtual possesses the reality of a task to be performed or a problem to be solved: it is the problem which orientates, conditions and engenders solutions, but these do not resemble the conditions of the problem. ... Difference and repetition in the virtual ground the movement of actualisation, of differenciation as creation. They are thereby substituted for the identity and the resemblance of the possible, which inspires only a pseudo-movement, the false movement of realisation understood as abstract limitation.[36]

So far in this chapter I have argued that the more familiar terms of Deleuze's vocabulary – virtual, actual, multiplicity – are elements of his attempts to transform his Spinozist inheritance into a robust philosophy of difference. We saw in Chapter 2 that Deleuze inherits from Spinoza a form of holism in which the one and the many are generated dynamically as the forms and objects of attributive expressions. By virtue of this dynamism, the whole is conceived as a virtual multiplicity with no existence outside or beyond the many by which it is expressed. However, Deleuze still considers Spinoza's ontology problematic because it conceives the production of the modes as the expression of the constitution of the essence of something other than themselves. Consequently, the differentiation of the modes is reduced to the arrangement of diversity, and this diversity is always referred to an external identity. Deleuze's philosophy of difference, however, demands that substance correspond to an actuality that expresses it without resembling it. In other words, Deleuze wants differential relations to drive his ontology – the genesis of beings and identities must be expressions of difference – and so the whole and individuals must be qualitatively distinct. This is why Deleuze characterizes the relationship between the virtual and the actual as a dialectic of problems: the constitution of a virtual multiplicity – a problem or an Idea – is a step in a dialectical relationship wherein neither term resembles the other. This is why we must turn at this point to examine Deleuze's famous *three syntheses of time*; the simultaneity of the past and future, and their synthesis in a complex process of differen*t*/*c*iation, enables Deleuze to conceive the actual present as the 'disjunctive synthesis'[37] of two movements of differentiation.

The three syntheses of time and correspondence without resemblance

In the *Ethics*, Spinoza argues that '[t]he essence of things produced by God does not involve existence'.[38] Spinoza is here referring to the ontological argument which he had deployed earlier to argue that the existence of God follows necessarily from his essence; this time, however, insofar as the things produced by God are the finite modes, existence does not follow from their essence – that is, the degree of power that characterizes a finite mode does not cause its existence. We saw in Chapter 2 that this was an important part of how Deleuze argued that God's self-causation was simultaneously the production of a modal universe, and it is an insight that continues to be important as his ontology transforms. This is why, when Deleuze recasts a mode and its essence as a solution and a problem, he argues that the two correspond, and respond to and determine each other, in a dialectical relationship, even though their correspondence never entails causation. That is, actual solutions *respond* to virtual problems, but the problems never cause their solutions. Thus, Deleuze attempts to account for their reciprocity in a way that portrays their correspondence as a dialectic driven by differentiation. When he challenges himself to conceive time as a series of repetitions that would realize univocity, he does so in an effort to carry out the categorical reversal necessary to transform Spinoza's ontology. Of course, working out this concept is also crucial to the reciprocity of individuals and the whole in the Bergsonism of the *Cinema* books; this dialectic of problems enables Deleuze to characterize individuals as the expression of a differential relationship which simultaneously generates a whole.

Deleuze begins his formulation of this correspondence in *Difference and Repetition* when he grounds the three syntheses of time in the present understood as a concrete particular that assumes a power of thinking in a living body that functions as the site of temporal syntheses. With this move, Deleuze reformulates the degrees of power of *Expressionism* as the folding of immanent powers into the constitutive events of living bodies. The way Deleuze proceeds in this reformulation of the Spinozist image of the whole owes significantly to his claim in *Expressionism* that the attribution of an essence to substance must be apprehended as such by substance; in other words, attribution must not only be an attribution *to* substance but also be an attribution *for* substance. The way Deleuze deploys this duality of *to* and *for* bears a remarkable similarity to his description of the first synthesis in terms of the anticipatory behaviour of the imagination. The deduction of this anticipatory behaviour is suggested in his early reading of Hume's anti-Cartesian view of the mind and its faculties – the first chapter of *Empiricism and Subjectivity* – and this influence reappears in the second chapter of *Difference and Repetition*. Deleuze begins his reflections on time with the Humean suggestion that repetition is not a case of change undergone by a thing but, rather, a transformation brought about in the mind which contemplates the thing.[39] Deleuze names the first synthesis *habit*, even though it is not a situation where a mind is in the habit of doing something. Rather, this habit is constitutive of the mind that contemplates. We must not make the mistake of assuming the priority of a mind that contemplates. Deleuze argues that the necessary precondition of a lived present is a passive synthesis of previous experiences into an anticipation that is geared towards the future. It is this synthesis, this *contemplation*, that earns the name *habit*.[40] Habit gives time its direction from the past to the future. As Deleuze says, 'Passive synthesis or contraction is essentially asymmetrical: it goes from the past to the future in the present, thus from the particular to the general, thereby imparting direction to the arrow of time.'[41]

When Deleuze describes this synthesis as contraction, he means it quite literally. The imagination is defined as a 'contractile power'.[42] Deleuze reads Hume as saying that similar cases (cases similar to the one at hand in the present) are grounded in the imagination that 'like a sensitive plate, ... retains one case when the other appears. It contracts cases, elements, agitations or homogeneous instants and grounds these in an internal qualitative impression endowed with a certain weight.'[43] Deleuze's claim here is appropriately concrete: given the traces of previous experiences that remain within the imagination, there will be the anticipation that future cases of similar events will be consistent with previous experiences. Deleuze calls the contraction of these traces into an anticipation *passive* because it is an automatic synthesis that makes the contemplative mind possible, not an anticipation that is generated by an already existing contemplating mind. This synthesis, however, has numerous levels and, as such, goes beyond the mere passive contraction of past events into an anticipation of the future. Deleuze argues that

> [w]e must ... distinguish not only the forms of repetition in relation to passive synthesis but also the levels of passive synthesis and the combinations of these levels with one another and with active syntheses. All of this forms a rich domain of *signs* which always envelop heterogeneous elements and animate behaviour. Each contraction, each passive synthesis, constitutes a sign which is interpreted or deployed in active syntheses.[44]

The first synthesis accounts for the passive contraction in the imagination of previous sensations into an anticipation of a future state of affairs. At the same time, this synthesis also accounts for the ways in which levels of contraction are themselves synthesized in a series of signs that determine the problem to which actions respond. Deleuze offers a preliminary description of active syntheses at this point: the manner in which sensation and perception – as well as all the traits of an entity that are superimposed onto a given passive synthesis: 'need and heredity, learning and instinct, intelligence and memory'[45] – combine in the generation of an action that the entity in question enacts as a response to a certain *problem* arising from a contemplation or habit. This connection between the first synthesis of time and the determination of problems is crucial. In *Difference and Repetition*, Deleuze suggests precisely this direction: 'To contemplate is to question. Is it not the peculiarity of questions to "draw" a response?'[46]

The second synthesis concerns the passive synthesis of the whole of the past that has no immediate importance to the synthesis of habit. Deleuze claims that in order for the synthesis of habit to occur, there must also be a simultaneous synthesis of the entirety of the past such that the past retains its reality while remaining distinct from the contraction that occurs in the imagination. It is only by virtue of this distinction of the whole of the past from the passive synthesis of habit that the elements synthesized in habit are themselves differentiated from all of the other virtual sensations from which the present contraction must distinguish itself. Put simply, the past, as a dimension of the present, must go unattended and the present must pass in order for time to have a direction more proper than that established by the anticipatory contractions of the first synthesis: 'It is not that the present is a dimension of time: the present alone exists. Rather, synthesis constitutes time as a living present, and the past and the future as dimensions of this present. This synthesis is none the less intratemporal, which means that this present passes.'[47]

The second synthesis is concerned with the limits of a present present and the way the conditions of a passive synthesis relate to the needs and power of a being: 'The present extends between two eruptions of need, and coincides with the duration of a contemplation.'[48] Deleuze claims that 'we must distinguish the foundation from the ground'[49] and so, while this originary synthesis of habit 'constitutes the life of the passing present', it is still grounded by another, 'fundamental', synthesis which 'constitutes the being of the past' and in so doing causes the present to pass.[50] This, of course, is the notorious discussion of 'a "past in general" that is not the particular past of a particular present but that is like an ontological element, a past that is eternal and for all time, the condition of the "passage" of every particular present'[51] that appears in all of Deleuze's discussions of time from *Bergsonism* on. Where the first synthesis is concerned with the operations of habit, the second concerns the passive synthesis of memory against which habit distinguishes itself. This issue is grounded in an element of Deleuze's reading of Bergson; in order for the present to pass – if the present is to become past – then there must be an element to its characteristic relations which constitute it as having already passed. In other words, if the present is to pass, it must already contain its past as a dimension of itself. Deleuze notes in *Bergsonism*: '[O]f the present we must say at every instant that it "was", and of the past, that it "is".'[52] If the present is the site of activity and of pure becoming, then the past is impassive and does nothing, but it *subsists*

– with all the reality proper to that which subsists – in the present as the being of the present:

> [T]he present *is not*; rather, it is pure becoming, always outside itself. It *is* not, but it acts. Its proper element is not being but the active or the useful. The past, on the other hand, has ceased to act or be useful. But it has not ceased to be. Useless and inactive, impassive, it IS, in the full sense of the word: It is identical with being in itself. It should not be said that it 'was', since it is the in-itself of being, and the form under which being is preserved in itself.[53]

The meaning of the past in general is then to give a milieu in which the present expresses itself as past present (representation) or present present: '[I]t is as if the past were trapped between two presents: the one which it has been and the one in relation to which it is past. The past is not the former present itself but the element in which we focus upon the latter.'[54]

Thus, when Deleuze conceives the second synthesis of time, he characterizes it as the passive synthesis of the whole of the past in general such that it constitutes the milieu of the being of the present becoming. We expect then that the third synthesis – for all its infamous difficulty – must deal with a very specific problem; how is it that a contraction of the past corresponds to a future-oriented action? In other words, the first and second syntheses address two issues; the past must be contracted as what persists and subsists in the present (second synthesis) and simultaneously must be organized in such a way that certain elements of the past are contracted into an anticipation of the future (first synthesis). For Deleuze there are then two levels or two repetitions, the first being 'a repetition of successive independent elements or instants' (*habit*) and the second 'a repetition of the Whole on diverse coexisting levels' (*memory*).[55] And with these two syntheses Deleuze continues to develop his conception of active synthesis: 'Active synthesis, therefore, has two correlative – albeit non-symmetrical – aspects: reproduction and reflection, remembrance and recognition, memory and understanding.'[56]

How then do these syntheses relate to each other and generate an action? No answer to this question will yield the ground for predicting which actions will come about. The actions to come are indeterminate in the sense that the determination of a future is, in fact, the actualization of that future. Consequently, the third synthesis does not concern a specific determined action; it concerns, rather, an action's determinability, and it is for this reason that the third synthesis can only be described in terms of the conditions it gives to the first and second syntheses such that their correspondence or association is expressed in an action. This is why Deleuze emphasizes that '[r]epetition is a condition of action before it is a concept of reflection'.[57] Certainly, this third synthesis – the 'empty form of time'[58] – concerns the necessary openness of the future with regard to habit and memory. James Williams notes that the openness characteristic of the third synthesis of time is a necessary presupposition precisely because it is the condition for generating the genuinely novel,[59] and so the third synthesis turns on a radical cut, a 'caesura', between past events that are representable and a future that is not given.

Deleuze describes this synthesis as having three characteristics. The first is the caesura that has just been described. The second characteristic of this cut is the need for *all* the events synthesized in the pure past to be cut from *all* the events that can become the future. In other words, the caesura must affirm the difference between the actual past – its image and representations – and the virtual in response to which the future will emerge. Deleuze describes the cut as generating a movement towards the genuinely new by invoking metaphors – the explosion of the sun, patricide or deicide – that describe the genesis of time's direction in virtue of the way 'the symbolic image ... draws together the caesura, the before and the after'.[60] But this image is so radical that it is incomprehensible – 'too big for me'[61] – and consequently the calling forth of a future which cannot be given. Indeed, Deleuze says that it 'matters little whether or not the event itself occurs ... so long as [those involved] experience the image of the act as too big for them'.[62] It is not the radicality of the event that matters in some objective sense; it is the experience, the apprehension and comprehensibility of the caesura that is crucial.

Finally, the third characteristic of this synthesis is that time is synthesized into two series with respect to the caesura. What is synthesized in the genesis of these series is the ordering of the events that, on the one hand, cannot return; that lack the power to be of any consequence to what is to come. And, on the other hand, there is the series of events that return; the events that, in virtue of being relived in the cut, are affirmed by it. These moments, whether they return or not, are events both of the past (*memory*) and of the future (*anticipation*), but they must not be confused with the past and future events of a historical time. Rather, what returns, whether it is the memory of something actual or what subsists virtually, is that which expresses a power of difference.

To understand why Deleuze affirms degrees of difference as the criteria for selection in repetition, we must return to his discussion of Ideas and the virtual and the actual. Of course, this is difference as it has always been discussed and therefore must be designated not as *something* which is affirmed but as a set of relations affirmed by the third synthesis. Difference in this case is the complex process of different/ciation: 'Whereas differentiation determines the virtual content of the Idea as problem, differenciation expresses the actualisation of this virtual and the constitution of solutions.'[63] When Deleuze describes the virtual and the actual – the differen*t*iated and the differen*c*iated – he does so by describing an object as double and characterized by asymmetrical 'images' that do not resemble each other.[64] On the one hand, differentiation – the determination of the Idea insofar as it is virtual – is complete but acts only on the existence and the distribution of the singular points that constitute the Idea. The nature of these points is determined by the shape and distribution of actual beings. On the other hand, the progression and determination of the virtual determine the form of an already operative actual side of the object whose constitutive parts are differenciated to express a response to a given Idea. What is differenciated then connects with other differenciated objects and generates a higher order being:

> [C]omplete determination carries out the differentiation of singularities, but it bears only upon their existence and their distribution. The nature of these singular points is specified only by the form of the neighbouring integral curves – in other words, by virtue of the actual or differenciated species and spaces … every structure has a purely logical, ideal or dialectical time. However, this virtual time itself determines a time of differenciation, or rather rhythms or different times of actualisation which correspond to the relations and singularities of the structure and, for their part, measure the passage from virtual to actual. … Each differenciation is a local integration or a local solution which then connects with others in the overall solution.[65]

It is with this logic of different/ciation, and the deduction of these three passive syntheses that are implicit in the dialectic of problems, that Deleuze discovers that underneath historical, linear time lies a profound notion of cyclical time. This cyclical time, in virtue of its Nietzschean heritage, is called eternal return. However, this is not return in the sense of a repetition of what has come before but an expression of power insofar as it is an affirmation of difference (different/ciation). But, of course, this is not 'merely' a philosophy of time, it is a description of what and how beings become in an ontology that always implies a differentiated whole: 'In this manner, the ground has been superseded by a groundlessness, a universal ungrounding which turns upon itself and causes only the yet-to-come to return.'[66]

While there are many ways of approaching this discussion of time that I have necessarily excluded from this discussion,[67] I will close this chapter with a brief discussion that enables us to anticipate a move to the *Cinema* books. The ontological issue which unites the concerns of *Deleuze and Ethology* is Deleuze's changing conception of the reciprocity of individuals and the whole. And so, we must consider how this chapter's discussion of some well-known Deleuzian concepts – the virtual, multiplicity and a philosophy of time – transform Spinozist concepts – essence, univocity, substance – in order to enact a categorical reversal of being and becoming.

Conclusion: Syntheses and the renewal of holism

Given that substance can no longer be conceived as a univocal being that is independent of the expressions that modify it, how must we describe the whole? Deleuze argues that the answer is *multiplicity* provided that we understand it in its 'substantive form':

> In this Reimannian [sic] usage of the word 'multiplicity' (taken up by Husserl, and again by Bergson) the utmost importance must be attached to the substantive form: multiplicity must not designate a combination of the many and the one, but rather an organisation belonging to the many as such, which has no need whatsoever of unity in order to form a system.[68]

If there is anything to justify this comparison between multiplicity and substance, it is a moment in *Bergsonism* where Deleuze, echoing Spinoza, claims that 'duration is like a naturing nature (*nature naturante*), and matter a natured nature (*nature naturée*)'.[69] Deleuze characterizes the second synthesis (the past in general) as an active sense of the world, or the world described in terms of the infinite attributes – that is, the attributes of substance that express an eternal and infinite essence. On the other hand, by comparing matter with nature understood as passive, Deleuze identifies matter with the modes that correspond to the sense of these attributive expressions of the essence of substance. This is to say that Deleuze's interpretation of Bergson employs a distinction between duration and matter that is comparable to the conception of the distinction between an actual mode and the degree of relational power that characterizes it that is at the heart of his reading Spinoza. This comparison is instructive because it suggests that, just as a mode expresses a degree of power in an actual state of affairs, we should read matter as the determinate expression of duration. However, there is an important difference as well; in reading Spinoza, Deleuze has the univocity of the attributes to guarantee the correspondence between modal essences and existing modes. Conversely, with the schema he adapts from Bergson, Deleuze turns to the logic of multiplicities to develop the third synthesis that guarantees the correspondence between matter (*habit*) and duration (*memory*).

If matter and the whole are equivalent to the correspondence between existing modes and their essences, we must bear in mind Deleuze's comment in *Difference and Repetition* where he at first seems to dismiss talk of essences when he says that '[i]deas are by no means essences. In so far as they are the objects of Ideas, problems belong on the side of events, affections or accidents rather than on that of theorematic essences.'[70] However, Deleuze quickly qualifies this remark by redefining the work essences must do in the ethology he seeks to develop:

> The events and singularities of the Idea do not allow any positing of an essence as 'what the thing is'. No doubt, if one insists, the word 'essence' might be preserved, but only on condition of saying that the essence is precisely the accident, the event, the sense; not simply the contrary of what is ordinarily called the essence but the contrary of the contrary: multiplicity is no more appearance than essence, no more multiple than one.[71]

This passage does not undermine the importance of essences to this schema. What it does, rather, is gesture towards how the constitution of a modal essence – a degree of power – is itself an event. That is, the degree of power expressed in an actual mode – the problem as such – is not given but rather is the expression of a degree of a *becoming*. The juxtaposition of a virtual becoming of the degree of power with the actual becoming of the mode requires repeated emphasis if we are to understand how the renewed conception of the whole collaborates happily with the categorical reversal of being and becoming that Deleuze undertakes in light of Nietzsche. 'The whole', Deleuze states, 'constitutes a virtuality' and, understood as such, the whole – being neither one nor multiple – is a multiplicity.[72] Or, to be more precise, the whole is both one and multiple because the whole is an indefinite, yet wholly determinate, structure: '[T]he many is a multiplicity; even the one is a multiplicity. That the one is *a* multiplicity ... is enough to reject back-to-back adjectival propositions of the one-many and many-one type.'[73] The description of the whole as a virtuality recalls Chapter 2's invocation of a form of distributive holism wherein the whole was described as lacking qualitative unity – a whole that concerned the 'the "each" rather than the "all"',[74] to borrow Christian Kerslake's phrase – in order to suggest a universality that was concerned more with the distribution of particulars than with a supervening collectivity. Deleuze argues that 'a monistic field is indeed a field inhabited by multiplicities ... there is nothing that is one, there is nothing that is multiple, everything is multiplicities'.[75]

To put it another way, when Deleuze read Spinoza, he extracted a concept of the whole – substance, or, God *or* nature – that was constituted in the same event and in the same sense as the modal universe was produced. But, as we have seen, the problem with this conception is that the identity of the whole determines the differentiation of the modes. He returns to Hume, Nietzsche and Bergson in *Difference and Repetition* – for he had written on all three before writing *Expressionism* – in order to confront the challenge of reversing this categorical hierarchy of identity and difference. I have argued in this chapter that he undertakes this reversal through the conception of a being and its power as reciprocal – the virtual and the actual; association as the juxtaposition of events that determine the structure of the space of their association in the event of their association – multiplicity; and the association of the whole and individuals as occurring through complex processes of different/ciation – repetition in the syntheses of time. This means that the identity of the whole is determined as the distributive systematicity that is immanent to the differentiation of its parts. In the *Cinema* books, Deleuze characterizes the immanence of the whole as the reality of the relations that subsist in the affective continuum differentiated by actual lives. Indeed, from the point of view of the Bergsonism of the *Cinema* books, the definite article in *the whole* is misleading. In his reading of Bergson's theses on movement, Deleuze argues that the distinctions between actual beings are 'artificial'[76] and that the whole is the subsistence of the reality of the relational nature of these artificially delineated beings that stops their separation from each other ever becoming too robust. He argues that the whole 'is not a closed set, but on the contrary that by virtue of which the set is never absolutely closed, never completely sheltered, that which keeps it open somewhere as if by the finest thread which attaches it to the rest of the universe'.[77]

That is, in the *Cinema* books, Deleuze takes the subsistence and immanence of the whole to the point of arguing that it is not a closed set which contains all but is an element or sense of the reality of a set that guarantees its attachment to the sets around it, the sets with which it is always already in a relationship. In *Cinema*, Deleuze talks about bodies as relatively closed systems, or, more correctly, he describes relatively closed systems as bodies; a body in an ontological sense is any set of affective relations expressed – *embodied* – empirically in a relatively closed system. The whole is the virtual side of a body which guarantees that its delineation is relative and never absolute. The argument Deleuze makes in *Cinema* is that bodies are the site of the interaction and reciprocal determination of virtual and actual relations: on the one side is the determination of a degree of power and on the other is the actualization of this degree in a set of sensible relations. To make more sense of these ideas, Chapter 4 will explore how *affection* replaces *attribution* in Deleuze's horizontal holism. Central to this discussion will be an elucidation of how affection connects a degree of power with an empirical body.

4

Images and affect

The *Cinema* books written by Deleuze in the 1980s introduce a concreteness to his metaphysics and transform the philosophy of being into a philosophy of life – mark his philosophy's transition from ontology to ethology, that is – by presenting an account of the affective relations of finite beings. What is significant about the *Cinema* books is that, through the turn to cinema, Deleuze has the tools to describe his ontology from the point of view of the particular beings who inhabit the world, and it is this shift in emphasis that I suggest ought to be at the heart of philosophical ethology. *Cinema 1* focuses on sensible relations that are presented in terms of the continuity of perception, affection and action, and, from the point of view of the evolution of Deleuze's ontology, affection is presented as doing the work attribution did in his reading of Spinoza. Even with this grounding in his work on Spinoza, however, this chapter explores the ways in which the *Cinema* books deepen and extend Deleuze's reading of Bergson. Indeed, the following discussion turns on one of the most crucial concepts Deleuze adopts from Bergson: *images*. Bergson begins *Matter and Memory* with praise for George Berkeley who 'proved … that the secondary qualities of matter have at least as much reality as the primary qualities'.[1] Bergson praises Berkeley for arguing against the habit of assuming that the secondary properties of matter – the sensible properties that are '*immediately perceived by sense*'[2] (temperature, taste, odour, sound, colour, etc.) – are properties of objects and are independent of the subject of experience. Berkeley's mistake, according to Bergson, was to think this led to the denial of material objects per se. The concept of images that Deleuze inherits from Bergson was originally developed in response to this precise problem – that is, the problem of how to conceptualize the nature of an 'existence placed half-way between the "thing" and the "representation"'.[3] As such, Bergson's concept of images is crucial to the conversion of Deleuze's ontology into an ethology concerned with a relationality grounded in sensibility and affect.

This is an important step because it brings this narrative about his transforming ontology back into contact with the ethical side of the ethological project that interests this book. In Chapter 3, we saw how Deleuze qualified his holistic ontology by developing the conceptual tools to talk meaningfully about the whole as a multiplicity constituted as the expression of the degrees of power determined by the differentiation of the individual lives that participate in the whole. In other words, Deleuze developed the conceptual tools to 'make substance turn around the modes'.[4] In the Bergsonism of the *Cinema* books, Deleuze further transforms this holism, even as its logic continues to resemble the one he argues for in Spinoza insofar as it retains the logic of a doubly expressive operation. In Spinoza's case, it was the attributes that were doubly expressive – they simultaneously constituted the essence of God and contained the essences of the modal universe that was produced as an expression of the degree of the constitution of God. In the *Cinema* books, affection takes centre stage and constitutes the whole by expressing the affects that occupy the interval between perception and action. The other side of this expression is that, expressed as affects *as such* – that is, as affects per se rather than the experience of an event tied to a subject – they are expressed as degrees of power which subsist in the differentiation of actual lives and, taken together, these degrees of power constitute an immanent, heterogeneous multiplicity.

Consequently, each element of this chapter is focused on either explicating the sensible elements developed in this conversion of his ontology into a peculiar form of distributive holism – that is, the elements that make this a concrete philosophy of sensible relations – or elaborating how they are deployed in order to achieve this conversion. The fundamental element of this conversion is the image and, to understand how the image functions in this project, we need to begin with the way Deleuze develops a Bergsonian conception of division and continuity. This conception is developed in Deleuze's reading of Bergson's analysis of movement because it is here that Deleuze sets out the context for conceiving the continuity and relationality that underpins his entire ontology, and, with it, his ethology.

Movement and distinction

The Bergsonism of *Cinema 1* echoes Deleuze's treatment of Spinoza. His concern in relation to both philosophers is to conceptualize the nature of the qualitative variation of a virtual whole, the quantitative division among actual things, and

Images and Affect

the reciprocity between the two. In Bergson, Deleuze finds a theory of divisions that is similar to Spinoza's theory of distinctions. His reading of Bergson emphasizes the concept of images developed in *Matter and Memory* because it provides a conceptual vocabulary for describing the actual world as an affective continuum. Deleuze appropriates Bergson's conception of images as a tool that enables him to argue that the division between actual objects is quantitative but not real – 'artificial'[5] – because these existents presuppose a continuous, relational whole whose transformations they express. The similarity between Deleuze's Spinozism and his Bergsonism is that, in both cases, ostensibly distinct actual existents presuppose a qualitatively heterogeneous whole and express the relational degrees of this whole's constitution and transformation. The theory of divisions that Deleuze finds in Bergson's analyses of movement in the final chapter of *Creative Evolution* allows us to understand how images give him this conception of a transforming affective continuum. In the first chapter of *Cinema 1*, Deleuze presents these analyses as three theses which together set out an initial formulation of the reciprocity of individuals and the whole that grounds the ontology of images that he adapts from *Matter and Memory*.

Bergson's first thesis on movement concerns the problem that follows from a critical response to what Bergson sees as 'the absurd proposition, that movement is made of immobilities'.[6] Bergson argues that movement is poorly understood when it is conceived as the accretion of discrete units in space. Movement is not, for Bergson, 'a mere instantaneous juxtaposition in space'.[7] He argues that movement must be conceived continuously, as the '*transition*' between the points which express this transition.[8] The second thesis follows directly from this discussion and appears as part of Bergson's confrontation with historical and contemporary conceptions of system and their relationship with this inadequate conception of movement. For Deleuze, the crucial moment here is Bergson's massaging of the critique of movement that constituted the first thesis in order to identify two illusions. On the one hand, classical philosophy gives us a conception of movement that 'refers to intelligible elements ... Forms or Ideas which are themselves eternal and immobile'.[9] These elements are then more or less accurately actualized in the entities in the world. As Deleuze puts it, 'Movement ... will thus be the regulated transition from one form to another, that is, an order of poses or privileged instants, as in a dance.'[10] On the other hand, modern science gives us movement that is still composed from abstract intervals; however, '[I]t [is] no longer recomposed from formal transcendental elements (poses), but from immanent material elements (sections)'.[11] Deleuze calls this immanent material section an *any-instant-whatever* and argues that, where antiquity had conceived movement as a synthesis of poses, modern science infers movement, *qua* recomposition, from an in-principle infinitesimal analysis of moving-matter. The illusion in both cases is to think that movement occurs in the juxtaposition of these points or sections. For Deleuze these two illusions amount to much the same thing and are fraught with the same problem:

> In fact, to recompose movement with eternal poses or with immobile sections comes to the same thing: in both cases, one misses the movement because one constructs a Whole, one assumes that 'all is given', whilst movement only occurs if the whole is neither given nor giveable. As soon as a whole is given to one in the eternal order of forms or poses, or in the set of any-instant-whatevers, then either time is no more than the image of eternity, or it is the consequence of the set; there is no longer room for real movement.[12]

The word *eternity* is a reference to a discussion in *Creative Evolution*. In an illusion Bergson calls *cinematographical*, 'the forms … are … only snapshots of the changing reality'[13] which are conceived by virtue of a process of abstracting forms from their duration – distinguishing 'agents' from 'processes' – such that 'past, present and future shrink into a single moment, which is eternity'.[14] In other words, because this cinematographical illusion abstracts movement from the objects which move, it reduces time to a single moment without duration. This reduction leads to either of the two illusions Deleuze describes. On the one hand, the classical illusion conceives movement as composed through the juxtaposition of privileged poses, and on the other hand, in the modern incarnation of this illusion, movement is composed from the accretion of 'immanent material elements'. Insofar as each illusion takes the respective poses and sections as given and thus overlooks the whole's variation every time there is a translation in space, they both lead us into the error of taking the whole to be a consequence of the actual and to be like the actual.

In Deleuze's reading, however, the whole cannot be given, 'because it is the Open'[15] and, because it is open, its nature is constant change, or the production of the new. Hence Deleuze's presentation of a third and final thesis on movement; movement is double insofar as it is simultaneously the translation or rearrangement of parts in space, as well as the openness of these parts to a whole which changes qualitatively. In *Cinema 1*, Deleuze conceives movement as facing in two directions, or rather, as a process that has two elements: '*It is the relationship between parts and it is the state of the whole*.'[16] On the one hand, movement involves a communication – an interaction and translation in space, a '*rapport*'[17] – between parts; on the other hand, movement also entails the relationship of this spatial translation to the whole. Since Deleuze defines the whole as relational[18] and, since the divisions between sets are artificial, the translation in space is not the reality of movement, even though it is its actual expression. The reality of movement is the qualitative change in the relational whole in which the translation of parts participates and which it explicates. Still, even though Deleuze is fond of saying that relations are external to their terms, this heterogeneous whole does not exist outside or independently of the sets that express it. To explain the subsistence of the virtual whole in actual being, Deleuze adapts the Bergsonian vocabulary of images. His discussion of the relationship between movement and images and, ultimately, affection, focuses on how the actual and the virtual are immanent to the sensible relationality of images.

Bergson's theses on movement enable Deleuze to transform the ontology he develops through his reading of Spinoza by converting it into a discussion of objects, movement and the transformation of the plane across which they move. This transformation turns on an identity of movement and continuous multiplicities insofar as the former, as Constantin Boundas observes,

> require[s] that the distinction between movement (the process) and moving (the agent or patient) be abandoned. Movement affects both space and the bodies moving through it. To move is not to go through a trajectory which can be decomposed and recombined in quantitative terms; it is to become other than itself, in a sense that makes movement a qualitative change.[19]

Boundas's identification of the logic of continuous multiplicities is vital because, as Deleuze argues, movement is not a relation that occurs between abstract, autonomous objects; it is not a reconstitution of 'movement with the space covered, that is, by adding together instantaneous immobile sections and abstract time'.[20] Just as with continuous multiplicities, the composition of the space through which bodies move is not really distinct from the bodies themselves. As such, the spatial translation of a body contributes to the composition of the whole of the space which contains the moving body. At the same time, the moving body is a function of the composition and transformation of the space through which it moves and, as such, it does not merely move from one point to the next unaffected by the transformations of the space across which it moves. The moving body becomes, as Boundas puts it, 'other than itself' insofar as it undergoes continual transformations reciprocally with the transformations of its milieu. To understand how Deleuze converts the problematic of sections and poses into one of centres within a relational, continuous universe, we must unpack the pivotal Bergsonian concept to which Deleuze appeals: *images*.

Images and representation

The term *image* might initially seem strange insofar as it evokes some sort of distinction between the objects of perception and objects as they actually are. However, in appealing to the notion of the image, Bergson and Deleuze are in critical dialogue with the traditional philosophical distinction between external objects and mental representations. As Bergson famously puts it at the start of *Matter and Memory*, an image is more than a 'representation' and less than a 'thing'; it is 'an existence placed half-way between the "thing" and the "representation"'.[21] In section XII of his *An Enquiry Concerning Human Understanding*, Hume articulates the problem by noting that even 'the slightest philosophy' assumes that 'nothing can ever be present to the mind but an image or a perception'.[22] Hume is interested in the peculiar problem that arises when we realize that, though the object of our perception changes as we continue to relate to it, the object itself, we presume, remains constant. Thus there arises a peculiar problem and an 'extreme embarrassment' to philosophy: that the natural instinct to believe that the external world causes, and is present in, our perceptions is naive and untenable, and yet equally untenable is the rationalist belief that the images born of our senses are distinct from an external world with which they cannot be reconciled.[23]

There have, of course, been many, varied attempts to negotiate this problem, but here I am interested in the way Deleuze, in his reading of Bergson, defends a nuanced version of a belief that Hume takes to be an immediate consequence of 'a natural instinct or prepossession'. For Hume, we 'always suppose the very images presented by the senses, to be the external objects, and never entertain any suspicion, that the one are nothing but the representations of the other'.[24] Bergson begins *Matter and Memory* by considering this natural instinct. He asks his readers to rise above the habitual assumption of a substantial distinction between the object and our perception of it and to inhabit a 'point of view of a mind unaware of the disputes of philosophers'.[25] This does not mean Bergson is guilty of any special pleading when it comes to accepting the hypotheses he puts forward in *Matter and Memory*. On the contrary, he suggests that any hostility that will arise with respect to his hypotheses is a product of our habitual deference to the idea that the contents of the mind are in some sense representations of some external object. Bergson's obvious frustration in the first chapter of *Matter and Memory* is directed at this representationalist thesis insofar as it seeks to conjure the external world from the mind's ideas or vice versa. In spite of this frustration, Bergson concedes that states of affairs in the world cannot help us decide between these theses, especially since pure perception – that is, perception idealized and considered without memory – 'bears, by definition, upon *present* objects ... and because everything always happens ... *as though* our perceptions emanated from our cerebral state'.[26] While he grants the intuition that the objects of our perceptions are dependent in some way on our perceptions (the point that motivates both eighteenth-century idealism and twentieth-century phenomenalism), Bergson argues that his thesis regarding the continuity of mind and world is to be preferred to the representationalist hypothesis on the grounds of its 'greater intelligibility'.[27] The problem for Bergson is that, even if experience operates as though our perceptions emanate from within us, representationalism remains unintelligible because it will inevitably run into the problem of how, if our perceptions do spring from our minds, the content of our minds ever coincides with the world intuition tells us we inhabit.

Thus, the most immediate point of connection between Deleuze's reading of Spinoza and his reading of Bergson is their respective attempts to outmanoeuvre particular species of dualism, whether post-Kantian dualism in Bergson's case, or Cartesian dualism in Spinoza's case. Similar to Spinoza's conception of body and mind as different systems of reference for the same event – that is, parallel modifications of substance – Bergson describes an image as being equally able to be understood from an objective point of view where, 'related only to itself', it contains an absolute value, or, from a subjective point of view, 'the world of consciousness, wherein all the images depend on a central image, our body, the variations of which they follow'.[28] On the one hand, following Descartes, Spinoza endeavours to provide an objective description of mind and body where the body is the modal expression of the constitution of substance and mind is the idea of the body. On the other hand, Bergson argues that the problem is to understand how images simultaneously operate for a subjective world – consciousness – and also operate for an objective world; in this case, the problem is how these worlds are correlative expressions of a sensible continuum. For both Spinoza and Bergson, matter and mind are expressions of degrees of change in a relational whole in which there is no substantial gap to be bridged between the material and ideal. Each world, ideal and actual, is a different system of reference for expressing a whole undergoing constant modification.

Bergson describes images as emerging from the gap between pictorial representations and their objects: '[B]y "image" we mean a certain existence which is more than that which the idealist calls a representation, but less than that which the realist calls a thing, – an existence placed half-way between the "thing" and the "representation".'[29] Bergson uses this term to flatten his ontology so that my body, the 'external object' and the affects which mediate their relations are all the same *type* of thing. This is why the relational world Deleuze articulates throughout his project is here described as a universe of continual movement, and this continual movement is equivalent to a universe of images: 'We find ourselves ... faced with the exposition of a world where IMAGE=MOVEMENT. Let us call the set of what appears "Image."'[30] Thus, in talking of images, Deleuze is not referring uniquely to cinema; rather, he is building upon Bergson's conception of a universe that constitutes the subjects and objects of perception by virtue of a series of continuous sensible relations. Bergson, indeed, begins *Matter and Memory* by describing images in terms of the mise en scène of the field of our perceptions: 'Images perceived when my senses are opened to them, unperceived when they are closed.'[31] Images describe what Bergson takes to be primitive: an experience of being immersed in a world of representations (and here Bergson is playing on the idea of images in the mind) and corresponding external objects. The way Bergson describes it, there are images which are referred to me and which vary with the modifications of my being, and there are images which refer to themselves and vary occasionally in their relations with other images but do not change for my sake. Such images do not form distinct series but constitute distinct systems of reference for the same order of images: 'The same images can enter at the same time into two distinct systems, one belonging to [*material*] *science*, wherein each image, related only to itself, possesses an absolute value; and the other, the world of *consciousness*, wherein all the images depend on a central image, our body, the variations of which they follow.'[32]

Bergson does not defend his starting position; rather, by starting from what he takes to be a fact about existence – that we constantly find ourselves 'in the presence of images'[33] – he begins in medias res and aims to show that such a beginning puts the lie to the split between consciousness and external things. Bergson wants to show that, by starting with the immediate presence of images, we will understand the world in such a way that the rift between materialism and idealism will never be opened. Bergson thus proposes a plane of images within which our bodies constitute a variable centre and, consequently, the fulcrum of relations – what Bergson calls a 'centre', itself an image – is neither privileged nor derided relative to the position it maintains on the plane on which it appears. As Suzanne Guerlac notes, Bergson talks in terms of images so as to 'interrupt our usual habits of thought';[34] he wants us to stop considering sensory information in terms of a more or less fallible epistemological engagement and think in terms of perception's relationship with action. For Deleuze, this means developing a model of the universe in which perception and movement 'would be ... a state of things which would constantly change, a flowing-matter in which no point of anchorage nor centre of reference would be assignable. On the basis of this state of things it would be necessary to show how, at any point, centres can be formed which would impose fixed instantaneous views.'[35]

The determinism of Bergson's description of this universe initially appears almost Laplacean; if we are content to describe them from the point of view of perception, then all these images seem to act and react upon each other in consistent ways, according to constant laws and, if we had perfect knowledge of these laws, we could predict all future states of these images.[36] This being the case, it would seem that the future states of images consist of nothing that is not already contained in their present state. However, there is an image which I can take from a different point of view: my body. This image, claims Bergson, can be known not only from an external point of view but also 'from within by affections'.[37] For Bergson, my body can be viewed in two ways, from the point of view of its external relations or from an internal point of view in terms of how those external relations are enfolded into affective states:

> The distinction between the inside and the outside will then be only a distinction between the part and the whole. There is, first of all, the aggregate of images; and then, in this aggregate, there are 'centres of action', from which the interesting images appear to be reflected: *My body* is that which stands out as the centre of these perceptions; *my person* is the being to which these actions must be referred. ... My body, then, acts like an image which reflects others, and which, in so doing, analyses them along lines corresponding to the different actions which it can exercise upon them.[38]

Bergson's claim seems clear, if counterintuitive; if I am to distinguish between the inside and outside of my body, then I will do so by virtue of a distinction between the parts of a system and that system as a whole. Deleuze's understanding of this Bergsonian concept of the image leads to an affirmation of the equivalency of the object and the image, which entails that the *object* and the *representation* are distinct only by virtue of the set of relations to which they are referred. The image called *perception* is not a representation of the object, nor is it some ideal mental content derived from the object; it is the object/image related to a particular image which frames it, selects out particular information and reacts to it mediately. Thus, we can provisionally say that the body, *my* body, is the special image to which the object relates mediately. Bergson emphasizes the fact that the body is not an impersonal object; when objects are referred to it, their relation is mediated by the *being* of the special image. This is why he says that 'my person is the being to which these actions must be referred'.

Even though Deleuze argues that moving bodies are indistinguishable from the executed movement, he still needs to carry out a deduction of the various degrees to which the affective continuum can be differentiated. Just as his Spinozism has its way of describing the expression or actualization of modifications of the whole, *Cinema* has its own way of describing the elements of an actual set. In this sense, Deleuze talks about three types of image, the *avatars of the movement-image*,[39] that express degrees of the whole's transformation in actual occurrences.

The movement-image and its avatars

I argued in Chapter 3 that Deleuze invokes the geometry of Bernhard Riemann and his concept of a continuous multiplicity – a space determined by the events that occur across it – as a way of articulating Bergson's formulation of *durée*. The reciprocal determination of a space and the events that populate it is, both for Deleuze and Bergson, a way to conceive the one and the many such that they are no longer opposed to each other. For Bergson this means understanding the two terms (one and many, part and whole) as points of view on the folding of continuous processes into the actions characteristic of bodies. Deleuze takes up this theme in *Cinema 1* when he describes movement in terms of the relationship between Bergson's bodies – now renamed 'relatively closed system[s]'[40] – and the plane of immanence – the set of what appears, the manifold of relations, *or*, the mise en scène of perception – that animates them. If we return to a passage from *Cinema 1*, we can see that what interests Deleuze is how Bergson's extension of the discussion of images makes possible an ontology wherein the movement of an object is inseparable from the constitution and transformation of the object itself:

> We find ourselves in fact faced with the exposition of a world where IMAGE = MOVEMENT. Let us call the set of what appears 'Image'. We cannot even say that one image acts on another or reacts to another. There is no moving body which is distinct from executed movement. There is nothing moved which is distinct from the received movement. Every thing, that is to say every image, is indistinguishable from its actions and reactions: this is universal variation. Every image is merely a road by which pass, in every direction, the modifications propagated throughout the immensity of the universe. Every image acts on others and reacts to others, on all their facets at once and by all their elements.[41]

In this sense, then, Deleuze takes up Bergson's ontology of images in order to critically reformulate the relation between objects and movement. The type of image around which Deleuze formulates his affective ontology is the *movement-image*. Insofar as the objects that fill out the universe are sections cut from a continuum, Deleuze, like Bergson before him, wants a way to refer to these objects that recognizes the fact that they were always already in motion. It is the concept of a movement-image that makes this possible: 'Cinema does not give us an image to which movement is added, it immediately gives us a movement-image. It does give us a section, but a section which is mobile, not an immobile section + abstract movement.'[42]

In *Matter and Memory*, Bergson suggests 'that the movements of matter are very clear, regarded as images, and [so] there is no need to look in movement for anything more than what we see in it'.[43] Deleuze cites this remark in his discussion of Bergson's critique of the traditional distinction between objects and the movements they execute.[44] And, in this context, Deleuze offers an insight that will be key to understanding how perception and action fit into the universe he describes. He begins by citing Bergson:

> 'You may say that my body is matter or that it is an image.' The *movement-image* and *flowing-matter* are strictly the same thing. ... The plane of immanence is ... therefore a section; but, ... it is not an immobile and instantaneous section, it is a mobile section, a temporal section, a temporal section or perspective. The material universe, the plane of immanence, is the *machine assemblage of movement-images*.[45]

Thus, the universe is a composite of movement-images – that is, of mobile sections of duration. In other words, the entities that inhabit the universe presuppose a relationality that they express. Everything we see is an image but it is not a representation by which an object is apparent to consciousness. It is a perception of the objects around us; the objects of our perceptions are the movements – *flowing-matter* – of the world and both the perceptions and the movements are images. There are no entities *as such* but rather, as Deleuze puts it in *Difference and Repetition*, 'being[s] of becoming'.[46] This idea appears in *Cinema 1* when Deleuze employs Bergson's vocabulary of a system of double references:

> An essential consequence follows – *the existence of a double system, of a double régime of reference of images*. There is firstly a system in which each image varies for itself, and all the images act and react as a function of each other, on all their facets and in all their parts. But to this is added another system where all vary

principally for a single one, which receives the action of the other images on one of its facets and reacts to them on another facet.⁴⁷

Consequently, moving bodies cannot be distinguished from the movements they execute, nor can affected entities be distinguished from what affects or moves them. This appropriation of Bergson allows Deleuze to be more forceful about the relational nature of the entities that fill out his ontology. Fundamental to this appropriation is Bergson's articulation of the universe as a plane of immanence with movements that run 'from the periphery to the centre, and from the centre to the periphery'.⁴⁸ This description appears in the context of Bergson's discussion of the continuity of perception and action and, as such, it is *perception* that travels from the periphery to the centre and *action* that travels from the centre to the periphery.⁴⁹ In both cases we are dealing with movement-images, the difference is the status of the centre to which the movement-image is referred. This continuity of perception and action, and the status of the centre, what Deleuze will call an affection-image, leads Deleuze to describe the movement-image as composed of – *as differentiated into* – three avatars, three types of image: '*Movement-images divide into three sorts of images when they are related to a centre of indetermination as to a special image*: perception-images, action-images and affection-images. And each one of us, the special image or the contingent centre, is nothing but an assemblage of three images, a consolidate of perception-images, action-images and affection-images.'⁵⁰

In the discussion of the three avatars in *Cinema 2: The Time-Image*, Deleuze is explicit about the way that the perception-image – 'the degree-zero in the deduction which is carried out as a function of the movement-image'⁵¹ – grounds the continuity of the other avatars and is the condition of the genesis of a whole. This is why Deleuze argues that the avatars 'are not simply ordinal – first, second, third – but cardinal: there are two in the second to the point where there is a firstness in the secondness, and there are three in the third'.⁵² These avatars, moreover, are types of images that in their relationships constitute a 'movement-image [that] gives rise to a sensory-motor whole'.⁵³ These types are an affection-image (firstness), an action-image (secondness), a relation-image (thirdness), and respectively they constitute 'something that only refers to itself, [a] quality or a power ... that refers to itself only through something else ... and something that refers only to itself by comparing one thing to another'.⁵⁴

If the movement-image is the continuity of a thing and its relations this is because it is the relationality which folds from an exteriority of objects into a centre of indetermination by virtue of a selection among virtual actions and the actualization of movement. Deleuze devotes much of *Cinema 1: The Movement-Image* to discussing the components of the movement-image, and to showing that the movement-image is not a set of relations between pre-constituted components. In doing this he again follows Bergson who suggests that 'because of the invincible tendency to think on all occasions of *things* rather than movements'[55] we misinterpret this relationship; we think of one agent passively receiving impressions from another and are thus unable to reconstruct the passage by which the impression, or image, travels from one point to another. In this sense, Bergson is concerned to highlight the operations of the faculty for receiving impressions: perception. Indeed, its importance and primacy as the ground of the subject of perception is what leads Deleuze to describe perception as the 'degree zero' in the cardinal relationship of the avatars.[56] Bergson describes a particularly tight relationship between perception and action such that 'perception … is … entirely directed towards action, and not towards pure knowledge'.[57] Thus, perception does not reflect upon an object in order to know it, but sifts relevant data from irrelevant data en route to the determination of action. To appreciate why Deleuze sees the avatars of the movement-image as expressing qualitative changes to the whole, we must consider the way in which Bergson's understanding of perception as posing a question to my body is taken up by Deleuze in his effort to characterize the relationship between perception and action as progressing dialectically through affection.

Perception and action, problems and solutions

Perception is, for both Bergson and Deleuze, so bound up in its relationship with action that the best way to describe it is in terms of how it operates. Indeed, it is the reciprocity of perception and action that leads Bergson to offer provisional definitions of matter and the perception of matter as, first, '*the aggregate of images*' and second '*these same images referred to the eventual action of one particular image, my body*'.[58] Deleuze takes this to mean that the only difference between the perception of an object and the object as such is the point of view – the system of reference – to which it is related. In this cinematic ethology, the image is the material object and, as such, the only distinction between an object and the idea of the object concerns our method of understanding the relation. When referring to the image in itself, 'as it is related to all the other images to whose action it completely submits and on which it reacts immediately',[59] we can say that the image is the object. When we refer the image to another image which frames it, it is a *perception-image*. For example, when I look at the tree outside my window, there is a point of view from which the tree is a thing among other things and, insofar as it is an object, the tree is submitted entirely to the other images/objects around it, relative to which it reacts immediately. In this case, the tree is referred to as an object. Conversely, when I describe the tree insofar as it induces certain behaviours on my part, I call it a perception of the tree. In both cases there is only one image; on the one hand, we can refer to it objectively, in its immediate and complete relations with other images, and on the other hand, we can refer to it as relative to a special image which frames it, a special image by which the reactions are mediated. Both Deleuze and Bergson argue that, defined this way, perception escapes the peculiar problem of representation. By defining perception as a process of framing and mediation it is a fundamentally subtractive process; that is, there is strictly less in the perception than in the object per se:

> From the point of view which occupies us for the moment, we go from total, objective perception which is indistinguishable from the thing, to a subjective perception which is distinguished from it by simple elimination or subtraction. It is this unicentred subjective perception that is called perception strictly speaking. And it is the first avatar of the movement-image: when it is related to a centre of indetermination, it becomes *perception-image*.[60]

Within the context of the *Cinema* project, the idea that perception is a process of elimination or subtraction is central to Deleuze's formulation of the dialectic of problems. What Deleuze calls 'the image as it is in itself'[61] is the world Bergson describes as posing challenges to my body. That is, Bergson offers a conception of perception as the posing of a problem when he claims that, '[a]s many threads as pass from the periphery to the centre, so many points of space are there able to make an appeal to my will and to put, so to speak, an elementary question to my motor activity. Every such question is what is termed a perception.'[62]

Insofar as Bergson considers perception to be a subtractive process, he argues that if we conceive living beings as centres of indetermination, and if 'the degree of this indetermination is measured by the number and rank of their functions, [then] we can conceive that their mere presence is equivalent to the suppression of all those parts of objects in which their functions find no interest'.[63] From the objects that transmit the data that finds a response in the centres, only part of what is reflected from their surface is relevant to the responses the centre can formulate. The information that is not relevant passes by unacknowledged and what is relevant is subtracted and converted into action. The centres of indetermination 'allow to pass through them ... those external influences which are indifferent to them; the others isolated, become "perceptions" by their very isolation'.[64]

For Bergson, the body, or, rather, the nervous system that characterizes it, is 'a mere conductor' which is lodged between the objects that affect it and those it can influence, thus the nervous system works to transmit, reflect or inhibit movement.[65] Deleuze suggests that, from the point of view of this influence and transmission, '[w]e are still in the perception-image, but we are already entering the action-image as well. In fact, perception is only one side of the gap, and action is the other side. What is called action, strictly speaking, is the delayed reaction of the centre of indetermination.'[66] If we refer to what Bergson calls a special image – what Deleuze variously calls a 'special image', 'my body', 'a centre of indetermination', and 'an interval' – we can see why Deleuze's ethology does not go far enough if it is limited to an objective account of the world. The subject – the *being* of the special image – stands out precisely because, insofar as I am a subject, I am able to take a more nuanced point of view on the being of the special image. In the most concrete terms, the special image is my body and I am able to view it internally, that is, *subjectively*. For Bergson this issue is clear; when we consider action in these subjective terms, we see an indetermination which is implied in the structure of the nervous system – 'an indetermination to which this system seems to point much more than to representation'.[67] This indetermination is why, for Deleuze, the interval between perception and action, between incoming information and an outgoing response, is not empty:

> The interval is not merely defined by the specialisation of the two limit-facets, perceptive and active. There is an in-between. Affection is what occupies the interval, what occupies it without filling it in or filling it up. It surges in the centre of indetermination ... between a perception which is troubling in certain respects and a hesitant action.[68]

The interval that generates action is characterized by a series of affections, and we know from the cardinal interrelationship of images that affection does not so much precede action as ground it. Every action is grounded in an affection, and action contains the affections that form it. This is why Deleuze says that affection 'surges in the centre of indetermination ... between a perception which is troubling in certain respects and a hesitant action. It is a coincidence of subject and object ... It relates movement to a "quality" as lived state.'[69] Because affection occupies the interval between the received perception and the reflected action, it suggests a coincidence of subject and object. As Ronald Bogue explains, to say that subject and object coincide is to say 'that the object of perception is felt in conjunction with a bodily sensation'.[70] So, when Bergson says that affection is 'that part or aspect of the inside of our body which we mix with the image of external bodies',[71] he affirms that we are 'embodied perceivers'[72] insofar as the affection-image is the coupling of an object with a body – *my body* – that responds to the perception of the object. This Bergsonian conception of affection offers a way to approach what Deleuze calls 'the second part of difference'[73] – differenciation – insofar as it constitutes solutions to the questions posed by perception. Thus, the importance of the action-image consists in the way it 'expresses the actualisation of this virtual'[74] through the coincidence of an object and a subject in a living image.

When Bergson turns to consider the nature of affection, he does so in order to address the hypothesis that 'affection *must*, at a given moment, arise out of the image'.[75] Bergson is interested in how affection operates in our bodies as the reduction of the distance between the object to be perceived – where perception remains the measurement of our 'possible action upon things, and ... [their] possible action ... upon us'[76] – and our own body. For Bergson, the issue is the selection or actualization of an action from a series of possible actions; as the distance between the object and my body approaches zero, the number of possible actions diminishes and an actual action is expressed.[77] However, we can formulate this same issue in Deleuzian terms by describing the reciprocity of the problem and the solution. Bergson describes this reduction of distance in terms of the way an imminent danger becomes increasingly urgent for an organism or the way a promise between object and subject becomes immediate.[78] This is precisely the type of situation Deleuze refers to when he describes '*the organism as a biological Idea*'[79] insofar as it 'is nothing if not the solution to a problem'.[80]

Affection in this case occurs at the horizon – affection is the threshold – where the diversity of sensory data is reduced to the degree that perception is formulated as a problem that is relevant to the body, and the body is the expression of a solution as an action. Of course, insofar as the action-image and the perception-image it transforms are both actual, the continuity of the movement-image does not move from one term to another. In this sense, the objects of perception are *not* the problem: the problem is formulated and expressed virtually as the object enters into a relationship with a special image. The actions my body expresses can resemble the actions of the object; however, *neither* can resemble the problem that is formulated by the relationship between the object and my body. There is thus an intensive transformation in the interval between perception and action such that the transformation of the flow of moving-matter corresponds to a transformation of power.

Affection and the reciprocal presupposition of individuals and the whole

The deeper connection between the conversion of ontology – what beings *are*, and how they relate to their own Being as well as to others' Being – into ethology – a robust attempt to think through ontological problems from the point of view of those living beings – in the *Cinema* books and Deleuze's early work can be seen in his description of the affection-image in terms of intensive series and individuation.[81] The interrelationship between intensive series and individuating events is first elaborated in *Expressionism* where Deleuze presents Spinoza's individual as the actualization of a degree of power,[82] but in this analysis, Deleuze responds to the problem of internal difference that he first formulated in his 1956 essay on Bergson.[83] This problem drives Deleuze's interpretation of the reciprocity of substance and modes, of the whole and its expression in individuating events, and it returns in *Cinema 1*'s description of the affection-image.

For Deleuze, the affection-image is synonymous with the close-up and the close-up is synonymous with the face. It would be a mistake to interpret 'the face' in human, or even subjective, terms, however. For Deleuze, the face or the close-up is a bipolar process of 'faceification'.[84] On the one hand, the face is, as Deleuze puts it, a sacrifice of the centre's movement. That is, the centre, or some facet of it, becomes immobile and instead functions as a unified, receptive surface on which the perception-image is etched. Deleuze calls this a 'receptive plate of inscription'.[85] In a phrase that recalls the first synthesis of time's anticipatory contraction of the past, this first pole is also called a site of 'impassive suspense'.[86] The affection-image also has a second pole: the constitution of an intensive series or 'a pure Power ... which carries us from one quality to another'.[87] This is why Deleuze says that '[t]here is no close-up of the face. The close-up is the face, but the face precisely in so far as it has destroyed its triple [individuating, socializing and communicating] function – a nudity of the face much greater than that of the body, an inhumanity much greater than that of animals.'[88]

While there seems to be a striking similarity between the way attribution works and the way affection works, affection does not mediate the perception/action dynamic in the way that attribution mediates the dynamic between substance and modes. *Difference and Repetition*'s criticism of Spinoza would seem to amount to the discovery of a vertical organization of substance and modes – where modes turn on an already given identity that is mediated by the doubly expressive operations of attribution. However, while affection has a similar, doubly expressive operation that relates the virtual whole to actual entities, it does so by flattening the relationship such that there is a horizontal, *reciprocal* relationship between the whole and particulars. It is just this double expressivity Deleuze refers to when he sets up a distinction between 'pure singular qualities or potentialities – as it were, pure "possibles" ... [and] the state of things, which are, as it were, [the] causes [of these singularities]'.[89] And yet, in reference to Hungarian film critic Béla Balázs, Deleuze still affirms a Humean scepticism about causation: 'However much the precipice may be the cause of vertigo, it does not explain the expression it produces on a face.'[90] That is, however much the two poles of the face reciprocally determine each other, their relationship is not *causal*: 'The precipice above which someone leans perhaps explains his expression of fright, but it does not create it.'[91]

This conception of the affection-image as bipolar enables Deleuze to convert the double expressivity of attribution into a doubly expressive operation of affection. The description of affection as bipolar is problematic, however, because it too often invokes the idea of a spectrum along which one moves; in this case the idea would be of a spectrum with affection alternating between the expression of a power for itself and a state of affairs in which the power is actualized. Instead, affection is bipolar insofar as it is an image with two distinct but interrelated senses. My body, insofar as it is the special image that is constituted as an interval between perception and action, is 'filled out and extended'[92] by an affection-image that is simultaneously actual – that is, it is the actual state of my body to the extent that it is entangled in an affective encounter – and it is virtual – it is the sense of this state of affection, abstracted from the actual encounter and expressed for itself. Following on from his Humean scepticism, these two senses of the affect, the two poles of the affection-image, obviously do not cause one another. To say they do not cause each other does not, however, necessitate claiming that these two poles do not interact. Even though it is virtual, the expression of the affect *as such* is still an expression of the sense of the encounter, and so it describes the encounter as an actual occurrence, and thus the virtual pole of the affect is determined by the actual. Similarly, the actual pole of the affect is determined by the virtual to the extent that the interval, *my body*, is not merely the site of passive reaction and, as such, its eventual action is determined by the degree to which its power *makes sense*.

With this in mind, we can see why Deleuze describes the two poles of the affection-image as the two sides of the expression of a 'power-quality'.[93] It is not merely the case that the interval is occupied by an image which is alternatively an immobile receptive plate and then the expression of a power in its passage from one quality to another. There is one side of the affection-image that is the receptive facet of the centre, but its relationship with the production of an action is a complex, double expression. The close-up abstracts its object, the affect, '*from all spatio-temporal co-ordinates*, [and] raises it to the state of Entity'[94] and, by virtue of this abstraction, the affect is also the generation of an actual state of things. When the affect is taken as an entity torn from spatio-temporal coordinates, the 'affection-image is power or quality considered for themselves, as expressed', and although its existence is not independent of the state of affairs in which it is actualized, 'it is completely distinct from it'.[95] It is in this sense that the second pole of the affection-image is expressed as 'ideal singularities and their *virtual conjunction*'.[96] In other words, the virtual side of the affect circulates within a multiplicity of ideal events that is distinct from the actual states of affairs that respond to it. The discussion of the actual side of the affection-image takes us into the action-image. The action-image is, after all, the actualization of a power-quality 'in an individuated state of things and in the corresponding real connections (with a particular space-time, *hic et nunc*, particular characters, particular roles, particular objects)'.[97] Insofar as it is the expression of a power-quality for itself, abstracted from an actual, individual state of things, it is clear how affection is doubly expressive. Expressed for themselves, affects are 'ideal singularities' – that is, the singularity of problems distinct from the actualities that express their solution and these ideal singularities constitute the whole.

When Deleuze outlines the interrelationship between the two forms of pluralism that characterize the constitution of monism in *Bergsonism*,[98] he anticipates how the *Cinema* project will reformulate the third thesis on movement by confronting the relationship between the infinity of actual entities and the virtual whole onto which the entities open. An important consequence of talking in terms of images is that Deleuze is finally able to concretely describe actual beings as points within a continuous becoming. Thus, it is hardly surprising that in *Cinema 1*'s elaboration of Bergson's critique of movement, Deleuze describes 'movement [as having] two facets ... *it is the relationship between parts and it is the state of the whole*'.[99] What is telling in this passage is the appearance of *affection* in the original, such that movement is the transformation of the whole: '*il est rapport entre parties, et il est affection du tout*'.[100]

In his reading of Spinoza, Deleuze describes affection as 'a state of the affected body that implies the presence of the affecting body'.[101] Moreover, we can distinguish between three senses of affection in Spinoza: modes are the affections of substance; affections are *what happens* to a mode; and, finally, affections are 'transitions ... or variations of perfection',[102] that is, actual changes in a mode. These affections are just what Deleuze calls images: 'Images are the corporeal affections themselves, the traces of an external body on our body.'[103] When we return to a basic point of Deleuze's – that '[m]ovement is a translation in space [and that] each time there is a translation of parts in space, there is also a qualitative change in a whole'[104] – we see an emphasis on the relationship between the parts and the whole. Affection does a double job; on the one hand, it is the interaction between actual bodies (the traces of an external body on my own), and on the other, it is the participation of the actual bodies in the whole they modify (the modification of substance as it moves to a different degree of perfection). From *Bergsonism*, through his work on Spinoza, and into the first volume on cinema, Deleuze retains a strikingly consistent conception of part–whole relations insofar as actual beings undergo constant reorganization relative to each other and simultaneously express the transformation of the whole.

Conclusion

It is the process of affection that drives the dialectic at the heart of Deleuze's ontology. On the one hand, affection is the immobilization of some facet of my body such that this surface functions as the point of communication between my body and the 'external' world. That is, affection is the process of enfolding these external relations into the composition of my body. On the other hand, affection also refers to the abstraction of this relation. That is, affection separates the relation from its terms and context, and expresses it *for itself*, as an intensive degree. What is the object of this expression? What is it a degree *of*? It is a degree of the constitution of *a* whole, of *a* multiplicity – a system that is numerically unique but qualitatively heterogeneous and is constituted as a whole of relations. Insofar as the sense of these expressions – that is, what they express of their object – is a degree of power, the whole thus constituted, turns around actual lives. In other words, the whole is constituted through the expression of power, but that power is always the power that subsists in the differentiation of the movement-image into its avatars. To the extent that this differentiation of the movement-image is an ontological formulation of a discussion that concerns actual beings, the transformation of power and modes of life, it is one facet of a discussion that is *ethological*. This means that, corresponding to this chapter's ontological formulation, the philosophy of the *Cinema* books could also be rendered as an ethical discussion that proceeds in terms of the bodies that are constituted as centres of indetermination between the formulation of the perception-image as a problem and the expression of the action-image as the actualization of a solution.

Elizabeth Grosz argues that Bergson's attitude to ethics and the sense in which humans are constituted by their freedom changes across his project:

> In his later works, Bergson focuses less on freedom as the exclusive attribute of a self, concentrated on only the one, conscious side of the distinction between the organic and the inorganic, as he did in his earlier *Time and Free Will*, and more on the relations between the organic and the inorganic, the internal constitution of freedom through its encounters with the resistance of matter.[105]

This is to say that Bergson ultimately affirms a freedom that is not a predicate of a self – in the sense of *a free agent* – but is located in actions that relate or respond to a material environment. Deleuze adapts this theme in *Bergsonism*, when he identifies freedom with the constitution of problems. Deleuze works to shift the discussion of freedom away from aspiring to conditions in which an agent would be freed to act more voluntarily – more wilfully – and characterizes it as the degree to which an individual participates in, as Paul Patton explains, 'the critical points at which some state or condition of things passes over into a different state or condition'.[106] The sense in which we might meaningfully describe an individual as free depends on how she makes sense of her embeddedness in the relationality of the world – *does she affirm this embeddedness, or does she resent it?* – and the degree to which this sense leads her to participate in the events that transform the whole of which she is a part. This is why Deleuze argues that '[t]rue freedom lies in a power to decide, *to constitute problems themselves*'.[107] The 'power to decide' is not the appearance of a wilful agency that makes conscious decisions; it is the selection and affirmation of the elements that constitute problems.

In the next and final chapter, I will argue that the *Cinema* project presents a conceptualization of how the conditions of freedom, that is, the conditions of participating more actively in the constitution of problems, are immanent to experience. This chapter has argued for an interpretation of the Bergsonism of the *Cinema* books as a crystallization of Deleuze's ethology as one in which actual lives constitute the whole of which they are a part by virtue of the degree of power that subsists in their affective relations. Following on from this, Chapter 5 will argue that a sophisticated conception of how individuals participate in the determination of problems illuminates the sense in which the conditions for the enhancement of their power are immanent to experience and affective relations.

5

Subjectivity, experimentation beyond the action-image and an 'art of living'

Discussions of the place of ethics in Deleuze often centre on issues of thinking differently, of transforming modes of life and enhancing power. Indeed, Deleuze himself tends to describe ethics as a matter of *formulating new problems*. In *Bergsonism*, Deleuze identified the constitution of problems with a power to decide,[1] and he returns to this theme in *Cinema*: 'It is characteristic of the problem that it is inseparable from a choice[;] … when the problem concerns existential determinations … we see clearly that choice is increasingly identified with living thought, and with an unfathomable decision. Choice no longer concerns a particular term, but the mode of existence of the one who chooses.'[2] To make his point, Deleuze refers to Blaise Pascal's famous wager concerning the existence of God. Deleuze argues that the significance of the wager is not its terms – belief, non-belief or abstention – but the mode of life entailed by the affirmation of particular terms: 'It is as if there was a choice of choice or non-choice. If I am conscious of choice, there are therefore already choices that I can no longer make, and modes of existence that I can no longer follow – all those I followed on the condition of persuading myself that "there was no choice".'[3] In other words, the question is not the terms of the wager, nor which one you ought to affirm, but that each term implies a mode of life that follows from the sense one makes of the possibility of choosing. As Deleuze says, 'I choose to choose, and by that I exclude all choice made on the mode of not having the choice.'[4] The significance of Deleuze's argument is that the ethical problem does not lie with the choice one makes between the terms of the wager, but the mode of life that follows from how one relates to, that is, *makes sense of*, the power to choose. In anticipation of discussions in this chapter, we can phrase this differently. The ethical situation is not about the elements of a particular problem in themselves, as though these elements exist outside their formulation in a problem; rather, the ethical imperative is about the way those elements are *framed* such that they formulate a problem that will generate a particular solution.

This conception of the relationship between choice and the formulation of problems makes sense in light of the Bergsonian conception of the continuity of perception and action discussed in Chapter 4. The objects of a perception, that is, the elements of a problem posed to my body, are only quantitatively distinct from 'nascent' action, the actions that my body will perform in response to the perception.[5] In other words, the elements of a problem – the objects of perception or the terms of a choice – are significant because of the actions and behaviour that follow from a particular framing of them. That Deleuze aligns the significance of this with situations which concern the existential determination of problems makes it clear that this cannot be exhausted by an ontological discussion, it also entails the ethical problem of the affective conditions of the determination and transformations of a being's capacities; in other words, the existential determination of problems is an *ethological* concern. Accordingly, the ethical orientation of Deleuze's analyses in the *Cinema* project can be expressed in terms of a properly ethological question: Under what conditions does an individual participate in the constitution of problems, and thus the genesis of modes of life, that go beyond the clichés of the action-image? These clichés, as I will argue in this chapter, concern the determination of a problem according to a character's belief that her actions have the power to disclose the truth of, or modify, a situation.

In keeping with Deleuze's insistence on immanence, the conditions under which an individual participates differently in the constitution of problems are immanent to experience *as such*. In other words, if there is to be any modification in how an individual participates in the determination of problems, the conditions of this modification must follow from the affective relations involved in her existence. This immanence of the conditions of change is vital to Deleuze's steering ethics away from a conception of individuals who behave voluntarily. To the extent that the subjects of the cinematic universe are produced as expressions of the becoming of the whole, modifications to a subject's power – even modifications that enhance her power – cannot come from the subjects' spontaneous transcendence of the relational plane of which she is a product. Modifications to her power must proceed from her relational embeddedness. As such, this chapter focuses primarily on the place and transformation of perception in the constitution of cinematic subjects. Because it concerns the determination of a problem through the differentiation of the movement-image, this attention to the subject as the product of perception will illuminate the sense in which the action-image is the actual expression – that is, the actual side – of the constitution of a problem as the synthesis of memories, expectations and multiple points of view on a set of relations. This entails a radical transformation in our conception of subjects, and so we will start this discussion with a brief look at Deleuze's ambivalence to phenomenology in order to maintain the anti-humanist context that we set out for Deleuze's project at the very beginning of this book. Moreover, through these discussions, it will become clear why Deleuze wrote about his encounter with cinema. Just as the differential logic of his ontology could not be described without his engagement with Spinoza, the significance of Bergson's philosophy of images for Deleuze's project could not have been properly articulated without an encounter with the techniques and technologies of the cinema.

Resisting the privilege of a human point of view: Bergsonism contra phenomenology

Deleuze claims that the Bergsonism of the *Cinema* books is 'the opposite of what phenomenology put forward'.[6] Deleuze opposes the phenomenological presupposition of subjectivity as a point of anchorage for the deduction of empirical phenomena. He argues that, because consciousness is immanent to the processes and structures that determine experience, consciousness is an insufficient starting point for undertaking the challenge that Husserl's reduction hoped to face.[7] Thus he turns to the conception of an anonymous viewpoint as a way of responding to phenomenology's focus on the content of a first-person perspective.[8] Deleuze takes phenomenology to task for its reinstatement of a dative to whom the plane of immanence is referred. This challenge is critical to an understanding of what Deleuze sets out to achieve in the *Cinema* books' exploration of a subject's status as a centre of indetermination. Insofar as a dative is a being 'to whom things appear',[9] Deleuze's issue with phenomenology is that, as Lawlor puts it, it 'relates the plane of immanence back to a subject that constitutes the given'.[10] Lawlor's analysis highlights the problem we have continually returned to, the problem that Deleuze describes as early as *Empiricism and Subjectivity*:

> We embark upon a transcendental critique when, having situated ourselves on a methodologically reduced plane that provides an essential certainty – a certainty of essence – we ask: how can there be a given, how can something be given to a subject, and how can the subject give something to itself? ... The critique is

empirical when, having situated ourselves in a purely immanent point of view, ... we ask: how is the subject constituted in the given?[11]

The 'methodologically reduced plane' to which Deleuze refers is the transcendental field accessed through Husserl's famous reduction, his bracketing of the contingencies of experience in order to deduce the transcendental structures of consciousness.[12] Deleuze argues that this methodology 'makes it possible to treat the plane of immanence as a field of consciousness [and, consequently] Immanence is supposed to be immanent to a pure consciousness, to a thinking subject'.[13] For Deleuze, this inevitably violates an ontology of immanence insofar as it 'discovers the modern way of saving transcendence: this is no longer the transcendence of a Something, or of a One higher than everything ... but that of a Subject to which the field of immanence is only attributed by belonging to a self that necessarily represents such a subject to itself'.[14]

In this context it becomes clear why Deleuze outlines the Bergsonism of his *Cinema* project in terms of its opposition to phenomenology. Deleuze argues that the radically decentred immanence of Bergson's ontology challenges phenomenology's methodological fixation on a subjective centre of perception. The crucial passage comes in the course of his discussion of Bergson's famous antipathy towards cinema – an antipathy grounded in cinema's apparent repetition of the fallacy of movement and perception as composed of poses or frames:

> [Bergson's ontological] model would be ... a state of things which would constantly change, a flowing-matter in which no point of anchorage nor centre of reference would be assignable. On the basis of this state of things it would be necessary to show how, at any point, centres can be formed which would impose fixed instantaneous views. It would therefore be a question of 'deducing' conscious, natural or cinematographic perception. But the cinema perhaps has a great advantage: just because it lacks a centre of anchorage and of horizon, the sections which it makes would not prevent it from going back up the path that natural perception comes down. Instead of going from the acentred state of things to centred perception, it could go back up towards the acentred state of things, and get closer to it. Broadly speaking, this would be the opposite of what phenomenology put forward.[15]

Deleuze engages with Bergson's ontology precisely because it enables him to challenge phenomenology's resurrection of the transcendent. As Levi Bryant put it, from the point of view of the ontology Deleuze develops, 'the human and its relation to the world can no longer be treated as a privileged starting point for philosophical investigation. Humans are among beings, rather than a privileged point around which being is organized.'[16] It is only from within this context that Deleuze can approach the Humean problem of the subject's constitution in the given. For Deleuze, an exploration of the constitution of subjectivity cannot hinge on the view of the subject as a dative case to whom the plane of immanence is given; his response is, simply, that the installation of the subject as a dative, that is, as the indirect object of empirical processes, reduces the plane of immanence to its immanence to a subject. To reinstate immanence as immanent only to itself,[17] Deleuze builds an ontology in which the subject is understood as an event on the plane of immanence: the subject corresponds to a fixed point of view in a universe of flowing movement-matter. Against the criticism Bergson offers in *Creative Evolution*, Deleuze argues that cinema does not merely reproduce the illusions of natural perception. Cinema, according to Deleuze, presents exactly this model of a universe of 'flowing-matter in which no point of anchorage nor centre of reference would be assignable'.[18]

In order to demonstrate how cinema forms subjects as 'centres ... which would impose fixed instantaneous views', we must explore how Deleuze conceives the subjects of the cinematic universe as immanent to the world they experience and condition. Gregory Flaxman suggests this approach when, in his contribution to the seminal collection *The Brain Is the Screen: Deleuze and the Philosophy of Cinema*, he writes that

> the subject is the extraction, the process of drawing order from [the universe as an aggregate of images] as if through a sieve ... this implies a 'cooling down' of the universe, for the world of images has begun to settle into a semblance of 'bodies' and 'rigid lines'. ... In a sense, the subject is a point at which the universe sees itself: the subject synthesizes the world from a particular point of view, but the subject also derives from that world, each perspective constituting a self-synthesis.[19]

Subjectivity is, then, the product of the synthesis which constitutes a point of view immanent to the processes of the flow of movement-matter. This requires an exploration of how Deleuze's interpretation of cinematic techniques for composing and associating images entails the emergence of fixed, instantaneous points of view from a synthesis of differing points of view. In particular, this entails two questions: First, how does Deleuze understand an image as being composed – *framed* – such that it has specific relevance to the point of view from which it is encountered? Second, how do different perspectives immanent to the same point of view constitute a form of subjectivity through their synthesis? These questions are closely related to what Deleuze calls cinema's 'great advantage'. For Deleuze, cinema circumvents phenomenology's privileging of the subject as a 'centre of anchorage' in the relationality of the actual world. The cinematic composition of centres, intervals and sections of movement does not present the problems of natural perception which join, according to Bergson, 'several clear images that represent states and which serve to distinguish all becomings from each other'.[20] The great advantage of cinema is, for Deleuze, that it bypasses the illusion that movement is composed of immobilities because its specific techniques compose an acentred universe. The immobile elements of cinema, the sequence of frames that run through the projector, imply a virtual whole which associates the immobile elements and ensures that their closure – their apparent independence from each other – is only ever partial; the sequence of which they are parts always gestures towards the law of association – the subsistence of problems – that assembles them as this or that sequence. With this in mind, we will turn in the next section to Deleuze's conception of the association and synthesis of images and how this association constitutes the 'immobilities', that is, the centres, of this universe of flowing movement-matter.

Bipolar perceptions: Analysis, description and semisubjectivity

For Deleuze, perception is bipolar. That is, any particular perception consists of two elements or senses: it is double. The subject – the subject of an action, the being of the interval – is a process in which the two poles of perception are conjoined in the determination of a problem. To develop a vocabulary for this discussion, Deleuze appropriates the concept of a semisubjective (or 'associated') image from Jean Mitry's classic *The Aesthetics and Psychology of the Cinema*. The semisubjective image is a total image, not in the sense that it provides the most total view of a scene – an objective or omniscient view – but instead in the sense that it produces the most meaning or, rather, the most total association between the viewer and the scene. This species of image emerges from the tension between two poles of the perception-image: an analytic image and a descriptive image. These images would typically be called subjective and objective images, respectively; however, since Deleuze's concerns are focused on what it would mean for an image to be either subjective or objective, we need to be careful with such adjectives. Indeed, Mitry ultimately reserves the term *subjective* for images which create memory relationships, since an image of this type necessarily relates us to the experiences of a filmic subject.[21] Since the subjectivity of this image is 'merely visual', he prefers to employ the term *analytic*. An analytic image is so named because it is always in place to show us what a specific character sees and to analyse the set of relations from that character's point of view. Opposed to this is a descriptive image through which we see the scene from outside and are privy to a point of view which has no particular investment in the set of relations it describes. Thus, 'analytic' and 'descriptive' denote respectively an analysis of the scene from a particular, internal point of view and a description of the scene from a general, external point of view. Following Mitry's lead, we will use 'analytic' and 'descriptive' because they allow us to reserve the terms *subjective* and *objective* for those instances when we are discussing relations *to* or *of* subjects or objects. Compared to *subjective* and *objective*, *analytic* and *descriptive* are more accurate adjectives for the poles of perception. The former pair, 'subjective' and 'objective', always risk relating a perception to a subject who perceives or an object that is perceived. 'Analytic' and 'descriptive', however, connote the role of perception in constituting its subject and object insofar as these adjectives describe the processes that occur at each pole. That is, they tell us whether a particular pole of perception presents us with a descriptive or an analytic point of view.

According to Mitry, neither the analytic nor descriptive image provides a total or exhaustive view on a scene; it is the semisubjective image which is a total image. Without this semisubjective image, film could not develop its stories and narratives because it would be limited to the opposition or juxtaposition of description and analysis. A dialectical juxtaposition of analysis and description presents an either/or proposition – a shot would be *either* analysis *or* description – and would thus preclude the possibility of seeing the reaction of a character to a situation at the same time as seeing the situation from the point of view of the character. And so it needs a special kind of image to associate analysis and description. As Mitry puts it, in such a situation, '[i]t is not possible to see both object and subject simultaneously'.[22] Limited to description and analysis, film cannot present a character's reaction to an analysis of a description. Mitry finds a solution to this dilemma in the semisubjective, a species of image exemplified in a scene from William Wyler's *Jezebel* (1938). The scene is of a central character, Julie, in a cleaning frenzy and the camera, framing her in midshot, follows her as she works:

> [I]n order to 'experience' the feelings of a given character, all the audience had to do is be with the character, alongside him. ... Thus instead of the camera taking the place of the character, there were images framing the hero, either from head to toe or from the waist up, following him as he moved, seeing with

him and at the same time as him. The image remained descriptive but shared in the character's points of view. ... Thus, as we see her acting, we feel as though we are acting with her; moreover, the agitation of the camera movements, prompted by the nervousness of her movements, conveys her agitation to the audience, which thereby experiences the same feelings of impatience and irritation and shares in her emotion.[23]

The semisubjective is, for Mitry, a species of image that goes further than a typically subjective or analytic image ever could. He argues that a shot which is ostensibly from a first-person point of view does not itself carry the information necessary to relate its content to any particular character and, as such, a subjective image is so only insofar as the image is referred to a character already established in the film. In this way, a subjective image is only 'a complement to another image ... [and] has meaning only insofar as it relates to a character already objectively described and placed'.[24] The semisubjective image is therefore an image which conveys to the audience the character's various affective states and engagements – that is, an *analysis* of a set of relations from the character's point of view – while simultaneously tracking, or, *describing*, the relative position and movements of the character within the relevant set.

There is, however, an important difference between Deleuze's use of this concept and Mitry's presentation. Mitry is interested in the semisubjective image because of its capacity to create an affinity between the character and the viewer whereas Deleuze, true to his Bergsonian heritage, is interested in the synthesis of analytic and descriptive points of view in the interval between perception and action. For Mitry, the affinity created between a character and an audience through the semisubjective image allows the audience to 'project *onto* [the character] feelings which *might have been ours* in similar circumstances'.[25] Deleuze, meanwhile, is concerned with cinema's, or more precisely, the *camera's*, capacity to show us an internal point of view on the set without that point of view belonging to a specific character, even though it tracks the character's movements within the set. Even with this difference in mind, Deleuze's use of Mitry's concept bears an important mark of its origin in the latter's work. For Mitry, the purpose of the semisubjective image is not to represent the psychological reality of the character, but to give 'the audience ... the impression that it is seeing or feeling "as though" it were the character in the drama'.[26] While Mitry presents this image as facilitating a rapport between characters and viewers, Deleuze's attention is focused elsewhere; for him, the semisubjective image is the synthesis of two points of view that are both immanent to the field of relations framed by the screen. The semisubjective image is not its content as such; it is, rather, the cinematic mode constituted in the syntheses of ostensibly distinct points of view. Deleuze sets out from this apparent distinction between two points of view and sets up provisional definitions of subjective/analytic images – 'the thing seen by someone "qualified", or the set as it is seen by someone who forms part of that set' – and objective/descriptive images – 'the thing or the set … seen from the view point of someone who remains external to that set'.[27] Deleuze stretches these definitions and argues for a situation in cinema wherein the distinction between descriptive and analytic is overcome in favour of 'a pure Form which sets itself up as an autonomous vision of the content'. It is a situation in which 'we are caught in a correlation between a perception-image and a camera-consciousness which transforms it'.[28]

To explain this correlation, Deleuze turns to Albert Lewin's *Pandora and the Flying Dutchman* (1951). The film's establishing shot exemplifies an objective shot: a wide shot of groups of people running along a beach towards a fishing boat that has run aground. But the camera withdraws and progressively expands the shot of the beach to take in a telescope on the balcony of a nearby house and then a character watching the beach scene through the telescope. Even though this shot never offers an analytic point of view – that is, we never see from the point of view of someone within the set – it is not a strictly objective point of view either because the inclusion of the character in the shot gives the scene significance to the viewer, especially when the camera follows the character inside her house where she discusses the fishing boat with her uncle. Deleuze, too, is interested in the determination of significance; however, his interest is not in the significance of the scene for a viewer as it was for Mitry. Rather, it is in the relationship between the analysis of the scene from the point of view of the character and the point of view of the camera itself – a point of view which accompanies the character but is not attributable to it.

Because this situation has no analogue in natural perception, Deleuze turns to linguists Pier Pasolini and V. N. Vološinov to provide tools for analysis. Vološinov argued for a phenomenon called 'Reported speech': 'speech within speech, utterance within utterance, and at the same time also *speech about speech, utterance about utterance*'.[29] Deleuze focuses here on what he calls an assemblage of enunciation:

> [T]here is not a simple combination of two fully-constituted subjects of enunciation, one of which would be reporter, the other reported, it is rather a case of an assemblage of enunciation, carrying out two inseparable acts of

subjectivation simultaneously, one of which constitutes a character in the first person, but the other of which is present at his birth and brings him on to the scene. There is no mixture or average of two subjects, each belonging to a system, but a differentiation of two correlative subjects in a system which is itself heterogeneous.[30]

The importance of this phenomenon in language is, Deleuze argues, that 'this differentiation of the subject' also occurs in thought. He argues that the cogito as 'an empirical subject cannot be born into the world without simultaneously being reflected in a transcendental subject which thinks it and in which it thinks itself'.[31] At this point, Deleuze turns to Pasolini who argues for a formal common ground between linguistics and cinema. In reading Pasolini, Deleuze contends that the significance of free-indirect discourse (Pasolini's name for reported speech) is that it presents a situation in which the

> character acts on the screen, and is assumed to see the world in a certain way. But simultaneously the camera sees him, and sees his world, from another point of view which thinks, reflects and transforms the view point of the character. ... But the camera does not simply give us the vision of the character and of his world: it imposes another vision in which the first is transformed and reflected.[32]

When we first considered the nature of the image in Chapter 4, it turned on a distinction between the image as object – a universe in which '*all the images vary in relation to one another, on all their facets and in all their parts*' – and the image as a subjective perception of the object, the situation where '*the images vary in relation to a central and privileged image*'.[33] More than merely recapitulating Bergson's concept of the image, however, Deleuze's conception of semisubjective images allows him to emphasize that, far from object and subject being distinct *types* of image, the distinction between the objective and subjective senses of the image provides 'a real definition of the two poles, or of the double system' of perception.[34] This definition of the objectivity and subjectivity of the image as poles of perception highlights the possibility of moving between the objective and subjective. Deleuze characterizes this diffuse form of perception as a liquid perception. In this case, perception is, as Bogue puts it, 'no longer constrained by bodies';[35] it is the image 'in the process of becoming liquid, which [flows] through or under the frame'.[36] In this case, then, there are three moments within the perception-image; two – the two poles, objective and subjective – which express the composition of specific perceptions, and a third, unique to cinema, that presents a third sense of the perception-image, a liquid form which expresses the genesis of perception.[37] In other words, the perception-image is generated as the mixing of the two poles, but when it is actualized as this or that perception, it is expressed as a specific ratio of analysis and description.

To move from this discussion of the bipolar composition of the perception-image to the determination of the perception-image as problematic, we must turn to the discussion of framing that Deleuze undertakes early in *Cinema 1*. 'Framing' is a name for the unconscious, or *passive*, processes that make perception possible, and it provides the context for Deleuze's analysis of contemplation and its role in the genesis of a uniquely cinematic subjectivity. Contemplation here is not a subject's reflection on an object; it is the passive process by which previous experiences are contracted into an anticipation of the future,[38] and so any discussion of perception necessarily presupposes a discussion of framing.[39] That is, insofar as an image is only an image to the extent that it is demarcated from the flux of which it is a part, an image is always framed.

Framing and the determination of problems

Framing is the technique by which a body selects out relevant data from the flux of movement-matter. As Deleuze puts it, '[F]raming is limitation. But, depending on the concept itself the limits can be conceived in two ways, mathematically or dynamically: either as a preliminary to the existence of the bodies whose essence they fix, or going as far as the power of existing bodies goes'.[40] Framing is a crucial component of the determination of problems because it defines the boundaries of the image to which a body responds. But there is also a second reason contemplation is significant to Deleuze's understanding of the determination of problems. The framed image comes into contact with an *opaque* screen.[41] This is why Bergson, in *Matter and Memory*, argues that the body is not an indifferent recipient of sensation. In other words, the power and capacities of a body direct it towards action, and the sensations of memory – that is, the affects which characterize the body's relationship to the whole – 'tend to bring about, within the body, all the corresponding sensations'.[42] Bergson's point is that an individual does not merely *receive* information, as though the body has no vested interest in the content and form of the information with which it is presented. Rather, the power and capacities of a body contribute significantly to the *framing* of the information it receives. This is why Deleuze calls the body an opaque screen; the structure and content of the facet of the body which receives information from the world – the screen on which the perception-image is reflected – determines the sense in which the perception-image is problematic insofar as it *frames* it.

This is the meaning of Bergson's argument that sensory modifications are not the cause of the sensations which affect the body, even though they determine the form of the action that follows from the body's transformations. Just as Deleuze was sceptical about the precipice causing the character's vertigo, Bergson argues that 'modifications in the centres called sensory ... are, then, less the real cause of the sensation than the mark of its power and the condition of its efficacy'.[43] Contemplation – the contraction of previous experience into an anticipation of the future – is vital because it determines the boundaries of the frame. Taken together, contemplation and framing determine the extent to which a particular perception constitutes a problem for a living image.

All of this is to say that Deleuze's conceptualization of cinematic subjectivity is actually an elaboration of the determination of *centres of indetermination* within a continuum of moving-matter.[44] 'Indetermination' here describes the centre as a being for whom the response to the problem presented by perception is not yet given; as D. N. Rodowick puts it, indetermination 'is the range of responses available for selection as the appropriate response or action with respect to analysed stimulus or perception'.[45] Subjectivity emerges from the interval between stimulus and response, between perception and action; however, the interval, the special image, insofar as it is an image which can be viewed from the inside, is not merely reactive in the ways sometimes implied by the vocabulary of stimulus and response. While it is not the case for every image, perhaps even the majority of images, the interval which generates a subject constitutes a rupture in which the content of a moving image is constituted as a perception-image. It is framed in particular ways, and its content is contemplated, apprehended and sifted such that it poses a problem for the being of the interval. These operations couple with the synthesis of points of view on the image and constitute a subject at the same time as they determine its action.

To understand the difference between Deleuze's Bergsonian model and a deliberative model of action, we need only turn to the famous cone that appears in the third chapter of *Matter and Memory* (Figure 2).[46] While he never develops the vocabulary in as robust a way as Deleuze, Bergson is still concerned with a 'conversion from the virtual to the actual'.[47] Bergson's discussion centres on 'the clearly defined form of a bodily attitude' at the point S, and the base of the cone, AB, as 'the aspect, no less defined, of the thousand individual images into which its fragile unity would break up'.[48] Simply put, at the base of the cone, AB, is the multiplicity of images, memories, sensations and affects, which together constitute the virtual background which determines the problems faced by my

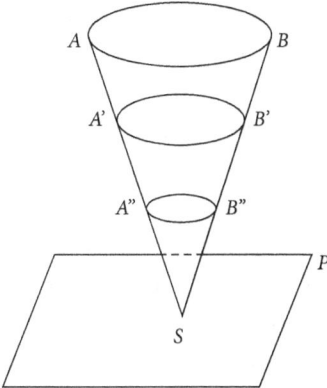

Figure 2 Bergson's 'second great schema', *Matter and Memory*'s famous cone with 'virtual circuits ... which contain all our past as [it] preserved in itself'. Deleuze, *Cinema 2*, 294; Bergson, *Matière et mémoire*, 168.

body. At the summit, S, is the contraction of these images into the determination of an action. Of course, the movement from perception to action, from AB to S, is infinitely divisible: A'B', A"B" and so forth. The base of this cone, or, rather, its determination, is not actual and neither are the slices excerpted from the passage from AB through S. These sections are, as Deleuze notes, virtual;[49] the only element of this image that represents something actual is S, the contraction of all images into the determination of an action. This is the crucial distinction between Deleuze's model and a deliberative model of action; a deliberative model of action would want to empower a subject, given at S, to choose between equally viable, *equally possible*, alternatives given at AB, whereas Deleuze's Bergsonism rejects the thought that any given slice is as possible as any other slice. Only S is actually possible, and the movement from AB to S, from base to summit, constitutes the determination of what is possible.

In *Difference and Repetition*'s interpretation of Bergson's essay 'The Possible and the Real', Deleuze repeatedly emphasizes that the actual cannot resemble the set of possibilities it actualizes.[50] Consequently, the sections AB, A'B', A"B" and so on do not present as collections of possibilities with greater or lesser chance of being realized at S. Instead, these sections are virtual multiplicities: assemblages of virtual elements undergoing progressive framings, descriptions and analyses en route to the formulation of a problem. Of course, it is not the problem itself which is framed at AB and so on; the elements of the multiplicity are framed and reframed until, at S, they are formulated as a problem. This problematic formulation, however, occurs simultaneously with the expression of the solution to the problem. In other words, the specific determination of the problem and the expression of its solution as 'the clearly defined form of a bodily attitude' occur simultaneously. This is what Deleuze means when he says that 'the virtual must be defined as strictly a part of the real object'.[51] Deleuze's model of the constitution of action is distinguished from a deliberative model by virtue of the fact that the specific conditions of a specific action are determined simultaneously with the expression of the action itself. While the elements of the multiplicity are not subordinate to their status as elements of a problem which corresponds to what actually occurs, talk of possibilities or options among which an agent can choose is nonsensical precisely because what is possible, in the sense of a virtual power, is determined at the same time as its expression in an actual occurrence.

Importantly, the sheets of the cone are sheets of the past – that is, of *memory*.[52] This is not the past of a particular individual but the past in general – the past as the ontological condition for the present. When Deleuze discusses this issue in *Cinema 2*, it echoes a theme that is present throughout his oeuvre: the production of subjectivity is a process that is internal to time. In this case, the constitution of a subject of action at S is internal to time insofar as it is actualization of the organization of the whole of *durée*. To the extent that the organization of the past *as such* is the ontological condition for the passing present, the action which characterizes this or that particular present is an intrinsic mode of the whole. Importantly, the sense in which the constitution and transformation of a subject is internal to time is how Deleuze conceives the passive contraction of the past, that is, *habit*, as a condition for the subject's action. As such, in the next section, we must explore the sense in which the dialectic of problems is temporal. The significance of this temporal sense of the dialectic of problems is that, insofar as the particular, actual present is the actual expression of the whole of *durée*, it gives us a more sophisticated view of the reciprocity of the individual and the whole of which it is a part.

Memory, perception and temporal series

Against Kant, who argues that time is an ideal category imposed on things by a transcendental form of subjectivity, Deleuze argues that the subject is constituted in time as a function of the whole of *durée*:

> That we are in time looks like a common-place, yet it is the highest paradox. Time is not the interior in us, but just the opposite, the interiority in which

we are, in which we move, live and change. ... Subjectivity is never ours, it is time, that is, the soul or the spirit, the virtual. The actual is always objective, but the virtual is subjective: it was initially the affect, that which we experience in time; then time itself, pure virtuality which divides itself in two as affector and affected.[53]

This passage gives us a provisional hypothesis: the Whole is temporal – indeed, it is time itself – and the bodies which both constitute and express the Whole are internal to time. As Deleuze notes, this whole is virtual, and we are internal to it in the sense that it is the reality of the relations that give content to our lives. The final section of this passage, however, illuminates the deceptive simplicity of this hypothesis. Deleuze's claim is that our experience shifts so that a new image – the time-image, *time itself* – becomes the object of experience. This is what he means when he says that the actual is objective and that the virtual is subjective; when our experience is directed at our affective relations, our being affected correlates with actual objects that do not cause the affects. However, as experience undergoes this transition, the object of experience changes, and time itself – virtuality or the being of relations – becomes the object of experience, the 'affector', even as we continue to be intrinsic expressions of time; therefore, time itself is simultaneously the subject of experience, the 'affected'.

What does it mean to say that '[t]ime ... is the interiority in which we are'? To answer this question we need to elaborate the sense in which the sections of *Matter and Memory*'s cone are *temporal*, that is, the sense in which they are 'sheets of the past'.[54] For Deleuze these sheets are contracted into an actual present and so, to understand how the past – embodied habits born of previous experiences, memories and so on – are contracted into something actually occurring in the present, we must turn to a model of time that envisions paradoxes of simultaneity as the conditions for chronological or serial time. Deleuze provides us with a model of this when he writes that

> [i]t is true that these regions ... appear to succeed each other. But they succeed each other only from the point of view of former presents which marked the limit of each of them. They coexist, in contrast, from the point of view of the actual present which each time represents their common limit or the most contracted of them. ... These are the paradoxical characteristics of a non-chronological time: the pre-existence of a past in general; the coexistence of all the sheets of past; and the existence of a most contracted degree.[55]

In his reading of Bergson, Deleuze argues that 'the "present" that endures divides at each "instant" into two directions, one oriented and dilated toward the past, the other contracted, contracting toward the future'.⁵⁶ These two hypotheses clearly echo the first two syntheses of time. On the one hand, the second synthesis outlined in *Difference and Repetition* concerns the passive synthesis of the whole of the past that has no direct importance to the synthesis of habit; the model offered in *Cinema 2* is, on the other hand, concerned with a past-oriented dilation of time that Deleuze calls *memory*. Deleuze had discussed Bergson's concept of memory in *Bergsonism*, and he returns to it here to conceptualize the ontological conditions of the passing of the present. Following Bergson, these conditions are called memory; however, they must not be confused with psychological recollection. In cases when the past is actualized in us, it is actualized as recollections; however, the past is not its actualizations. Memory, or the past, for Deleuze treats them as synonyms, is the in-itself, '*l'en-soi*', of being; it is the ontological condition of our lives.⁵⁷ As Deleuze puts it, 'Memory is not in us; it is we who move in a Being-memory, a world-memory'.⁵⁸

The argument Deleuze presents here is structurally similar to the arguments for the second synthesis in *Difference and Repetition*. As Williams argues, this synthesis is grounded in an effort to make sense of why it is that the passing present passes at all.⁵⁹ In order for the present to pass, Deleuze argues, it must be grounded in a past that subsists in it. However, this subsistent past is not a prior present, it is a form of time that exists for itself and as the condition for the serial time we experience. Thus, when Deleuze calls it *past*, he does not mean it in the same sense that a former present is past. On the one hand, it is the past in the sense that it is our relationship to what has been, the potential for our recollection and, therefore, memory. On the other hand, it is the condition under which the present passes in order to become this or that particular past. He writes that

> [t]he past is 'contemporaneous' with the present that it *has been*. If the past had to wait in order to be no longer, if it was not immediately and now that it had passed, 'past in general', it could never become what it is, it would never be *that* past. If it were not constituted immediately, neither could it be reconstituted on the basis of an ulterior present. The past would never be constituted if it did not coexist with the present whose past it is.⁶⁰

This is why Deleuze says that the present 'divides' at each instant. The present is not a divisible quantity; it is, rather, an occurrence that is double. On the one hand, it is the actual presence of the images with which we engage,⁶¹ and on the other hand, it is invested in a continually dilating and transforming past in general. In other words, the past in general that Deleuze describes is the virtual, expanding history of actual occurrences such that it functions as a set of heterogeneous conditions for the actual.

This leaves us with Deleuze's other hypothesis; the present is not merely dilated towards the past in general but also contracted towards the future. This hypothesis bears a marked similarity to the first synthesis of time, concerned as it is with habit or the imagination's passive contraction of previous sensations into an anticipation of a future state of affairs. The future towards which the present is contracted is, as Williams argues, constituted through *anticipation*.[62] That is, the genesis of the future is the contraction of past particulars into an anticipation that something will happen. However, the constitution of this anticipation is passive and, as such, has no object; being passive there is no mind or consciousness which anticipates and so the anticipation has no content to attach it to an object. The focus of Deleuze's second hypothesis is thus the aspect of the living present which synthesizes or contracts the past into the anticipation that constitutes the future. 'An activity', Williams argues, that 'must synthesise earlier movements and later ones'.[63]

Clearly, then, *Cinema 2* returns to a model of time that has its origins in *Empiricism and Subjectivity* and appears more or less explicitly in every subsequent work. However, one element that initially seems absent from *Cinema*'s presentation of time is a version of the third synthesis of time, the empty form of time that brings the first two syntheses together such that the heterogeneous assemblage of series of virtual events determines the actual instantiation of a mode of life. Even though Deleuze does not signpost it as such, there is a concept in the *Cinema* books which does this work. Deleuze talks about the present as the shortest circuit between an actual image and its virtual image: 'The actual image and *its* virtual image thus constitute the smallest internal circuit, ultimately a peak or point, but a physical point which has distinct elements. ... Distinct, but indiscernible, such are the actual and the virtual which are in continual exchange' (Figure 3).[64]

By appealing to an illustration that Bergson offers in *Matter and Memory*, Deleuze argues that the actual present is not simply an actual object, action or image; it is the minimally contracted circuit between the object and its virtual image. In other words, the living present is the locus of two tendencies, past-oriented dilation and future-oriented contraction.[65] Consequently, the question of the third synthesis of time can be given in cinematic terms: Why do the circuits of the actual image and its virtual image expand and contract? Deleuze's claim is that it is a *sensory-motor schema* that is the affective motor of the contractions and dilations of these circuits between an actual image and its virtual image. In other words, the sensory-motor schema is the motor by which particular signs differentiate and specify the movement-image as this or that particular sequence of perceptions, affections and actions. This is not to suggest that *Cinema* presents a model of time with a repetition of the first two syntheses and the sensory-motor schema as a replacement for the complexity of the third synthesis. Rather, this Bergsonian concept allows Deleuze to emphasize the role played by sensory-motor linkages and interactions in synthesizing the two tendencies of the living present such that something actually occurs.[66] As such, in classical cinema's treatment of the movement-image, montage entails action. The sensory-motor schema is not a prescriptive rule for how the movement-image is to be differentiated into the coupling of perception and action; it is, rather, a set of conditions that must be met in order for the double expressivity of affection to connect a perception with an action.

Deleuze does not say a lot about the sensory-motor schema in itself; in fact, he devotes more space to its breakdown, and I will discuss this in the final section of this chapter. For now, however, there are still inferences to be made once we treat it as the condition of the immanent logics that determine an action on the basis of the relationship between perception, memory and affection. In *Cinema 2*, Deleuze couples his broader discussion of semiotics with a critique of the standard view that film is primarily a narrative medium, and, on the back of his

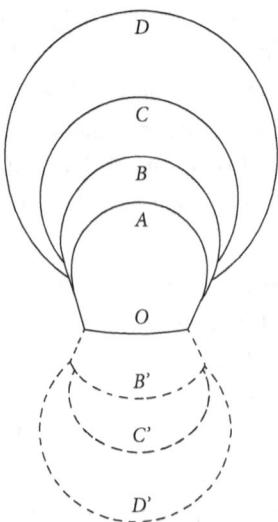

Figure 3 Bergson's 'first great schema', the circuits of memory and perception. Deleuze, *Cinema 2*, 289; Bergson, *Matière et mémoire*, 109.

conception of semiotics as the system of signs which associate types of image, Deleuze describes montage as the condition which determines narrative:

> [N]arration is only a consequence of the visible images themselves and their direct combinations – it is never a given. So-called classical narration derives directly from the organic composition of movement-images [*montage*], or from their specification as perception-images, affection-images and action-images, according to the laws of a sensory-motor schema. ... Narration is never an evident [*apparent*] given of images, or the effect of a structure which underlies them; it is a consequence of the visible [*apparent*] images themselves, of the perceptible images in themselves, as they are initially defined for themselves.[67]

Before it is anything else, the universe is, for Deleuze, the composition and arrangement of movement-images.[68] And so, when he claims that *Matter and Memory*'s presentation of the universe as an assemblage of images is a description of the universe as a 'cinema in itself', Deleuze names this assemblage *montage*. Narration, the narrative sequence of events, is then a consequence of montage because it is only the surface effect of images being cut together and assembled according to a logic that is not grounded in the film's narrative. Accordingly, Deleuze argues that classical cinema is concerned with sensory-motor situations. Action-images have two possible concerns; on the one hand, a situation is either deduced or disclosed through an action or, on the other hand, a situation is transformed through an action.[69] In any case, all of these concerns involve the passive retention and contraction of past particulars into future-oriented anticipations; that is, the generation of the action-image always entails contemplation. Thus, Deleuze argues, 'The action-image ... was inseparable from acts of comprehension through which the hero evaluated what was given in the problem or situation, or from acts of inference by which he guessed what was not given.'[70] In this context, Deleuze borrows a phrase from Spinoza, *spiritual automaton*, to, as Bogue puts it, 'stress the involuntary nature of thought's response to the moving image'.[71] As Deleuze argues, '*Automatic movement* gives rise to a *spiritual automaton* in us, which reacts in turn on movement. The spiritual automaton ... designates ... the circuit into which [thoughts] enter with the movement-image, the shared power of what forces thinking and what thinks under the shock.'[72] Deleuze's point is that thought is as determined as action. Action, insofar as it develops according to a sensory-motor schema, is determined by how a character *makes sense* of the situation in which she finds herself. That is, action is determined according to the way that elements of the past – recollections, habits, the portion of history and memory accessible to the character – interact with new information such that the movement-image is specified as a perception or a problem: 'The cinema of action depicts sensory-motor situations: there are characters, in a certain situation, who act ... according to how they perceive the situation. Actions are linked to perceptions and perceptions develop into actions.'[73]

Serial or chronological time is thus an expression of a collection of virtual elements assembled and arranged according to a logic whose specific content is determined immanently to its actual expression. Deleuze's use of cinema's vocabulary makes it clear which element is epiphenomenal. The flux of movement-matter is differentiated relative to my body, a centre of indetermination, such that part of it corresponds to a determined problem, and the remainder passes by unattended. According to an immanent logic – the laws of a sensory-motor schema – this virtual problem corresponds to the determination of an action-image. This process, the differentiation of the movement-image into its avatars, and their organization into this or that particular assemblage, is what Deleuze calls montage. The superficial expression, the narrative, the sequence or chronology of occurrences is epiphenomenal in the most literal sense of being a by-product of montage. However, to understand the means and consequences of the transition from a perception of objects to a direct experience of time, we need to understand how the movement-image is differentiated relative to my body and for that we must turn to Deleuze's semiotics.

Signs and the differentiation of the image

As opposed to interpretative methods which treat film as a symbolic language, the semiotics of *Cinema* is concerned with the relations between the elements that compose images; as Deleuze says, '[T]he various types of image don't already exist, they have to be created. A flat image or, conversely, depth of field, always has to be created or re-created ... all images combine the same elements, the same signs, differently.'[74] However, this creation of images through the relations among signs is not a creation ex nihilo. In *Cinema 2*, Deleuze argues that, insofar as distinct types of image appear when the movement-image is referred to an interval, the components of the movement-image together form a 'plastic mass ... [that] is formed semiotically, aesthetically and pragmatically'.[75] This plastic mass undergoes a constant process of specification and differenciation. From this point of view there is a '*signaletic material*'[76] – an entire ecology of signs, of 'modulation features' – which, relative to an interval, differentiates and specifies the movement-image as a perception, an affection and an action. In this sense, signs are the compositional elements of the image.[77]

However, signs do not merely compose and differentiate images; they also facilitate their relations. This is why Deleuze at first offers a sympathetic presentation of C. S. Peirce's understanding of the sign; on Deleuze's account, signs, for Peirce, 'make relations efficient'.[78] According to Bogue, signs generate this efficiency insofar as they make possible associations between images.[79] However, Deleuze ultimately criticizes Peirce for subordinating images to their linguistic sense insofar as this efficiency is grounded in knowledge; that is, the referential function through which signs associate images is essentially cognitive. For Deleuze, this means that Peirce occasionally finds 'himself as much a linguist as the semiologists … [insofar as] he would have given up trying to make semiotics a "descriptive science of reality" (logic)'.[80] Instead, Deleuze defines the sign as 'a particular image that refers to a type of image, whether from the point of view of its bipolar composition, or from the point of view of its genesis'.[81] Importantly, then, the legibility and eventual problematic structure of images are not issues of interpreting semiological references; Deleuze's semiotics treats signs as the objects of affective encounters. It is in this sense that John Mullarky argues that 'this "signaletic" material has direct, sensory affects on the brain, not the symbolic imagination'.[82] This is why Deleuze argues that '[s]omething in the world forces us to think. This something is an object not of recognition but of a fundamental *encounter*. … It is not a quality but a sign.'[83]

Cinema's semiotics is significant because it foregrounds the importance of contemplation. As Williams argues, '*[E]ven in activity the present is contemplation, that is, passive absorption and transformation of retained particulars beyond the set considered in an action*.'[84] Crucial to Deleuze's ontology here is a claim that any action will exhibit various general and particular selections and these selections presuppose the continuum of moving-matter from which they are drawn. This, Williams argues, leads to the argument that conscious action is grounded in passive, unconscious processes of retention and expectation.[85] In this sense, the semiotics described by *Cinema* sets out the role of understanding, of the agent's making sense of its milieu,[86] in the differentiation of images and the determination of problems. This issue takes us straight to the significance of the philosophy of time as Deleuze presents it in *Cinema 2*, which exhibits the same concern with the role of differen*t/c*iation in the determination and actualization of time as a series of repetitions as Deleuze's encounter with Bergson in the 1960s. However, in *Cinema 2*, Deleuze foregrounds the ethological sense of his philosophy of time by emphasizing that the past is the virtual subsistence of memory and that the present is the world which gives content to conscious experience. The processes by which the sensory-motor schema determines expansions and contractions in the circuit between an actual image and its virtual image are essentially semiotic. We have discussed the sensory-motor schema, or more accurately, its clichés, as habit, that is the contemplative process which grounds the determination of action in the contraction of the whole of the past. However, the issue that concerns this work, the issue that I contend is ethologically significant, is the sense in which the failure of the sensory-motor schema is the derailing of this habit, the shattering of its efficacy, insofar as *new* actions, ones not informed by clichés, become possible. As such, we must turn to an exploration of the sense in which the failure of the sensory-motor schema is also semiotic.

On the failure of the sensory-motor schema and an art of living

Post-war cinema, Deleuze argues, entails a transition from affects to time as the object of experience. In *Cinema*, Deleuze is interested in sensible experiences; that is, experiences which have as their object the ways in which an external body interacts affectively with my own. Deleuze is interested in the way that, in cinema's post-war transition, there are particular types of sensible experiences that are too great for habit to synthesize into a coherent idea. When this occurs, imagination, the faculty in which these syntheses occur, is taken to its limit by an experience which Deleuze, following Kant, calls *sublime*. In the experience of the sublime, reason intervenes and produces a new idea, a new problem, with the whole itself as its object. What follows when our actions, our modes of life, are determined by new types of ideas? To respond to this question, we will need to explore the type of existential experimentation that Deleuze presents as the consequence of contemplation failing to generate an expectation of the future, of habit being unable to make sense of an experience. Deleuze argues that post–Second World War European cinema is the site of a crisis in the production of action-images, and so in genres such as Italian Neo-Realism and French New Wave, there appear characters who

> hardly believe any longer that a global situation can give rise to an action which is capable of modifying it [anymore] than [they] believe that an action can force a situation to disclose itself. The most 'healthy' illusions fall. The first things to be

compromised everywhere are the linkages of situation-action, action-reaction, excitation-response, in short, the sensory-motor links which produced the action-image.[87]

What breaks or compromises the sensory-motor links is a loss of faith in the power of an action to disclose or transform a situation. Unsurprisingly, this phenomenon first appears in Italian Neo-Realism with characters who are trapped and unable to make sense of war-ravaged cities. However, with later contributions to Italian Neo-Realism, and later genres, cinema further develops the crisis of the action-image and, as such, Deleuze's description of these circumstances goes beyond the historical contingency of the war. There are deeper aesthetic conditions which were actualized in the Second World War, and these conditions gave rise to a new species of image, the crystal image. This image emerges in the circuit between an actual image and its corresponding virtual image, and disrupts their discernibility by reflecting each in the other, and reversing their roles. Where the signs of an image usually facilitate the relations between images by referring them to each other, the signs of the crystal image, *opsigns* and *sonsigns*, refer only to the images as optical and auditory situations thus rendering the virtual and the actual sides of a circuit indiscernible. From this, Deleuze develops the theme of time as the object of experience. Time is not objectified; rather, the actual object cannot be distinguished from its virtual image and so experience takes the multiplicity of indeterminate meaning as its object and is unable to extract an intelligible, actual image. Deleuze argues that

> indiscernibility constitutes an objective illusion; it does not suppress the distinction between the two sides, but makes it unattributable, each side taking the other's role in a relation which we must describe as reciprocal presupposition, or reversibility. In fact, there is no virtual which does not become actual in relation to the actual, the latter becoming virtual through the same relation.[88]

The emergence of the crystal image does not necessarily require conditions as violently traumatic as a global war: 'Without recourse to violence, and through the development of an experimentation, something will come out of the crystal, a new Real will come out beyond the actual and the virtual.'[89] In one of his more explicit appropriations of a Kantian theme, Deleuze characterizes the conditions of this breakdown in terms of the sublime; as Valentine Moulard puts it, '[W]hen we are confronted with an excess of beauty or horror in images, with the sublime or the unbearable, our sensory-motor mechanisms jam.'[90] In the *Critique of Judgement*, Kant describes as sublime those experiences which have as their object something that is '*absolutely great*'; that is, the objects we can rightly judge as sublime are those whose greatness is without quantitative magnitude and beyond all comparison.[91] At this point, Kant sets out an argument that is crucial to Deleuze's argument that time's rupture is grounded in a subjective experience; with regard to the object of the judgement of the sublime, Kant argues that 'it is the disposition of soul evoked by a particular representation engaging the attention of the reflective judgement, and not the Object, that is to be called sublime'.[92] Kant argues that, because the greatness of the sublime is such that 'in comparison ... all else is small',[93] the objects of the senses cannot be called sublime. The magnitude of any object of sensation is measurable relative to some other object and, thus, there will always be something relative to which the magnitude of the initial object is smaller or larger. For Kant this argument is applicable to any object whose magnitude is subject to mathematical estimation. However, there are also objects which are beyond my capacity to experience completely in a single instant, and here Kant offers as an example the pyramids of Egypt. I cannot view the pyramids as a totality; by the time my eye moves to take in the summit, it will have lost sight of the base. However, as it is the task of the imagination to synthesize these sensations into a total image, this does not present a problem because 'the power of numbers extends to infinity',[94] and so there is nothing given or givable to the senses which could be called sublime. Contrary to this, it is the object's provocation of the judging subject which Kant calls sublime: '[F]or the aesthetic estimation there certainly is [a greatest possible], and of it I say that where it is considered an absolute measure beyond which no greater is possible subjectively (i.e. for the judging Subject), it then conveys the idea of the sublime, and calls forth that emotion which no mathematical estimation by numbers can evoke.'[95]

In the 'Analytic of the Sublime', Kant divides the operations of the imagination into either apprehension or comprehension. In his reading of Kant, Deleuze argues that apprehension is 'the successive apprehension of parts'; it is the synthesis of parts that is the condition for a future-oriented anticipation (*contemplation*).[96] According to Kant, there is no difficulty in extending such apprehension to infinity; however, the expansion of this operation takes comprehension to its limit. Once the imagination takes in so much information, adding further information corresponds with a loss. Consequently, while apprehension – the accretion of 'representations of sensuous intuition'[97] – can proceed to infinity, comprehension reaches a limit that the imagination cannot overcome. An important question follows from this: If the imagination reaches the limit of its power of comprehension in the experience of the sublime, what is it that pushes it to this limit? What is it that forces the imagination to extend its reach in an attempt to unite and comprehend the immensity of the world? It is *reason's Ideas* – Ideas produced by the faculty of reason – that can be thought but not known or imagined.[98] As Kant says, '[T]he sublime must in every case have reference to our *way of thinking*';[99] when we enlarge imagination, reason inevitably appears and 'compels us subjectively to *think* nature itself in its totality as a presentation of something supersensible, without our being able to effectuate this presentation *objectively*'. The imagination concerns itself with nature as a phenomenon through which is presented a nature-in-itself. This nature-in-itself is the idea of reason which we cannot determine any further and which cannot be given objectively to the imagination. The idea can only be thought as such; it cannot be cognized or comprehended in its presentation as empirical phenomena.[100]

Deleuze takes an important lesson from this; between these two faculties, imagination and reason, which initially suffer a sharp discord, a pleasure arises.[101] By confronting its limit, the imagination can, at least negatively, go beyond this limit insofar as it can represent to itself the inaccessibility of reason's Idea. Deleuze writes,

> At first sight we attribute this immensity, which reduces our imagination to impotence, to the natural object, that is to sensible Nature. But in reality it is *reason* which forces us to unite the immensity of the sensible world into a whole. This whole is the Idea of the sensible, in so far as this has as a substratum something intelligible or suprasensible. Imagination thus learns that it is reason which pushes it to the limit of its power, forcing it to admit that all its power is nothing in comparison to an Idea.[102]

Deleuze argues that the imagination presents to itself the fact that an unpresentable exists and '*it exists in sensible nature*'.[103] This lesson allows us to refine our earlier description of the sign. The disjunctive relationship between the faculties discloses a sensibility that receives and apprehends signs; however, these signs are not themselves sensible objects, they are the being of the sensible–sensibility's raison d'être. This is what it means to talk about signs as the genetic and compositional elements of images. From an empirical point of view, signs per se are not sensible precisely because the sign constitutes the limit of the faculty of sensibility (the imagination); however, from a transcendental point of view, the sign can only be experienced sensibly because it is accessible only to the faculty of sensibility in its transcendental exercise.[104] The sign is not a sensible object nor is it even a component quality of such objects, and so even though each species of image has its corresponding signs, we must not conflate the image with its signs. Signs are, however, always presupposed by the image;

they are conditions of the genesis and composition of the image, and to this extent are accessible only to the *specialized facet* on the surface of my body that receives information or has a sensory relationship with the image.

In the experience of the sublime, reason is forced to think nature as a totality; that is, as the syntheses of imagination become increasingly incomprehensible, the imagination presents to itself the fact that some element, *some sense*, of the field of sensible phenomena cannot be given objectively. In this case, however, a question remains: If reason, or, more accurately, its *Idea*, is present between imagination's crisis and epiphany, how does imagination experience this idea *as such*? Imagination experiences signs of the intensity of an experience, of 'pure' optical or sound situations (*opsigns* and *sonsigns*). The joy that arises in this instance is to be found in the crystal image to which these signs give rise:

> The crystal reveals a direct time-image, and no longer an indirect image of time deriving from movement. It does not abstract time; it does better: it reverses its subordination in relation to movement. ... What the crystal reveals or makes visible is the hidden ground of time, that is, its differentiation into two flows, that of presents which pass and that of pasts which are preserved. Time simultaneously makes the present pass and preserves the past in itself. There are, therefore, already, two possible time-images, one grounded in the past, the other in the present. Each is complex and is valid for time as a whole.[105]

Properly speaking, the crystal image is not an image in the sense that perception or action are images: the crystal has no actuality, no objectivity. It is a semiotic structure – a structure with its own relevant signs – where 'the actual optical image crystallizes with *its own* virtual image'.[106] Deleuze argues that we see in the crystal a rupture wherein time is no longer subordinated to movement. That is, time ceases to be reduced to an indirect representation as the measure of movement. The crystal discloses time as such; that is, it discloses the relational conditions of actual existence with its differentiation into past- and future-oriented tendencies. The crystal is the point where the virtual and the actual are reflected in each other such that their distinction becomes indiscernible precisely because each always reflects the other: 'The crystal-image is, then, the point of indiscernibility of the two distinct images, the actual and the virtual, while what we see in the crystal is time itself, a bit of time in the pure state, the very distinction between the two images which keeps on reconstituting itself.'[107] Thus an actual object cannot be distinguished from the virtual event which characterizes it.

Setting out from a discussion of the cinema of Jean Renoir, Deleuze argues that this situation breaks with automatic movement and becomes the means for experimenting with new modes of life:

> Without recourse to violence, and through the development of an experimentation, something will come out of the crystal, a new Real will come out beyond the actual and virtual. Everything happens as if the circuit served to try out roles, as if roles were being tried in it until the right one were found, the one with which we escape to enter a clarified reality. In short, the circuit, the round, are not closed because they are selective, and produce a winner each time.[108]

This theme of experimentation is crucial to Deleuze. If the characters in his ethology want to escape the reciprocity of automatic movement and the clichés of the action-image, something novel must be produced. At the same time, however, if Deleuze were to suggest that the form and content of this novelty could be determined in advance, that it could be prescribed, he would be repeating the clichés of automatic movement – he would be suggesting that the action or attitudes of a qualified observer could disclose and transform a situation – and violating his own philosophy of difference by suggesting that novelty is the actualization of an idea given in advance. Beginning with this idea of experimentation is crucial; in describing Renoir's work, Deleuze argues that life emerges from the crystal precisely insofar as it gambles on a mode of life which takes shape in the crystal. Deleuze argues initially for the possibility of the reflection and circulation of the indiscernibility of an actual image and its virtual image persisting indefinitely; however, he comes to argue that it is only the gamble made on an experiment that brings this circulation to completion: 'Now, in contrast, the dividing in two can come to completion, but precisely on condition that one of the two tendencies leaves the crystal, through the point of flight. From the indiscernibility of the actual and the virtual, a new distinction must emerge, like a new reality which was not pre-existent.'[109] And so, it is through three moments that novelty is produced beyond the clichés of the action-image; first is an experience that is beyond the capacity of habit to represent comprehensibly; second, because it is this experience which disrupts the schemata according to whose laws the action-image is generated, this experience confronts us with an idea of the whole *as such*, instead of subordinating it to the spatial translation of its parts; and, finally, gambling on one of the roles glimpsed in the image disclosed by the new idea of the whole.

Conclusion: The breakdown of the sensory-motor schema and experimentation

In recounting the Bergsonian ontology of the *Cinema* books over Chapters 4 and 5, we have seen that the sensory-motor schema is Deleuze's name for the immanent laws by which the doubly expressive processes of the affection-image determine an action in response to a problem posed by perception. In other words, the sensory-motor schema is the immanent logic by which sensible experience relates to its ideal conditions through affection, and vice versa. However, Deleuze's deployment of the Kantian conception of experiences of the sublime in the *Cinema* books allows him to suggest that there are experiences which disrupt this schema. These experiences are precisely those in which the faculty of imagination, in its habitual operation of synthesizing previous experiences into an anticipation of the future, fails to produce a concept of the objects of experience. Deleuze argues that this failure confronts the imagination with its own impotence and also with a new idea of the whole of nature. Even though it is reason's idea which exposes the imagination to the limits of its power, the object of the idea is sensible nature. That is, it is reason's idea of sensible nature which disrupts the sense-making habits of the imagination precisely by presenting the imagination with its limits in the form of a sensible, yet unrepresentable object. In *Deleuze and Ethology*'s conclusion, I will continue this discussion of the rupture in the operations of the imagination and how it brings about a new idea, a new conception of the body's relationship to its milieu. This discussion must be held over into another context because properly explicating the ethological significance of experiences of the sublime requires that we emphasize the nature of the relationship between the actual and the virtual – that is, the reciprocity between a being and its power, and I will do this in the first half of the Conclusion. I will subsequently return to the twin themes of *sense* and *umwelt* presented in Chapter 1 in order to explicate how and why the breakdown of the sensory-motor schema – experiences of the sublime – is a vital means for the transformative experimentation at the heart of Deleuze's ethology.

Conclusion

By way of concluding *Deleuze and Ethology*, I want to reflect on two themes that are beyond the remit of the present work, but which press on us nonetheless: the distinction between relationships of determination and causation, and the relationships between humans and other animals as a way of suggesting the sort of praxis that might follow from Deleuze's ethology. On the one hand, I have spent a great deal of time discussing the conditions under which an event – either an actual occurrence or a virtual idea – is determined, but this demands that, sooner or later, we attend to the role of causation in Deleuze's metaphysics. What I offer here is not intended as a definitive account of the relationship between concepts of determination and of immanent causation in Deleuze, but, rather, a theme that summarizes many of the key arguments presented in *Deleuze and Ethology*, while gesturing towards the significance of these themes. On the other hand, while *Deleuze and Ethology* is primarily an attempt to clarify the nature of Deleuze's metaphysical project by following a particular problem as it moves and transforms through his oeuvre, it would be remiss of this work to gesture towards philosophical ethology and never reflect on the relationship between humans and other animals as a case of the broader ethical problems to which Deleuze's ethology is connected. As such, we can take an ordinary, almost banal, example from the relationship between humans and their inter-species companions as a case study for imagining how Deleuze's emphasis on experimentation lends itself to a praxis that maintains his emphasis on the immanent determination of the logic and significance of an encounter. As an example, I want to consider the routine occurrence by which my feline housemate calls on me to open the door for her every morning. This example is one of many banal occurrences that could no doubt be described by anyone who shares their home with other species. This banality, however, is precisely the point. I want to close *Deleuze and Ethology* by suggesting one of the directions in which we might take this discussion as we progressively elaborate the practical details that are entailed by a Deleuzian ethology. The everyday fact that our worlds are shot through with threads connecting them to the worlds of myriad other species needs to be unpacked because in doing so we will understand that experimentation – the art of living described in *Cinema 2* – concerns reconceptualizing and reconfiguring the everyday encounters that constitute the bulk of our lives.

Even though *Deleuze and Ethology* has offered ethology as a way of characterizing a philosophical project that transforms both ontology and ethics as a way of producing a philosophy of life where modes of life are themselves implied in the qualification and transformation of being as such, such a project inevitably raises a question: What are the practical, ethical implications of such a philosophy? Of course, such a question cannot be definitively answered because, in the terms of the *Cinema* books, such answers will rely on habits and the reproduction of clichés, at least in part. The question about practical implications can only be answered by a further question: What are the conditions of genuine transformation? And that question can only be answered provisionally, relative to the circumstances of a particular affective encounter. Deleuze's insistence on experimentation is by now well known, but, in view of his treatment of experiences of the sublime, I would like to suggest eventually that this experimentation is in fact a way of reformulating ordinary experiences so that their objects are recast as strange or unfamiliar. In other words, experimentation is a way to introduce 'a little time in its pure state'[1] into everyday experience.

Immanence and expression between causality and determination

While the two topics of interest to this chapter – causation and practice – are inexorably bound, there are specific reasons to begin the discussion by looking at the issue of causation and determination. On the one hand, this discussion allows a crystallization of a theme that has persisted throughout *Deleuze and Ethology*: the reciprocity between individual beings and the ensembles of relations in which they participate. And, on the other hand, it clarifies precisely why we need to think about practice; that is, the clarity and significance of how this issue of how the practices of daily life will fit into Deleuze's ethology relies on the metaphysical question of the reciprocity of beings and their environments. So, we will begin the discussion of causation and determination with an issue that has run through *Deleuze and Ethology*: the interconnectedness of sense and affect. We will recall that the problem of sense begins from the problem of the internal differentiation of the absolute; affect, meanwhile, constitutes the two directions in which this differentiation is expressed. On the one hand, it is expressed as something actual; as actually existing bodies, the reality of which is their continuity. In virtue of the fact that it fills the interval between perception and action, affect is the entanglement of two bodies. Or, more correctly, affection is their continuity to the extent that the two bodies, insofar as they constitute perception- and action-images, cannot be clearly distinguished. On the other hand, the differentiation of sense is expressed virtually. In this case, affect is the abstraction of this entanglement, or, rather, its expression for itself, abstracted from the constraints of actual bodies, and expressed as a degree of power – as a degree of the transformation of the relational plane on which actual beings appear.

In order to talk about how this differentiation of sense clarifies the reciprocity between actual beings and the relational conditions of their becoming, we will turn in a moment to *The Logic of Sense*'s conception of quasi-causation. Before this turn, however, we need to consider a brief argument made by Bergson and cited by Deleuze as an exemplar of the false problem of the confusion of the more with the less. This argument concerns the habitual presumption that non-being is a condition for being and helps us clarify what we expect from discussions of causation. In the collection *The Creative Mind*, Bergson takes aim at the long-standing philosophical concern with the relationship between being and non-being. The idea of non-being, he argues,

> designate[s] a presence-the presence of a thing or an order which does not interest us, which blunts our effort or our attention; it is our disappointment being expressed when we call this presence absence. Consequently, to speak of the absence of all order and all things, that is, to speak of absolute disorder and absolute nothingness, is to pronounce words void of meaning.[2]

Bergson argues that the metaphysical habit of positing nothing as a condition for something – non-being as a condition for being – is vacuous. His argument shares much with the critique of the idea of possibility that we saw in Chapter 3; just as the idea of possibility presupposes the reality on which it is modelled, and is thus more than the reality it was supposed to birth, the idea of non-being presupposes being insofar as it begins from the presence of being, confuses our inattention or disinterest with lack in the object, and posits this lack as an absence which would give birth to presence. Non-being thus implies the presence of the being that it is supposed to negate. As such, non-being cannot be the condition of being's genesis. Deleuze glosses this argument in *Bergsonism* and suggests that it is a paradigm case of a false problem insofar as it confuses the more with the less.[3] How could existence come from non-existence when the idea of non-existence presupposes existence? Consequently, questions about causal relations are not automatically meaningful, because causal potency does not emerge ex nihilo. This means that we need to be very clear about what we mean when we set out to discuss causal relations in Deleuze; as before, if we want to make sense of Deleuze's understanding of causation, then we must begin by articulating the problem to which Deleuze's discussion of causation responds. If we are to take anything from Bergson's argument, it needs to be the idea that such questions presuppose the existence of those posing the question. For the sake of Deleuze's ethology, this means that the world and its inhabitants already exist; the pertinent question concerns the determination of the particular configuration that the world happens to have. The key consequence of this is that it establishes the necessity of the actual world. Not because it argues for the world's necessity but because it argues that the world's coming into being – or, more precisely, the non-being required in attempts to posit the world's coming into being – is simply a false problem.

In Deleuze's 1968 reading of Spinoza, it is not obvious what, if anything, guarantees the correspondence of the modes and their essences. The principle of univocity guarantees that the modal essences follow necessarily from the constitution of the essence of God, and, acting as their agency, the existence of the modes is caused by God. However, there can be no direct relation between the essence and the existence of a particular mode as this would, according to EIP24, lead to the absurd claim that a mode exists necessarily. In inverting the relations of substance and modes, however, Deleuze outmanoeuvres this problem. The actual world exists necessarily; not because existence pertains to its essence, but because attempts to argue that the world does not – or at some point, did not – exist confuse the more with the less. Substance, the absolute, also exists necessarily. Since the actual world exists necessarily, then the absolute exists necessarily insofar as it is nothing other than the sense of the world, expressed for itself. It is cause of itself insofar as its reality does not collapse into either its expression (this or that attribute) or its object (this or that mode).

To unpack this problem in relation to the expression of sense, let us return to an example from Chapter 1, the palm berries in my front garden that constitute a problem for the bird feeding on them, and consider further why *substance* is not an explanatory term – a noun with a concrete object – in the way that the modes are terms. Consider a particular berry. Some aspect of it – its colour, for instance – poses a problem for the koel that is deciding whether or not to eat it. This aspect is constituted by an ensemble of the berry's actual properties – the way that its skin refracts and reflects light – but its sense, expressed as a problematic idea, is particular to the ecological relations of which it is a part. Insofar as this idea constitutes an expression of the sense of the berry, the berry is the object of the idea, and the sense is what is expressed of the object. We know that sense does not collapse into its expression (the idea), nor does it collapse into its object (the berry). In this sense, the sense inheres or subsists in its expression. Thus, we have two objects to which we can refer, and one 'quasi-object' to which we cannot refer because as soon as we attempt to refer to this quasi-object, it becomes another object: the object of another proposition. The two objects and the quasi-object are thus a virtual idea, an actual object, and the sense that, expressed of the latter by the former, subsists in this expressive dynamic insofar as it has no external existence. If we maintain Chapter 3's argument that this virtual idea is the name that Deleuze gives to Spinoza's modal essences, then substance is a quasi-object in the same sense that sense is a quasi-object; it subsists in the expressive dynamic between an actual thing (a collection of relevant properties, or extensive parts) and its qualification as a virtual problematic within a particular relation (whether these properties signify a berry that is more or less desirable than the berries surrounding it). At this point we see precisely the problem to which a robust concept of immanent causality must speak. Causality is not the event from which new actions and situations spring; it is the complex dynamic through which existing actual beings are brought into a dialogue with the conditions of the transformation of the relations in which they participate.

The first thing we can say of substance or sense is that, as a quasi-object, it must be understood structurally. This means that we are mistaken if we think of substance as a concrete object or referent in its own right. There are only two objects or referents here, one virtual and one actual, and neither can be understood outside their reciprocity. In this sense, substance is to be understood as the movement between intensive degrees that constitute the transforming structure of this reciprocity. The second point is the most famous; the structural relation between virtual and actual terms must proceed via different/ciation. This is not as simple as saying that virtual ideas (problems) do not represent the states of affairs whose transformations they express, nor does it mean simply that the actual things (solutions) that respond to these problems do not resemble these ideas, although *Deleuze and Ethology* has consistently affirmed both of these points. Our point is a subtler one. The determination of the multiplicity that constitutes the field that gives structure to the reciprocity of virtual and actual terms proceeds via the differentiation of these terms.[4] This is what it means when Deleuze emphasizes that what 'is expressed has no resemblance whatsoever to the expression'.[5] Sense or substance – the multiplicitous structure that scaffolds the relation between the virtual and the actual – is expressed by a proposition and of an object but resembles neither.

The *Cinema* books' discussion of affect illuminates the problem of the internal differentiation of sense because it gives content to the actual and the virtual: the movement-image and its differentiation into perception, action, affection and relation, as well as the expression of the movement-image as a degree of transformation of a whole of relations. In this context, *The Logic of Sense*'s quasi-cause is the relation that guarantees the correspondence of these terms. Moreover, this problem also illuminates the significance of affect for understanding ethology from a Deleuzian point of view. We will recall from Chapter 4 that affection is not something that happens but is the horizon against which things occur. Affection, as Deleuze puts it, is simultaneously the intermingling of bodies insofar as it is the marking of one body with the traces and signs of another, and it is their interaction with the transforming whole that contains them. In this sense, affection affirms the dialectic of problems insofar as my body, while bearing the marks of another body, does not interact directly with the other body but has its response to this body determined by the problem that is expressed of the former body. Thus, affection is the horizon against which the ideal event – the problem – is expressed. Affection is also the threshold where the determination of some particular action is carried out as the solution of this problem. In both cases there is an expression (either the determination of some ideal problem or action as a bodily movement in space) but in neither case does the affection-image collapse into the expressions or objects. Affection thus affords us a robust scaffolding on which to build an interpretation of the double-causality discussed in *The Logic of Sense*.

Even though *Difference and Repetition* contains no explicit anticipation of the discussions that make up *The Logic of Sense*, the latter appeared only a year after the former with its dialectic of virtual problems and actual solutions recast as the complementarity between material occurrences and the singular events that populate a 'field of intensity'.[6] This suggests that the quasi-causality of *The Logic of Sense* must be understood with reference to the same dynamism by which the virtual and the actual do not causally interact but do obey a guaranteed correspondence by virtue of their simultaneous contribution to the production of an individual – that is, an intensive region that is distinguished by the virtual elements that make up a problematic idea (*The Logic of Sense*'s 'events') and is explicated by the extensity in which it is expressed. Key here then is the reciprocity between series of virtual events and series of actual occurrences. As Deleuze puts it, insofar as they are events or problems, 'Incorporeal effects are never themselves causes in relation to each other; rather, they are only "quasi-causes" following laws which perhaps express in each case the relative unity or mixture of bodies on which they depend for their real causes.'[7] Thus, where we have, on the one hand, actual occurrences – or, a phrase that anticipates *Cinema*'s definition of affect, the mixtures of bodies – on the other hand, we have the incorporeal effects that depend on these mixtures and express their sense for itself. In a famous theme that subtends almost the entirety of *The Logic of Sense*, these incorporeal effects do not occur at some depth inside bodies; rather, they subsist at the surface of bodies. Since, by definition, they are not actual, they bear no spatial relation to actual bodies. To the extent that these bodies are modal expressions of ecological relations, these incorporeal effects are the subsistent expression, *for itself*, of the sense of this bodily entanglement. But between these expressions is an intensive horizon that we have at various points called sense or substance.

Deleuze suggests that 'if sense as the double of the proposition is indifferent to affirmation and negation, if it is no more passive than active, then no mode of the proposition is able to affect it. Sense is strictly the same for propositions which are opposed from the point of view of quality, quantity, relation, or modality.'[8] In other words, while a particular actual mode will constitute either an affirmation or negation of a particular degree of sense, sense, expressed for itself, is indifferent to this affirmation or negation. The relationship of quasi-causation is therefore the juxtaposition or contraction of all sense which could be attributed to this or that affective encounter, even though this juxtaposition is indifferent to whether it is actually affirmed or negated. This is why Deleuze says that 'events are never causes of one another, but rather enter the relations of quasi-causality, an unreal and ghostly causality, endlessly reappearing in the two senses'.[9] Because sense is indifferent to the mixture of bodies that will or will not affirm it, it is always double: Alice will grow shorter, or she will grow taller. And because the relation of quasi-causality happens in time, the doubling of sense is always expressed in the infinitive: Alice drinks the potion to grow taller or to grow shorter. Jon Roffe offers an insightful commentary on this issue and affirms that, while the quasi-causal relation is not 'causal in the corporeal sense' neither is it a relation of logical necessity; these two senses belong together insofar as they make sense of each other.[10] The potion makes Alice shorter only insofar as the event 'to grow taller' persists, offering a position from which 'to grow shorter' can be sensibly expressed. As we know from Chapter 5, however, the double sense of the event, insofar as it constitutes an ideal expression of what actually occurs, does not present a collection of possibilities; 'to grow shorter' and 'to grow taller' must not be confused with logical possibilities. This is why

Deleuze goes on to argue that '[i]t is neither at the same time, nor in relation to the same thing, that I am younger and older, but it is at the same time and by the same relation that I become so'.[11] Alice could only grow shorter after drinking the potion, and she could only grow taller by eating the cupcake on the table. The two senses are not equally possible, and Alice cannot do both things; however, each sense is necessary to make the other sensible.

What we see here is that *The Logic of Sense*'s quasi-causality is not causality in the everyday, transitive sense; it is a relation that brings together the conditions for a meaningful expression of sense. It is not for nothing, however, that it is called quasi-causation. Insofar as the movement of mixed bodies necessarily communicates with the ideal expression of sense, quasi-causation is still a condition or degree of actual relations that are ostensibly causal. Indeed, much of *The Logic of Sense*'s discussion of Stoicism concerns the heritage of this splitting of causal relations. Thus, causal relations are the subject of a subtle, nuanced reconceptualization. Even Spinoza's claim at EIP17SII that modes are the causes of the existence of other modes, and its corollary that God is thus an efficient cause, as well as an immanent cause, does not mean that we can infer a relationship of direct transitivity between corporeal causes. We will recall from Chapter 3 that Deleuze argues that 'the genesis that takes place in time'[12] does not occur between one actual term and another but involves a movement through the virtual structures that subsist in the actual terms. To put it another way, the reality of the actual world is its continuity – hence there are only 'artificial' distinctions between affectively entangled beings – and yet the transformations of that continuity necessarily entail the ideal expression of the sense of bodily mixtures for itself. And, because this sense can neither be reduced to nor exhausted by the objects of which it is said, it constitutes an intensive horizon between the two that contracts the double sense through which the problematic idea is meaningfully attributed to this or that state of affairs.

Deleuze begins the second chapter of *Difference and Repetition*, 'Repetition for Itself', by citing Hume: '*Repetition changes nothing in the object repeated, but does change something in the mind which contemplates it.*'[13] Repetition, the non-chronological 'passage' of time that consists in the contraction of a state of affairs, an event and the intensive horizon that facilitates this contraction, does not repeat an already existing state of affairs. Rather, repetition synthesizes that state of affairs with an idea that forces the former's transformation. When Deleuze speaks of a 'mind which contemplates' repetition and draws a difference from it, he means precisely the ontological process by which an idea is attributed to a state of affairs and expresses its sense as the condition of its transformation.

Consequently, the causal relation that interests Deleuze is not a linear, transitive sense of causation; it is the determination of an idea that is appropriate to a given affective relation.

Towards a Deleuzian ethology

From here we can briefly consider how this relational metaphysics transforms ethics. This issue of the determination of ideas that are adequate to their objects does not mean that we need to produce ideas that more accurately represent their objects. A theme that *Deleuze and Ethology* has persistently returned to is that an idea is not the representation of some object in the mind of an observer; an idea is an ensemble of signs arranged according to the needs and capacities of some being so as to constitute some other being as a problem to which the former can respond. This problem is, as we saw in Chapter 1, never a question of epistemology, of how accurately the idea represents its object, but of ontology and the ways that the sense of its object transforms the capacities of its subject. Never is this issue clearer than the case of Pascal's wager, where Deleuze argues that the possible responses to its question about the existence of God only matter insofar as they effect some change in the mode of life of the one who wagers.

If, as I have just argued, the idea is the route through which the subject and object of an encounter participate in the transforming whole – substance pluralized and concerned with the each rather than the all – then we can see how ethics is, as Beistegui argues,[14] continuous with ontology. We can formulate a logic by which this or that being participates in the complication and explication of Being as such. But the lesson of the *Cinema* books is that if we want to attend to the calculus of affects that is immanent to actual beings and the particularity of their encounters, then we can only do so by factoring in their own points of view, as well as the histories, needs, beliefs, capacities and so on, that are entailed by those points of view. So, while the ontological register of Deleuze's ethology encapsulates questions about the logic of the reciprocity of beings and Being, the ethical register concerns the beliefs, power, needs and so on that each being involves in its encounters with other beings. Appropriately then, a key ethical theme in the transition from *Cinema 1: The Movement-Image* to *Cinema 2: The Time-Image* is the collapse of illusion and characters' loss of faith in the world:

> We hardly believe any longer that a global situation can give rise to an action which is capable of modifying it no more than we believe that an action can force

a situation to disclose itself, even partially. *The most 'healthy' illusions fall.* The first things to be compromised everywhere are the linkages of situation action, action reaction, excitation response, in short, the sensory-motor links which produced the action-image.[15]

These illusions are the large and small forms of the action-image: the expectation that action could either modify an existing situation or at least disclose its sense as coherent and ordered such that it is ripe for modification. Deleuze spends a considerable amount of the *Cinema* project reflecting on how the history of the cinema has articulated the history of these illusions as well as the conditions and consequences of their collapse. Insofar as Deleuze's interpretation of causation is actually a concern with the reciprocity between ideas and states of affairs, and the adequacy of the former to the latter, we see the significance of the failure of the sensory-motor schema. *Deleuze and Ethology* has argued that the sensory-motor schema is the immanent logic that operates in the interval and connects perceptions to bodily capacities for action. In the context of the discussion of causation, we could say that the sensory-motor schema is the logic by which the dual processes of the affection-image guarantee the correspondence of an idea and its object in the double expression of the internal differentiation of sense. In this case, the failure of the sensory-motor schema, and the concomitant collapse of the large and small forms of the action-image, is in fact the failure of an habitual response to the perception-image. It is the failure of given models of sense-making – models given in terms of past experience – to adequately respond to current states of affairs in their problematic sense.

To appreciate the ethological significance of this issue, as well as the broader problem of causation, we need to return to the issue which began Chapter 5: how one participates in the determination of problems. Deleuze famously called Spinoza the 'Christ of philosophers'[16] and never tired of emphasizing his importance; however, I would suggest that Deleuze's ethology is more Bergsonian than Spinozist if only because the former informs both the ontological problem faced by this ethology (how is Being disclosed through the operations of intensive difference?) and its corresponding ethical problem (how does the sense that beings make of the world participate in the determination of problems that drive the dialectic of positive difference?). In order to formulate the significance of this ethological problem clearly, as well as to eventually understand what the umwelt theory adds to a Deleuzian ethology, we need the theory of subjective constitution described in Chapter 5. We recall that what counts as a subject's point of view is in fact the synthesis of two points of view on a set of relations:

an analytic point of view which is internal to the set and a descriptive point of view which is external to the set and describes it impassively. This synthesis is not a psychological operation that the subject carries out; rather it is a passive ontological operation that constitutes the subjectivity of the centre. This is why Deleuze describes semisubjectivity as the correlation constitutive of subjectivity – the correlation of an empirical subject with a 'transcendental subject which thinks it and in which it thinks itself'.[17] If we were to phrase this in terms more aligned to *Bergsonism* than the *Cinema* books, we might say that this synthesis is the synthesis of a subject that is concerned with the immediate demands of a present situation with an empty form of subjectivity that connects the empirical subject with a whole-of-memory that will determine the significance of the present situation. Because experiences of sublime objects constitute a failure of the sensory-motor schema by which this double subjectivity would make sense of this object – formulate an idea that is adequate to the object, that is – then we can say that the resonance of these two points of view is crucial to the eventual determination of the conditions of a response to this object.

The sublime, then, is not a question of the object itself, but the degree to which it invokes a dissonance or disharmony between the faculty which concerns an internal point of view on the relation I have with the object (imagination), and reason, the faculty which presents an idea which is supposed to make sense of the object and capture its significance. When such a discord arises, reason is forced to produce a new idea that expresses an immensity that is attributed to sensible nature. Even though this discord leads reason to produce a new idea, we are compelled to attribute it to something supersensible in nature. In short, while this disruption to our attempt to make sense of an object of experience is a problem that arises in the imagination and is taken up by reason, reason produces a new idea of the whole of nature. In this context we can pose precisely the question with which a Deleuzian ethology challenges us. How, or by what method, do affective encounters generate the conditions for genuine transformation? Whether we invoke the 'too big for me' comment in *Difference and Repetition*, his comments about war in *Cinema 1*, or his wish to get drunk on a glass of water,[18] we know that for Deleuze the actual size of the object of our encounter does not necessarily correspond to the intensity of its presence, but in how we make sense of it. In this sense, any one of the innumerable wild geckoes living in my neighbourhood is as much the object of a potentially sublime experience as the pyramids.

And so, we can consider how everyday encounters between humans and the multitude of other species with whom they share their worlds takes on a renewed significance by illuminating a pragmatic interpretation of the failure of the sensory-motor schema. Indeed, these encounters present a fertile context for elaborating what Deleuze means by experimentation. The most explicit discussion of human–animal encounters in Deleuze's oeuvre comes in '1730: Becoming-Intense, Becoming-Animal, Becoming-Imperceptible …', the tenth plateau of *A Thousand Plateaus*. In her work *When Species Meet*, Donna Haraway offers a scathing rejection of Deleuze and Guattari's work because, ultimately, it offers only 'a symptomatic morass for how not to take earthly animals – wild or domestic – seriously'.[19] Ironically, Deleuze and Guattari are ultimately closer to the heart of *When Species Meet* than Haraway seems to realize, so the fastest way to articulate the significance of Deleuze and Guattari's interpretation of human–animal encounters is to juxtapose their discussion with Haraway's criticisms. Ronald Bogue has offered an excellent response to Haraway, so there is no need to rehearse a full response here;[20] all that we need concern ourselves with is the issue of how we ought to approach other animals. Consider, for example, that Haraway is persistently, and, I would argue rightly, opposed to anthropomorphism and the reductive humanization that humans too often impose on other animals: 'It seems to me that it is all too easy in dogland to forget that resistance to human exceptionalism *requires* resistance to humanization of our partners.'[21] In *A Thousand Plateaus*, Deleuze and Guattari famously celebrate wolf packs, while simultaneously rejecting overly familiar animals like lap dogs. Initially, theirs seems like an overly romanticized conception, which would allow Deleuze and Guattari a neat but false distinction between wild animals and Oedipal animals. Haraway, unfortunately, approaches Deleuze and Guattari in terms of this false distinction and criticizes them for failing to appreciate the intensity of the relationships people have with the animals that share their homes. But this is an unfair caricature of Deleuze and Guattari for two reasons. First, they affirm Haraway's point about anthropomorphism, not by affirming the point, but by going further and destabilizing the ground on which such erroneous analogies between humans and other animals are constructed. Second, Deleuze's ethology offers crucial insights into renewing human–animal relations once this ground has been disturbed.

When unpacked, the charge of anthropomorphism is a curious one and we ought to be wary of it. Haraway's point is that we cannot make sense of one mode of being (dog-being, say) through an analogy with another mode of being (human being). That is, we cannot take one mode of being and make sense of it by counting the ways it is or is not like a mode of being with which we are more familiar. Deleuze for his part would undoubtedly agree, provided we are careful not to beg the question in how we distinguish these modes of being. At its heart, the charge of anthropomorphism is relatively simple. A common, prosaic case might be the animal mascots of sports teams. These mascots are anthropomorphic in the sense that they take one type of being (a tiger) and characterize it in terms of the behaviour of another type of being (wearing uniforms or competing to cross a line while carrying a ball). Given the extent to which thought and writing rely on the possibility of playing with ontological predicates in this way, anthropomorphism is exceedingly common and not always problematic. However, as Haraway points out, to judge a dog in human terms is the fastest way to misunderstand both. A Deleuzian ethology would go further in that it challenges the conditions of distinguishing between types of being and warns us against invoking the charge of anthropomorphism when the distinction between types of being is precisely what is at stake.

We saw in Deleuze's 1966 reading of Bergson that he considers the distinctions between beings to be artificial; however, his most articulate handling of this issue follows from his 1968 reading of Spinoza and the use of the scholastic conception of real and numerical distinctions therein. Deleuze's argument that modes are distinguished numerically is entirely consonant with the Bergsonian claim that actual beings are only artificially distinct given that numerical distinctions are, by definition, not real distinctions. So, we know then that the distinctions between existents are quantitative, but quantities of what? In Spinozist terms, these quantities are expressions of the qualitative constitution or transformation of the whole of substance. In ethological terms, we might say that existents are relatively closed sets that constitute expressions of degrees of the transformation of intensive wholes – expressions, that is, of sense events. It is from this point of view that the charge of anthropomorphism is problematic; existents are not to be defined in qualitative terms, in terms, that is, of what they are, but in quantitative terms, as expressions of the transformations of the relationships in which they participate. So, if, as Deleuze and Guattari insist, a workhorse might have more in common with an ox than a racehorse, then there may be cases where anthropomorphism is appropriate insofar as a police dog may have more in common with her non-canine colleagues than she does with a toy poodle. Conversely, we might say that this is a call to cease anthropomorphizing humans insofar as Victor, the protagonist of François Truffaut's *The Wild Child*, has more in common with the beasts with whom he shared his childhood than he does with the doctor who attempts to save him. Ultimately, then, Deleuze and Guattari are less interested in particular types of animals than they are in relational logics. Or, more correctly, the various species that make up Deleuze and Guattari's famous bestiary (wolves, ticks, spiders, etc.) interest them not because of the type of animals that they are but because of the types of becoming they embody.

Appropriately, this brings us to a challenge that Haraway sets and that brings her closer to Deleuze and Guattari than her early criticisms anticipate. As her discussions of dog training progress, Haraway reflects on the necessity of meeting dogs as strangers[22] in order 'to craft atypical ways to interpret each other's specific fluencies and to reinvent their own repertoires through affective semiotic intra-action'.[23] Where Haraway heads into a rich discussion of the continuity of language across and within different species, there is also a Deleuzian theme that is present in Haraway's writing. This theme of approaching animal others as strangers is present throughout Deleuze and Guattari's discussion, even though it is less a celebration of strangeness than it is a critique of attempts to translate relational logics across different encounters. As they put it, 'Although there is no preformed logical order to becomings and multiplicities, there are *criteria*, and the important thing is that they not be used after the fact.'[24] In other words, for each being one encounters, the metric used to define and negotiate each encounter must be specific to that particular encounter. And so, the operative question concerns these criteria; anthropomorphism is less a problem of erroneously analogizing between species and more about using meaningful and appropriate criteria for a given encounter in order to be sensitive to its singularity. If, as Deleuze suggests, the specific form of these criteria cannot be used after the fact, then his ethology will not produce normative imperatives that will instruct our behaviour. We must ask instead how learning to meet other species as strangers fulfils these criteria for the emergence of a multiplicity and the determination of a new idea.

As we saw in Chapter 3, *Difference and Repetition* outlines three criteria for the emergence of a multiplicity. Such a multiplicity is the structure that scaffolds the determination of an idea. Thus, we are not looking at anything other than an expression of the sense or substance of an actual, affective encounter that would be sufficient for the determination of a new idea. The three criteria are, first, the affirmation of the multiplicity's qualitative difference relative to the actuality to which it corresponds; second, that the elements of the multiplicity be sufficient for defining the metric that will determine the idea; and, finally, that the multiplicity follow a differential relation. In order to flesh out how these criteria relate to meeting other species as strangers, I should like to consider a regular experience with my feline housemate, Penny. The previous tenants of our house installed a flap for their dog in the security screen at the rear of the house. This flap is big enough for Penny to use, but as it was installed for a dog, it is too heavy for

Penny to consistently open on her own, and so I have to prop it open so that she is free to come and go as she pleases. She has become sufficiently familiar with this situation that she seems to understand that my intervention is necessary to her making use of the flap. Hence, a frequent occurrence is that, in the morning when she is anxious to get out of the house, she will sit at the backdoor and, once I have entered the room, she will watch me until we make eye contact, at which point she begins pawing and scratching at the flap until I open it for her. It is this frequent experience that makes it clear that I am an element in how the world constitutes a problem for her. Just as the koel's world was composed as a complex involving wind, berries, leaves and so on – a complex which the koel made sense of – I am an element of the complex that Penny confronts as she makes sense of her encounter with the back door.

In a moment this anecdote will be considered in order to think through engaging with our inter-species companions as strangers. But first I must acknowledge Deleuze's well-known disdain for cats, including Deleuze and Guattari's comment that 'anyone who likes cats or dogs is a fool'[25] (a comment cited by Haraway as an entry into her invective against Deleuze and Guattari's supposed rejection of ordinary, everyday encounters with animals). Against this, however, is *Gilles Deleuze's ABCs* (the collection of interviews televised after his suicide in 1995) and his explanation of his dislike for cats as being a dislike of animals that rub against him. Moreover he concedes that, in principle, this does not amount to much since people who share their lives and homes with animals often have inhuman – *animal*, that is – relationships with these animals.[26] Indeed, in this vein, Deleuze and Guattari grant that it is 'possible for any animal to be treated in the mode of the pack or swarm. ... Even the cat, even the dog.'[27] What is important here is not the animal as such, but the specific relational mode through which we encounter it. In this sense, it is hard not to read Deleuze and Guattari against the caricature presented by critics like Haraway that implies that they are two elitists who 'disdain ... the daily, the ordinary, the affectional'[28] in favour of a sublime or otherworldly interpretation of life. To the contrary, the emphasis on affect that we explored in Chapters 4 and 5, the tenor of the 'Becoming-Animal' plateau or the concessions that Deleuze makes to the inhumanity of humans' relationships with their inter-species companions seems very much like a concern with the ordinary insofar as it challenges us to see the everyday with new eyes; to see the familiar in terms of its strangeness and wonder, its terror and its beauty – in short to experience the sublime in the everyday.

The formidable vocabulary of *A Thousand Plateaus* has taken on a life of its own so that its denunciation of the sentimentality of human–animal relations that amount to assimilating other species into Oedipal relationships gets mixed with a daunting, occasionally militant style to such a degree that its readers overlook the possibility that becoming-animal might involve what Guattari called 'a gentle deterritorialization' (*'une déterritorialisation douce'*).[29] I want to suggest that learning to encounter the non-human cohabitants of the everyday as strangers requires a 'new gentleness' similar to what Guattari argues is needed 'between the sexes, generations, ethnic groups, races ...'.[30] We would come 'to know them not through representation but through affective contamination. They [would] start to exist in you, in spite of you.'[31] This conception of a gentle deterritorialization is much closer to *Deleuze and Ethology*'s description of affection or the mixing or intermingling of bodies insofar as it is the coincidence of subject and object in the interval between perception and action.

Ethologist philosopher Vinciane Despret offers a beautiful description of ethology as 'a story of stories. ... [Y]ou have living animals, who have lives, who do things. They risk their life, they reproduce, they have babies. They take care of their babies. They meet someone, they have friends (and another being becomes "someone"), sometimes they enjoy living. ... And these are all stories – beautiful stories.'[32] And so, in the 'Umwelt' entry in her wonderful *l'Abécédaire*, *What Would Animals Say If We Asked the Right Questions?*, Despret suggests that the umwelt theory of Uexküll has as its aim the divesting of 'the objective world of its *familiarity* and to make ourselves feel *less* at home in it'.[33] Despret's claim is quite specific, and the way she nuances it will be insightful for transformation in my encounter with Penny. Borrowing an idea from Deleuze's discussions with Claire Parnet, that 'animals are "neither in our world, nor in another, *but with an associated world*"',[34] Despret conceives animal lives as the coexistence of worlds which are indexed to particular animals but shot through with threads connecting worlds with each other and ensuring their constant transformation. It is in this sense that the umwelt theory divests the objective world of its familiarity; it upends the world in which I felt at home and confronts me with the prospect that my world – the world I took to be *the* world – is littered with the signs of associated worlds that are woven into it. In other words, my world becomes alien to the extent that I intuit it as a multiplicity constituted as the association of associated worlds.

The facts which would constitute an 'objective' description of a particular cat (the colour and pattern of her fur, the sound of her voice, the sting of an impatient nip etc.) thus become the signs of an analytic perception of a person whose world is intermingled with my own. And she *is* a person, provided we reject the anthropomorphism of such an interpretation and replace it with the

Bergsonian sense of person (*personne*) as the being of the interval: the being to whom a perception must be referred in order to make sense. My daily encounters with this person are testament to the fact that I have a significance in an associated world, a significance that is unknowable to me. This unknowability is important. Despret, in reflecting on how the umwelt theory has been taken up by ethology as a science, comments on the mistake ethologists make when they test the capacities of animals by manipulating the objects that they expect to be significant in the animals' worlds.[35] The implication here is that, while I can infer that I am an element in how the world constitutes a problem for this cat, I do not – cannot – know how or to what extent I am a significant element of her idea of the world. Where the concepts of affect and gentle deterritorialization emphasized the intimacy of becoming-animal, the fact that my becoming with this animal also entails the unknowability of my significance for her means that how I experience my encounter with her requires a certain, humble curiosity, an open and careful attention on my part.

This is what Deleuze means when he refers to experiences that are too big for me or when he refers to the breakdown of the sensory-motor schema – an experience that seems banal – opening a door for my feline friend – contains a moment that confronts me with the inability of sensory-motor habits to exhaustively make sense of the association between two worlds. I am confronted with the incapacity of my habits and the necessity of reorienting myself to its signs and inducements. Thinking back to Deleuze's criteria for the constitution of a multiplicity, we see that what is crucial in this moment is the impossibility of making sense of this encounter in terms of habits I already have and being open to the production of an idea which is not merely a description of the encounter, but an idea that is an expression, *for itself*, of the sense and significance of this intuition of an object that escapes my knowledge. When Deleuze invokes the Kantian idea that being confronted this way forces the production of a new idea of the whole of nature, he does not mean that this brief moment with my inter-species companion leads me to formulate a novel description of the world. Rather, we must recall a description from Chapter 1; ideas – the ideal expressions of sense – are not representations of the world, they are a transforming way to plot a path through the world in terms of its significance, its problematic sense, for us. Consequently, the encounter with Penny presents a disruption to my habits and forces a transformation in how I orient myself to a world that I must acknowledge is connected to manifold other worlds. Insofar as these experiences happen daily, and involve myriad beings other than this one cat, they do not accumulate ordinally – they do not simply happen one after the other – but constitute an ongoing transformation of the means by which I orient myself to the diverse beings and worlds entangled with my own.

This is why Deleuze is so famously insistent on experimentation. In his discussion of the crystal image, Deleuze engages directly with instances where encounters become indistinguishable from the relational conditions of their occurrence – instances, that is, wherein an actual image can no longer be distinguished from its virtual image. If actualization is inseparable from an illusion that obscures its relationship to the virtual, then it is in transforming everyday experience that this illusion is disrupted. This is not to suggest that this illusion is finally done away with; rather, the ideal habits that sustain it (the large and small forms of the action-image) are confronted with their inadequacy in the face of worlds associated with my own. And, as Deleuze puts it, something new emerges from this scenario. What it is or will be cannot be given in advance, even though this disruption is a necessary element in an escape from habit.

To appreciate the broader ethological significance of this, we should return to the idea of the suprasystem articulated by Thure von Uexküll: '[W]e would say that the [semiotic structure of the umwelt] describes the structure of systems and that it is therefore valid within a system, but also valid between systems, once these have been joined together in a suprasystem.'[36] The whole, the suprasystem constituted as the multiplicity in which myriad *umwelten* are associated, does not supervene on the individuals who participate in its transformation. The whole transforms reciprocally with the becoming of the individuals who participate in it. Our becoming is a movement through the world that occurs simultaneously with, and in the same sense as, the qualitative transformation of a world constituted as the reality of the life-world that subsists in our quantitative movements through the world. In this sense, an individual becoming is always entangled in manifold other becomings insofar as the substantive content of the life-world transformed in my becoming is the intensive logic by which other life-worlds are articulated to mine. As the large and small forms of the action-image make clear, the becoming-actual of my movements through the world relies on effacing my entanglements with other worlds. In other words, relying on habit to make sense of how the world constitutes problems for me keeps me blind to the very conditions of novel modes of life. However, if the breakdown of the sensory-motor schema has anything ethological to teach us, it is the possibility that the conditions of novel – and so, by definition, unpredictable – modes of life appear in dissonant encounters: encounters, that is, that we fail to make sense of but that constitute our everyday experiences with other species, other modes of life.

Notes

Introduction

1 Gilles Deleuze, *Difference and Repetition*, trans. Paul Patton (New York: Columbia University Press, 1994), 216.
2 The most recent English translation of Uexküll's 1934 text *Streifzüge durch die Umwelten von Tieren und Menschen* renders his work as *A Foray into the Worlds of Animals and Humans*. Translator Joseph O'Neil explains this choice by suggesting that the traditional English translation, *A Stroll through the Worlds of Animals and Men*, fails to capture the radical re-envisioning of animal and human life that is presented in the work. Given that I cite this work throughout *Deleuze and Ethology*, it would be remiss of me to not be up front about my ambivalence about O'Neil's decision. While he is certainly correct to describe Uexküll's project as radical, this radicality is grounded in more theoretically dense works such as *Theoretische Biologie* (1920, translated as *Theoretical Biology* in 1926) and in the two editions of *Umwelt und Innenwelt der Tiere* (1909 and 1921, this work has never been fully translated into English; however, excerpts are available in the 1985 collection *Foundations of Comparative Ethology*). In this light, *A Stroll* is supposed to be unassuming; it is a work in which theoretical density takes a back seat to a whimsical exploration of the interrelatedness of animal worlds. Since the English word 'stroll' effectively captures this unassuming whimsy, changing a well-known title seems, at best, unnecessary.
3 For an exemplary discussion of the influences of these two thinkers on each other's work, see François Dosse's *Gilles Deleuze and Felix Guattari: Intersecting Lives*, trans. Deborah Glassman (New York: Columbia University Press, 2011).
4 For a robust overview of the place of Hyppolite's reading of Hegel in post-war France, and its influence on Deleuze's developing philosophy, see Gary Gutting, 'French Hegelianism and Anti-Hegelianism in the 1960s: Hyppolite, Foucault and Deleuze', in *The Impact of Idealism: The Legacy of Post-Kantian German Thought*, ed. Karl Ameriks, vol. 1: *Philosophy and Natural Sciences* (Cambridge: Cambridge University Press, 2013), 246–71.
5 Alfred North Whitehead, *Process and Reality* (New York: The Free Press, 1978), 39.
6 Gilles Deleuze, *Cinema 1: The Movement-Image*, trans. Hugh Tomlinson and Barbara Habberjam (Minneapolis: University of Minnesota Press, 1986), 12. Emphasis in original.

7. Levi R. Bryant, 'A Logic of Multiplicities: Deleuze, Immanence, and Onticology', *Analecta Hermeneutica* 0.3 (2011): 4.
8. Brett Buchanan, *Onto-Ethologies: The Animal Environments of Uexküll, Heidegger, Merleau-Ponty and Deleuze* (Albany: State University of New York Press, 2008), 4.
9. Examples of recent essays, collections and monographs that affirm the importance of ethics include *Deleuze and Ethics*, eds. Nathan Jun and Daniel W. Smith (Edinburgh: Edinburgh University Press, 2011); Rosi Braidotti, 'Nomadic Ethics', in *The Cambridge Companion to Deleuze*, ed. Daniel Smith and Henry Somers-Hall (Cambridge: Cambridge University Press, 2012); and Tamsin Lorraine, *Deleuze and Guattari's Immanent Ethics: Theory, Subjectivity, and Duration* (Albany: State University of New York Press, 2011).
10. Gilles Deleuze, 'Sur Spinoza', 21 December 1980. Transcripts of Deleuze's lectures are freely available in numerous languages online at www.webdeleuze.com
11. Dosse, *Intersecting Lives*, 119, 130.
12. Gilles Deleuze, *The Logic of Sense*, trans. Mark Lester (New York: Columbia University Press, 1990), 21.
13. Deleuze, *Difference and Repetition* 191.
14. For examples of the former, see Donna Haraway, *When Species Meet* (Minneapolis: Minnesota University Press 2008) and *Staying with the Trouble: Making Kin in the Chthulucene* (Durham: Duke University Press, 2016); Vinciane Despret, *What Would Animals Say If We Asked the Right Questions?* trans. Brett Buchanan (Minneapolis: University of Minnesota Press, 2016), or Jean-Marc Drouin, *A Philosophy of the Insect*, trans. Anne Trager (New York: Columbia University Press, 2019), and for examples of the latter, see George Monbiot, *Feral: Searching for Enchantment on the Frontiers of Rewilding* (London: Allen Lane, 2013); Michael McCarthy, *The Moth Snowstorm: Nature and Joy* (London: John Murray, 2015); and Marc Bekoff, *Rewilding Our Hearts: Building Pathways of Compassion and Coexistence* (Novato: New World Library, 2014).
15. Miguel de Beistegui, *Immanence – Deleuze and Philosophy* (Edinburgh: Edinburgh University Press, 2010), 114. Emphasis in original.
16. Ibid., 105.
17. Deleuze, *Cinema 1*, 10.
18. James Williams, *Gilles Deleuze's Philosophy of Time: A Critical Introduction and Guide* (Edinburgh: Edinburgh University Press, 2011), 160.
19. Ibid., 161.
20. Ibid.
21. Gilles Deleuze, 'Sur Spinoza', 25 November 1980.
22. Gilles Deleuze, 'Responses to a Series of Questions', *Collapse* 3 (2007): 42.
23. Gilles Deleuze, 'Bergson's Conception of Difference', in *The New Bergson*, trans. Melissa McMahon and ed. John Mullarky (Manchester: Manchester University Press, 1999), 42.

24 Christian Kerslake, *Immanence and the Vertigo of Philosophy: From Kant to Deleuze* (Edinburgh: Edinburgh University Press, 2009), 3–4.
25 Deleuze, *Difference and Repetition*, 89.

Chapter 1

1 Deleuze, 'Sur Spinoza'.
2 Gordon M. Burghardt, 'Darwin's Legacy to Comparative Psychology and Ethology', *American Psychologist* 64, no. 2 (2009): 102–10.
3 Richard W. Burkhardt, 'On the Emergence of Ethology as a Scientific Discipline', *Conspectus of History* 1, no. 7 (1981): 62–1, 65–8. Or, for a thorough history, including an account of Lorenz's interaction with Uexküll, see Burkhardt's magisterial *Patterns of Behavior: Konrad Lorenz, Niko Tinbergen, and the Founding of Ethology* (Chicago: University of Chicago Press, 2005), 154–8.
4 Konrad Lorenz, 'The Comparative Method in Studying Innate Behavior Patterns', *Physiological Mechanisms in Animal Behavior (Symposia of the Society for Experimental Biology)*, IV (1951): 221–54, 223. One could argue, as Lehrman does, that Lorenz's talk of innate or genetically fixed behaviour recapitulates a robust distinction between the interior of the organism and the exterior of the environment, and thereby obscures a properly processual understanding of the organism where the boundaries between interior and exterior are porous and the organism, understood as series of developmental process in time, periodically involves elements of its environment. D. S. Lehrman, 'A Critique of Konrad Lorenz's Theory of Instinctive Behavior', *The Quarterly Review of Biology* 28, no. 4 (1953): 337–63. This is an important point, and if this project entailed a full comparison of Deleuze's and Lorenz's contrasting conceptions of individuated organisms, we would need to engage with it more fully. However, as we will consistently be concerned with how Deleuze's account of individuals as expressions of affective continuities undermines an atomistic conception of individuals, and he has his own relational way to account for the persistence of individual's capacities, this is not a problem that seriously presses upon us at this juncture.
5 Jakob von Uexküll, *Theoretical Biology*, trans. D. L. Mackinnon (New York: Harcourt, Brace & Company, Inc. 1926), xv.
6 Ibid., 42.
7 Thure von Uexküll, 'The Sign Theory of Jakob von Uexküll', *Classics of Semiotics*, ed. M. Krampen K. Oehler, R. Posner, T.A. Sebeok and T. Uexküll (New York: Springer, 1987), 165.
8 Uexküll, *Theoretical Biology*, 146–7.

9 Gilles Deleuze, *Spinoza: Practical Philosophy*, trans. Robert Hurley (San Francisco: City Lights Books, 1988), 123.
10 Ibid., 123–4.
11 Ibid., 24; Uexküll, *Theoretical Biology*, 44–5.
12 Brett Buchanan, *Onto-Ethologies*, 156.
13 Carlo Brentari, *Jakob von Uexküll: The Discovery of the Umwelt between Biosemiotics and Theoretical Biology* (Dordrecht: Springer, 2015), 215–17.
14 Deleuze, *Cinema 2*, 29; Uexküll, *Foray*, 48–9.
15 Uexküll, *Foray*, 49.
16 Brentari, *Discovery of the Umwelt*, 98. Emphasis in original.
17 Uexküll, cited in Carlo Brentari, *Discovery of the Umwelt*, 99.
18 Uexküll, *Foray*, 47.
19 Ibid., 48–9.
20 Ibid., 48.
21 Ibid.
22 Uexküll, *Foray*, 69.
23 The text in which Uexküll most develops this discussion, *Umwelt und Innenwelt der Tiere*, has never been fully translated into English; however, chapter five of Carlo Brentari's *Discovery of the Umwelt* provides an excellent exploration of the relationship between the perceptive and operative worlds through a comparative reading of the 1909 and 1921 editions of Uexküll's work.
24 Uexküll, *Foray*, 126.
25 Jean Hyppolite, *Logic and Existence*, trans. Leonard Lawlor and Amite Sen (Albany: State University of New York Press, 1997), 191. Emphasis in original.
26 Ibid., 4.
27 Ibid., 192.
28 Ibid., 92.
29 Ibid., 97.
30 Ibid., 99.
31 G. W. F. Hegel, *Phenomenology of Spirit*, trans. A. V. Miller (Oxford: Oxford University Press, 1977), 113.
32 Hyppolite, *Logic and Existence*, 195.
33 Deleuze, *Difference and Repetition*, 246.
34 Ibid., 183.
35 *Essential Readings in Biosemiotics: Anthology and Commentary*, ed. D. Favareau (Dordrecht: Springer 2010) 2. See also Marcello Barbieri, "A Short History of Biosemiotics", *Biosemiotics* 2, no. 2 (2009): 221-45 and Jesper Hoffmeyer, "A Biosemiotic Approach to the Question of Meaning", *Zygon* 45, no. 2 (2010): 367-90.
36 Uexküll, *Foray*, 143.
37 Uexküll, 'Sign Theory', 300.

38 Buchanan, *Onto-ethologies*, 28.
39 Jakob von Uexküll, 'The New Concept of Umwelt: A Link between Science and the Humanities', *Semiotica* 134 (2001): 118.
40 Ibid., 119.
41 Uexküll, 'Sign Theory', 286.
42 See, for instance, the collection *Peirce and Biosemiotics: A Guess at the Riddle of Life*.
43 Gilles Deleuze, *Cinema 2: The Time-Image*, trans. Hugh Tomlinson and Robert Galeta (Minneapolis: University of Minnesota Press, 1989), 25-6.
44 Charles Saunders Peirce, *Collected Papers of Charles Saunders Peirce*, ed. Charles Hartsthorne and Paul Weiss (Cambridge: The Belknap Press of Harvard University Press, 1960). Following custom, references to Peirce's *Collected Papers* appear as *CP*, followed by volume and paragraph number. *CP* 1.302.
45 *CP* 1.322.
46 *CP* 1.324.
47 *CP* 1.325.
48 *CP* 1.337.
49 *CP* 1.341.
50 *CP* 1.339.
51 Deleuze, *Cinema 2*, 31.
52 Ronald Bogue, *Deleuze on Cinema* (London: Routledge, 2003), 68.
53 Deleuze, *Cinema 2*, 27.
54 Leonard Lawlor, 'Is It Happening? Or, the Implications of Immanence', *Research in Phenomenology* 44 (2014): 349.
55 Alfred North Whitehead, *Science and the Modern World* (New York: Pelican Mentor Books, 1948), 59.
56 Steven Shaviro, 'Transcendental Empiricism in Deleuze and Whitehead', in *Secrets of Becoming: Negotiating Whitehead, Deleuze, and Butler*, ed. Roland Faber and Andrea M. Stephenson (New York: Fordham University Press, 2011), 83.
57 Deleuze, *Difference and Repetition*, 78.
58 Ibid., 153.
59 Ibid., 154.
60 Ibid.
61 Ibid.
62 Deleuze, *Logic of Sense*, 12.
63 Ibid., 12-14.
64 Ibid., 15.
65 Ibid., 19.
66 Ibid.
67 Giorgio Agamben, *The Open: Man and Animal*, trans. Kevin Attell (Stanford: Stanford University Press, 2004), 41.

68 *Spinoza: Practical Philosophy* is the first time that Deleuze describes Spinoza as an ethologist, a description which persists throughout Deleuze's lectures of the 1970s and 1980s: 'Uexküll, one of the main founders of ethology, is a Spinozist when first he defines the melodic lines or contrapuntal relations that correspond to each thing, and then he describes a symphony as an immanent higher unity that takes on a breadth and fullness ("natural composition")' (trans. Robert Hurley, San Francisco: City Lights Books, 1988, 126).

Chapter 2

1 Robin Durie, 'Immanence and Difference: Toward a Relational Ontology', *The Southern Journal of Philosophy* 40, no. 2 (2002): 161–89, esp. 176. To the best of my knowledge, Durie's article is almost unique. Other English-language works that discuss the ontological significance of Deleuze's linguistic interpretation of expression are Wasser (Audrey Wasser, 'Deleuze's Expressionism', *Angelaki* 12, no. 2 (2007): 49–66.) and Nail (Thomas Nail, 'Expression, Immanence and Constructivism: "Spinozism" and Gilles Deleuze', *Deleuze Studies* 2, no. 2 (2008): 201–19.) and they too inform parts of the reading of Deleuze's Spinozism offered in this chapter.
2 Daniel W. Smith, 'The Doctrine of Univocity: Deleuze's Ontology of Immanence', in *Essays on Deleuze*, ed. Daniel W. Smith (Edinburgh: Edinburgh University Press, 2012), 32.
3 Deleuze, *Difference and Repetition*, 35.
4 Ibid., 35–6.
5 Ibid., 36.
6 Ibid., 38.
7 Ibid., 36.
8 Ibid., 66.
9 Ibid., 37.
10 Simon Duffy, *The Logic of Expression: Quality, Quantity, and Intensity in Spinoza, Hegel, and Deleuze* (Hampshire: Ashgate, 2006), 6.
11 Deleuze, *Difference and Repetition*, 36.
12 Ibid., 37.
13 Ibid., 37–8.
14 Ibid., 37.
15 Ibid., 38.
16 Ibid.
17 Ibid.
18 Given that this is a limited discussion of Deleuze's reading of Spinoza, I have necessarily omitted a significant aspect of Deleuze's conception of difference,

namely, his interest in the history of the differential calculus. In *Difference and Repetition*, Deleuze discusses at length the differential relation, dy/dx. Deleuze is interested in this operation because it is one where a subsisting relationship generates and sustains terms that would otherwise vanish. In his elaboration of the mathematics informing Deleuze's position, Simon Duffy argues that Deleuze is interested in the differential relation because in the relationship dy/dx the terms y and x can have values that are equal to zero; however, the differential relationship, dy/dx, sustains its terms precisely because of the relationship that subsists between them. As Duffy notes, the differential logic of the infinitesimal calculus is vital to Deleuze's philosophy of difference; indeed, as Deleuze develops his philosophy of relational individuals, he is drawing on this sense of differential relations that are positive insofar as they determine and sustain their terms. See Simon Duffy, 'Schizo-Math: The Logic of Different/ciation and the Philosophy of Difference', *Angelaki* 9, no. 3 (2004): 199–215 and Duffy, *The Logic of Expression*; as well as Aden Evans, 'Math Anxiety', *Angelaki* 5, no. 3 (2000): 105–15 and Daniel Smith, 'The Conditions of the New', *Deleuze Studies* 1, no. 1 (2007): 1–21.
19 Gilles Deleuze and Félix Guattari, *What Is Philosophy?*, trans. Hugh Tomlinson and Graham Burchill (London: Verso, 1994), 39.
20 Ibid., 48.
21 Deleuze, *Difference and Repetition*, 36.
22 Pierre Macherey, 'From Action to Production of Effects, Observations on the Ethical Significance of *Ethics* I', in *God & Nature: Spinoza's Metaphysics*, ed. Yirmiyahu Yovel (Leiden: E.J. Bill, 1991), 165.
23 Ibid., 163–4.
24 I will argue in this chapter that, in his reading of Spinoza, Deleuze argues that no being possesses power which is not expressed. For God, this power is an active 'potentia identical to his essence', whereas modes, produced necessarily as expressions of the affections, are identical to a power of being affected (*potestas*) which corresponds to God's *potentia*. Deleuze, *Spinoza: Practical Philosophy*, 97–8.
25 Macherey, 'Action to Production of Effects', 164.
26 Deleuze, 'Sur Spinoza'.
27 Gilles Deleuze, 'Immanence: A Life', in *Pure Immanence: Essays on a Life*, trans. Anne Boyman (New York: Urzone, 2001), 26. Emphasis in original.
28 Gilles Deleuze, *Expressionism in Philosophy: Spinoza*, trans. Martin Joughin (New York: Urzone, 1990), 175.
29 Ibid., 104.
30 Ibid., 43.
31 Durie, 'Immanence and Difference', 166.
32 EIP13C.
33 EIP13CS.

34 Durie, 'Immanence and Difference', 166.
35 Deleuze, *Expressionism*, 28.
36 EIP4.
37 EIP4D.
38 EIP18.
39 Deleuze, *Expressionism*, 32.
40 Ibid., 32.
41 Ibid., 33.
42 EID5.
43 Deleuze, *Expressionism*, 33.
44 Descartes states that what we understand by the name '*modes* [is] exactly the same thing as we understand elsewhere by *attributes* or *qualities*'. René Descartes, *Principles of Philosophy*, trans. Valentine Rodger Miller and Reese P. Miller (Dordrecht: D. Reidel Publishing, 1983), 24–5.
45 Deleuze, *Expressionism*, 29.
46 Durie, 'Immanence and Difference', 167.
47 Deleuze, *Expressionism*, 38.
48 Durie, 'Immanence and Difference', 172.
49 In Spinoza's formulation of the ontological argument, the existence of substance necessarily follows from its essence, and so we can say that substance acquires existence only in its essences being constituted by the attributes. It is this process that enables Deleuze to claim that substance, by being rendered as a qualitative multiplicity – a multiplicity of essences – by the attributes, exists. The attributes in this case are not static terms in need of a relation to substance but are, in fact, 'dynamic and active forms' that generate substance by actively attributing essence to it. Deleuze, *Expressionism*, 45.
50 Deleuze, *Expressionism*, 43.
51 Ibid., 43.
52 Ibid., 42.
53 Durie, 'Immanence and Difference', 172.
54 Ibid., 172.
55 We will turn to the question of qualitative and quantitative distinctions when we discuss the modes as degrees of power in a later section. The issue, essentially, is that the distinctions among the attributes, insofar as they constitute substance, are distinct from each other qualitatively. An attribute, insofar as it is a part of the constitution of substance relative to the other attributes, can be described *extensively*; that is, we can talk about *the extent to which a particular attribute participates in the constitution of substance*. The sense in which we can predicate *extensity* of a particular attribute is the intensive degree, the degree of power, that informs the numerical distinctions that characterize existing modes.

56 Deleuze, *Expressionism*, 44.
57 Durie, 'Immanence and Difference', 172.
58 Deleuze, *Expressionism*, 49.
59 EIP25S.
60 EIP25C.
61 Deleuze, *Expressionism*, 100–1.
62 Ibid., 62.
63 Durie, 'Immanence and Difference', 176.
64 EIIP3.
65 Deleuze, *Expressionism*, 100.
66 This is not a trivial point; a crucial element of Spinoza's argument that a single substance necessarily possesses an infinity of attributes is his argument that each attribute is infinite in its own kind – for example, the attribute of thought is infinite insofar as it constitutes a power of thinking – where substance, however, is absolutely infinite insofar as it possesses all attributes.
67 Durie, 'Immanence and Difference', 177.
68 Deleuze, *Expressionism*, 102–3.
69 Ibid., 104.
70 Deleuze, *Logic of Sense*, 21. Translation modified.
71 Durie, 'Immanence and Difference', 177.
72 For a concrete example, we can turn to Deleuze's discussion in *The Logic of Sense* of the white knight's song in *Through the Looking Glass*. In *Through the Looking Glass*, when Alice encounters the white knight, he offers to sing a song he has written; however, when the knight introduces the song, he and Alice have some difficulty: 'The name of the song is called "*Haddock's Eyes*".' 'Oh, that's the name of the song, is it?' Alice said, trying to feel interested. 'No, you don't understand,' the Knight said, looking a little vexed. 'That's what the name is *called*. The name really *is* "*The Aged Aged Man*".' 'Then I ought to have said "That's what the *song* is called?"' Alice corrected herself. 'No, you oughtn't: that's quite another thing! The *song* is called "*Ways and Means*": but that's only what it's *called*, you know!' 'Well, what *is* the song, then?' said Alice, who was by this time completely bewildered. 'I was coming to that,' the Knight said. 'The song really *is* "*A-sitting On A Gate*": and the tune's my own invention.' Lewis Carroll, *Alice's Adventures in Wonderland and Through the Looking Glass and What Alice Found There* (London: Vintage Books, 2007), 291. Deleuze is interested in this passage because it presents the relationships between 'a series of nominal entities'. In fact, in the various names, this passage presents four iterations of sense: what the song really is, '*A-sitting on a Gate*'; the name that denotes this reality, '*Ways and Means*'; the sense of this name, '*The Aged Aged Man*'; and the name which denotes or expresses the sense of this new name, '*Haddock's Eyes*.' In short, Deleuze is interested in this episode in Carroll's story

because it sets up a series from the song as it really is, through the expression of the reality of the song and the subsequent naming of the song to the sense of the song's name. Deleuze, *Logic of Sense*, 28–35.
73 Deleuze, *Expressionism*, 110.
74 Deleuze, *Difference and Repetition*, 35.
75 Deleuze, *Expressionism*, 175.
76 Ibid., 93.
77 Duffy, *Logic of Expression*, 6.
78 EIP34.
79 EIP11S.
80 Deleuze, *Expressionism*, 89.
81 Duffy, *Logic of Expression*, 6.
82 EIVP4D.
83 Deleuze, *Expressionism*, 91.
84 The linguistic sense of Deleuze's reading of modification as the expression of power is not the only way to read this issue. In his article 'Schizo-Math', Simon Duffy offers a compelling account of powers by elaborating Deleuze's calculus-inspired claim that '[p]ower is the form of reciprocal determination according to which variable magnitudes are taken to be functions of one another'. Deleuze, *Difference and Repetition*, 174.
85 Deleuze, *Expressionism*, 90.
86 Ibid., 183.
87 Ibid., 197.
88 Ibid., 47.
89 Ibid., 192.
90 Ibid.; Deleuze, *Spinoza: Practical Philosophy*, 78. See also, Benedict de Spinoza, 'Letter 12', in *The Collected Works of Spinoza*: Vol. 1, trans. and ed. Edwin Curley (Princeton, NJ: Princeton University Press, 1985), 202.
91 Deleuze, *Expressionism*, 193.
92 EIP24.
93 EIP25.
94 Deleuze, *Expressionism*, 196.
95 Ibid., 197.
96 Ibid.
97 EIP23.
98 Deleuze, *Expressionism*, 198.
99 Ibid.
100 Ibid., 125.
101 Ibid., 122–3.
102 Deleuze, *Difference and Repetition*, 40.
103 EIID5.

Chapter 3

1. Deleuze, *Expressionism*, 212.
2. Deleuze, *Difference and Repetition*, 304. Emphasis in original.
3. Ibid., 40.
4. Ibid.
5. Ibid., 41.
6. Ibid., 208–9. Emphasis in original.
7. Gilles Deleuze, *Bergsonism*, trans. Hugh Tomlinson and Barbara Habberjam (New York: Zone Books, 1988), 96–7.
8. Ibid., 97.
9. Henri Bergson, 'The Possible and the Real', in *An Introduction to Metaphysics: The Creative Mind*, trans. Mabelle L. Andison (Patterson: Littlefield, Adams & Co., 1965), 101.
10. Ibid.
11. Deleuze, *Bergsonism*, 97.
12. Deleuze, *Difference and Repetition*, 211.
13. Ibid., 211.
14. Deleuze, *Bergsonism*, 97.
15. Deleuze, *Difference and Repetition*, 211–12.
16. Ibid., 212.
17. Bergson, 'Possible and the Real', 102.
18. Keith Ansell-Pearson, *Philosophy and the Adventure of the Virtual: Bergson and the Time of Life* (New York: Routledge, 2002), 79.
19. Deleuze, *Bergsonism*, 97.
20. Deleuze, *Difference and Repetition*, 212. Emphasis added.
21. Ibid., 178.
22. Deleuze, *Difference and Repetition*, 178–9.
23. Simon Duffy, 'Albert Lautman', in *Deleuze's Philosophical Lineage*, ed. Graham Jones and Jon Roffe (Edinburgh: Edinburgh University Press, 2009), 365.
24. Deleuze, *Difference and Repetition*, 183.
25. The implication here that association and causation are opposed, mutually exclusive types of relationship is problematic. To elucidate why causation is not opposed to association – that is, why causation and association are not necessarily distinct types of relationships between existing relata – I will spend much of this and the next chapter focusing on a concept that is central to Deleuze's philosophy of time: *synthesis*. In *The Logic of Sense*, Deleuze argues that the virtual and the actual correspond to each but have their own respective causal orders; he suggests that there is an order of actual causes and an order of virtual 'quasi-cause[s]'. Deleuze, *Logic of Sense*, 94. However, neither order of reality – actual and virtual, body and

idea – contains relations of efficient causation. In other words, Deleuze does not reject the notion of causation and replace it with one of association; rather, he rejects the idea of efficient causation between discrete entities and develops a new logic of causation that sees it as a much more complex system of syntheses and correspondences. The actual is produced as an eternal living present characterized as a series of passive syntheses, that is, contractions of extensive parts into bodies characterized by intensive degrees – the degrees of power that subsist in the relations between bodies. Simultaneously, the virtual is constituted as the ideal expression of sense or significance of present occurrences synthesized as both the whole of the past and the future-oriented anticipations of the present. In a later section in this chapter, I will elaborate this conception of time, and in Chapter 4 I will pay extended attention to the particularity and interactions between these syntheses as they are relevant to the *Cinema* books. Still, this is a complex issue and I return to it in the conclusion of *Deleuze and Ethology* as a way of summarizing the metaphysical picture that Deleuze offers. Moreover, in *Deleuze's Philosophy of Time*, Williams offers an exemplary summary of the slippery interaction of *Difference and Repetition*'s and *The Logic of Sense*'s respective vocabularies, esp. 148–52.

26 Deleuze, *Difference and Repetition*, 98.
27 Gilles Deleuze, 'Dualism, Monism and Multiplicities (Desire-Pleasure-*Jouissance*)', *Contretemps* 2 (2001): 99.
28 The issue of the translation of manifold, *multiplicité* and multiplicity is a complex one which cannot be discussed in great detail in this context. It will suffice to suggest briefly what seems a likely origin of this anomaly. The conceptual content of 'plateau' 14 of *A Thousand Plateaus* – 'The Smooth and the Striated' – contains, as Plotnitsky points out, the almost unavoidable impression of Riemann's work. Arkady Plotnitsky, 'Bernhard Riemann', in *Deleuze's Philosophical Lineage*, ed. Graham Jones and Jon Roffe (Edinburgh: Edinburgh University Press, 2009), 206. However, Brian Massumi's English translation of *Mille Plateaux* appeared in 1987, before significant secondary work had been done in English on the extent of the debt Deleuze owes to the history of mathematics. Coincidently, Massumi translated *multiplicité* as 'multiplicity', even though it is translated as 'manifold' in mathematics. This choice, it must be said, is a perfectly understandable one, particularly in light of the prevalence of the term *multiplicity* in English language 'French Theory'. Furthermore, by the time English language commentators began paying serious attention to Deleuze's debt to mathematics in the late 1990s, most of his major work had already been translated into English and *multiplicity* had become the standard term. For the duration of this book, uses of the word *multiplicity* bear this Riemannian sense, particularly when used in the context of Bergson and in quotes from the *Cinema* books.
29 Plotnitsky, 'Bernhard Riemann', 198–9.

30 Gilles Deleuze and Félix Guattari, *A Thousand Plateaus: Capitalism and Schizophrenia*, trans. Brian Massumi (London: Continuum, 1987), 482–3.
31 Ibid., 485.
32 Miguel de Beistegui, *Truth and Genesis: Philosophy as Differential Ontology* (Bloomington: Indiana University Press, 2004), 249.
33 Deleuze, *Difference and Repetition*, 183.
34 In the original *Différence et Répétition*, Deleuze's line is '*Ces conditions sont au nombre de trois, et permettent de définir le moment d'émergence de l'Idée*' (237) and, in his English translation, Paul Patton renders this as '[t]here are three conditions which together allow us to define the moment at which an Idea emerges' (*Difference and Repetition*, 183). While Patton's translation makes sense, we must be aware that the English clause 'an Idea emerges' presents the subject of the verb as active in a way that is not present in the original clause '*d'émergence de l'Idée*'. I would argue that, insofar as it is the subject of the verb 'emerge', we must be careful not to present the Idea as having an activity it does not have; this is why I have opted for a passive construction. The subtlety of this point is important for the discussion of the passive syntheses of time where Deleuze insists that it is only the actual, living present that is active and that the multiplicitous Idea remains passive.
35 Deleuze, *Difference and Repetition*, 183.
36 Ibid., 212.
37 Disjunctive syntheses are a crucial component of Deleuze's conception of a dialectic insofar as it is the genesis of action in the process of different/*c*iation. Unlike, say, an Hegelian dialectic where the synthesis of terms is a *conjunction* en route to a higher unity, Deleuze's dialectic involves disjunctive syntheses that affirm the difference of the terms of a synthesis at the same time as synthesizing them. See, for instance, Williams's argument that '[a] disjunctive synthesis is not a reduction through abstraction but a transforming addition that connects by creating differences'. Williams, *Deleuze's Logic of Sense*, 27.
38 EIP24.
39 Deleuze, *Difference and Repetition*, 70.
40 Contemplation is the occurrence of this synthesis in the mind: '[Passive synthesis] is not carried out by the mind, but occurs *in* the mind which contemplates, prior to all memory and all reflection' (Deleuze, *Difference and Repetition*, 71). This contemplation moreover is the genesis of a 'question' that determines a response. But this determination draws us closer to the need for a fuller account of active synthesis as well to later syntheses.
41 Deleuze, *Difference and Repetition*, 71. With the phrase 'it goes from … the particular to the general', this discussion is obviously going to involve a confrontation with what is perhaps *the* classic issue associated with the contemporary reception of Hume's philosophy: the problem of induction. However, a standard formulation of the problem of induction – under what

circumstances could our anticipation of future events, given past events, ever be considered logically valid? – is not appropriate for Deleuze's account of Hume for a very straightforward reason: the empiricism of Deleuze's Hume is not primarily concerned with the epistemological problems traditionally associated with Hume. For Deleuze, the pressing problem with Hume concerns the genesis of subjectivity relative to the conditions of experience. Jon Roffe, 'David Hume', in *Deleuze's Philosophical Lineage*, ed. Graham Jones and Jon Roffe (Edinburgh: Edinburgh University Press, 2009), 68. Consequently, Hume's empiricism is not the standard formulation of empiricism that asks after the derivation of knowledge from experience; such a formulation, claims Deleuze, is neither appropriate to empiricism in general nor Hume in particular since, for Hume, to ask after the constitution of knowledge in experience (and with regard to our claims about future circumstances given past experiences) is question begging.

42 Deleuze, *Difference and Repetition*, 70.
43 Ibid., 70.
44 Ibid., 73.
45 Ibid.
46 Ibid., 78.
47 Ibid., 76.
48 Ibid., 77.
49 Ibid., 79.
50 Ibid., 80.
51 Deleuze, *Bergsonism*, 56.
52 Ibid., 55.
53 Ibid. Emphasis in original.
54 Deleuze, *Difference and Repetition*, 80.
55 Ibid., 84.
56 Ibid., 80.
57 Ibid., 90. Emphasis in original.
58 Ibid., 88.
59 James Williams, *Gilles Deleuze's 'Difference and Repetition': A Critical Introduction and Guide* (Edinburgh: Edinburgh University Press, 2003), 102.
60 Deleuze, *Difference and Repetition*, 89.
61 Ibid.
62 Ibid.
63 Ibid., 209.
64 Ibid.
65 Ibid., 210–11.
66 Ibid., 91.
67 Not only is James Williams interested in the three syntheses of time in Deleuze's ontology (2011); Keith Faulkner revitalizes the Freudian influence to elucidate

the syntheses' Bergsonian response to Kant. Keith Faulkner, *Deleuze and the Three Syntheses of Time* (New York: Peter Lang Publishing, 2006). Meanwhile, Jay Lampert explores their place in the philosophy of history that emerges from Deleuze's collaborations with Félix Guattari. Jay Lampert, *Deleuze and Guattari's Philosophy of History* (London: Continuum, 2006).
68 Deleuze, *Difference and Repetition*, 182.
69 Deleuze, *Bergsonism*, 93.
70 Deleuze, *Difference and Repetition*, 187.
71 Ibid., 191.
72 Ibid., 185.
73 Ibid., 182.
74 Christian Kerslake, 'The Vertigo of Philosophy: Deleuze and the Problem of Immanence', *Radical Philosophy* 113 (2002): 13.
75 Deleuze, 'Dualism, Monism and Multiplicities', 99.
76 Deleuze, *Cinema 1*, 10.
77 Ibid.

Chapter 4

1 Henri Bergson, *Matter and Memory*, trans. Nancy Margaret Paul and W. Scott Palmer (Mineola: Dover Publicans, Inc., 2004), ix.
2 George Berkley, *Three Dialogues between Hylas and Philonus*, ed. Robert Merrihew Adams (Indianapolis: Hackett Publishing Company, 1979), 11.
3 Bergson, *Matter and Memory*, viii.
4 Deleuze, *Difference and Repetition*, 304.
5 Deleuze, *Cinema 1*, 10; Bergson, *Matter and Memory*, 36.
6 Henri Bergson, *Creative Evolution*, trans. Arthur Mitchell (New York: Dover Publications, 1998), 308.
7 Ibid., 341.
8 Ibid., 313. Emphasis in original.
9 Deleuze, *Cinema 1*, 4.
10 Ibid.
11 Ibid. Emphasis in original.
12 Ibid., 7.
13 Bergson, *Creative Evolution*, 317. This discussion is itself a reference to Plato's *Timaeus*, hence Bergson's use of *forms*.
14 Ibid., 320. Bergson argues that this cinematographical illusion is the consequence of consciousness seeing 'clearly of the inner life what is already made, and only [feeling] confusedly the making'. Ibid., 273. In fact, this is a criticism of the

mechanistic illusion whereby consciousness confuses the divisibility of bodies for the conditions of their movement and life. Early in *Cinema 1*, Deleuze argues that Bergson mistook cinema's potential since the medium was still in its infancy when *Creative Evolution* was written in 1907. The problem, in sum, is the illusion that movement is an abstract relationship added to immobile forms; however, as we will see in the next two sections, Deleuze argues that 'cinema does not give us an image to which movement is added, it immediately gives us a movement-image. It does give us a section, but a section which is mobile, not an immobile section + abstract movement'. Deleuze, *Cinema 1*, 2.
15 Deleuze, *Cinema 1*, 9.
16 Ibid., 19. Emphasis in original.
17 Gilles Deleuze, *Cinéma 1: L'image-mouvement* (Paris: Les Éditions de Minuit, 1983), 32.
18 Deleuze, *Cinema 1*, 10.
19 Constantin V. Boundas, 'Deleuze-Bergson: An Ontology of the Virtual', in *Deleuze: A Critical Reader*, ed. Paul Patton (Boston, MA: Blackwell, 1996), 84.
20 Deleuze, *Cinema 1*, 3.
21 Bergson, *Matter and Memory*, vii–viii.
22 David Hume, *An Enquiry Concerning Human Understanding*, ed. Eric Steinberg (Indianapolis: Hackett Publishing Company, 1993), 104.
23 Ibid., 102–7.
24 Ibid., 104.
25 Bergson, *Matter and Memory*, viii. Leonard Lawlor offers an incisive and compelling discussion of how Bergson employs this artifice 'to "dissipate" the obscurity' of the false problems bequeathed to modern philosophy by the split between materialism/realism and idealism/spiritualism. Leonard Lawlor, *The Challenge of Bergsonism: Phenomenology, Ontology, Ethics* (London: Continuum, 2003), 1–4.
26 Bergson, *Matter and Memory*, 83.
27 Ibid., 83.
28 Ibid., 13–14.
29 Ibid., vii–viii.
30 Deleuze, *Cinema 1*, 58.
31 Bergson, *Matter and Memory*, 1.
32 Ibid., 13–14.
33 Ibid., 1.
34 Suzanne Guerlac, *Thinking in Time: An Introduction to Henri Bergson* (Ithaca: Cornell University Press, 2006), 112.
35 Deleuze, *Cinema 1*, 57–8.
36 Bergson, *Matter and Memory*, 2–3.

37 Ibid., 1.
38 Ibid., 44–6. Translation modified. Bergson wrote, '***Mon corps*** *est ce qui se dessine au centre de ces perceptions;* ***ma personne*** *est l'être auquel il faut rapporter ces actions.*' Henri Bergson, *Matière et mémoire: essai sur la relation du corps a l'esprit* (Genève: Skira, 1946), 49. Paul and Palmer's translation renders this as '*My body* is that which stands out as the centre of these perceptions; *my personality* is the being to which these actions must be referred'. I have rendered '*personne*' as '*person*' to try and avoid the psychological baggage that 'personality' has accumulated in the century since Paul and Palmer produced their translation.
39 Deleuze, *Cinema 1*, 64.
40 Ibid., 12.
41 Ibid., 58.
42 Ibid., 2.
43 Bergson, *Matter and Memory*, 9–10.
44 Deleuze, *Cinema 1*, 58.
45 Ibid., 59.
46 Deleuze, *Difference and Repetition*, 41.
47 Deleuze, *Cinema 1*, 62.
48 Bergson, *Matter and Memory*, 40.
49 Ibid., 40–1.
50 Deleuze, *Cinema 1*, 66.
51 Deleuze, *Cinema 2*, 31.
52 Ibid., 30.
53 Ibid., 32.
54 Ibid., 30.
55 Bergson, *Matter and Memory*, 154.
56 Deleuze, *Cinema 2*, 31–2.
57 Bergson, *Matter and Memory*, 21.
58 Ibid., 8.
59 Deleuze, *Cinema 1*, 63.
60 Ibid., 64. Quentin Meillasoux offers an incisive interpretation of the first chapter of *Matter and Memory*, the important distinction between an active selection and a passive reception of images therein, as well as the significance of this distinction for Deleuze's project. 'Subtraction and Contraction: Deleuze, Immanence and *Matter and Memory*', *Collapse* 3 (2007): 63–107.
61 Deleuze, *Cinema 1*, 63.
62 Bergson, *Matter and Memory*, 40–1.
63 Ibid., 28.
64 Ibid., 28–9.
65 Bergson, *Matter and Memory*, 40.

66 Deleuze, *Cinema 1*, 64. This question of indetermination recalls our ongoing discussion of why, for Deleuze, and for Bergson before him, the outcome of an event cannot be given in advance of its actually occurring. While the first synthesis of time is the expression of an anticipation of the future grounded in prior experience, this anticipation participates in the determination of the conditions of the future and, as such, the future cannot be given without participating in the determination of the actual future. This sense in which the future cannot, in principle, be given is the sense in which both Deleuze and Bergson call the centre a centre of indetermination. This indetermination cannot be overstated because it is a function of the constitution of subjects. The discussion in this chapter grounds an issue I will explore in more detail in Chapter 5; because of the way Deleuze describes the relationship between problems and solutions that constitutes subjectivity, indeterminacy is a condition of the subjects of Deleuze's ontology.
67 Bergson, *Matter and Memory*, 23.
68 Deleuze, *Cinema 1*, 65.
69 Ibid., 65.
70 Bogue, *Deleuze on Cinema*, 37.
71 Bergson, *Matter and Memory*, 60.
72 Bogue, *Deleuze on Cinema*, 37.
73 Deleuze, *Difference and Repetition*, 209.
74 Ibid., 209.
75 Bergson, *Matter and Memory*, 55.
76 Ibid., 57.
77 Ibid., 51–9.
78 Ibid., 58.
79 Deleuze, *Difference and Repetition*, 184.
80 Ibid., 211.
81 Deleuze, *Cinema 1*, 87.
82 Deleuze, *Expressionism*, 191.
83 He argues that 'if the being of things is … in their differences of nature, we can hope that difference is itself something, that it has a nature, finally that it will deliver Being to us'. 'Bergson's Conception of Difference', 42.
84 Deleuze, *Cinema 1*, 88.
85 Ibid., 87.
86 Ibid.
87 Ibid., 90.
88 Ibid., 99.
89 Deleuze, *Cinema 1*, 102.
90 Ibid.
91 Ibid. The distinction between causation and determination is crucial to Deleuze's project for a number of reasons. On the one hand, it is simply a problem he

inherits from his forebears; Hume is notoriously sceptical of efforts to infer causal relations from serial events, and famously distinguishes causal relations from the 'constant conjunction' of the objects of our experience. Spinoza, however, insists on God as immanently causing the essences of things in the world (EIP18), while, at EIP17SII, he argues that 'a man is the cause of the existence of another man, but not of his essence, for the latter is an eternal truth. Hence, they can agree entirely according to their essence. But in existing they must differ.' In other words, there is a distinction between the cause of the existence of the beings in the world and the determination of their essence. The importance of this distinction is clear in Deleuze's repeated affirmation that movements from the virtual to the actual and vice versa must proceed by differen*t*/ciation. In sum, the virtual *does not* cause the existence of the beings/fluxes that fill out the actual world; however, it *does* determine the actual form of a being's becoming at any given moment. Given that the virtual and the actual are reciprocal, we can say the same about the actual's determination of the virtual; the actual world is not the cause of the virtual, even though it determines its content. Even though a detailed account of this issue is beyond the scope of the current work, I will engage with it briefly in the conclusion to hold together a number of issues and suggest that an account of causation in Deleuze's ethology must be connected to topics I discussed in Chapter 2, particularly the claim that any individual being is caused not by its essence or by the power it expresses but that the necessity of its existence comes from God, or the whole in which it participates.

92 Ibid., 124.
93 Ibid., 102.
94 Ibid., 95–6.
95 Ibid., 97.
96 Ibid., 102.
97 Ibid.
98 'There is only one time (monism), although there is an infinity of actual fluxes (generalized pluralism) that necessarily participate in the same virtual whole (limited pluralism).' Deleuze, *Bergsonism*, 82.
99 Deleuze, *Cinema 1*, 19.
100 Ibid., 32.
101 Deleuze, *Spinoza: Practical Philosophy*, 48–9.
102 Ibid.
103 Ibid., 73.
104 Deleuze, *Cinema 1*, 8.
105 Elizabeth Grosz, 'Feminism, Materialism, and Freedom', in *New Materialisms: Ontology, Agency, and Politics*, ed. Diana Coole and Samantha Frost (Durham: Duke University Press, 2010), 148.

106 Paul Patton, 'Freedom', in *The Deleuze Dictionary*, ed. Adrian Parr (Edinburgh: Edinburgh University Press, 2010), 118.
107 Deleuze, *Bergsonism*, 15. Emphasis added.

Chapter 5

1 Deleuze, *Bergsonism*, 15.
2 Deleuze, *Cinema 2*, 176–7.
3 Deleuze, *Cinema 1*, 114.
4 Ibid., 114. For discussions of the ethical significance of Deleuze's interpretation of the wager, see Bogue's and Rodowick's respective contributions to *Afterimages of Gilles Deleuze's Film Philosophy*.
5 Bergson, *Matter and Memory*, 10–11.
6 Deleuze, *Cinema 1*, 58.
7 For all that Deleuze challenges phenomenology, we cannot overlook the extent to which Deleuze owes a debt to the phenomenological tradition. In an excellent essay, Lawlor discusses the impact of Husserl, by way of Jean Hyppolite, on Deleuze's project. Husserl famously argued for the necessity of a phenomenological *reduction*, a 'bracketing' of the actual world and intentional acts that assume the existence of the world, so that the phenomenologist might make her way back to a realm of transcendental subjectivity. Deleuze, as we shall see, is persistently critical of the idea of transcendental subjectivity; however, Lawlor is quick to remind us that the *Logic of Sense* 'takes place entirely under the sign of the phenomenological reduction'. Leonard Lawlor, 'The End of Phenomenology: Expressionism in Deleuze and Merleau-Ponty', *Continental Philosophy Review* 31, no. 1 (1998): 18. He argues that this reduction is a necessary condition for Deleuze's ontological project, concerned as it is with sensible phenomena and the plane of immanence. Put simply, if, as Lawlor suggests elsewhere, 'one could ... say that phenomenology consists in the immanence of the concept in life', then Deleuze's persistent concern with the immanence of thought in life, and the idea that cinema could return up the path that natural perception travels down, owes a tremendous debt to the phenomenological reduction as methodology ('A Miniscule Hiatus: Foucault's Critique of the Concept of Lived-Experience (*Vécu*)', in *Logos of Phenomenology and Phenomenology of the Logos. Book One: Phenomenology as the Critique of Reason in Contemporary Criticism and Interpretation*, ed. Anna-Teresa Tymieniecka (Dordrecht: Springer, 2005), 417). While an in-depth engagement with this debt is beyond the remit of *Deleuze and Ethology*, one of the most powerful lines we could mention of phenomenology's influence, or, at least,

Deleuze's common ground with phenomenology, is Merleau-Ponty. In her comparative study, *Thinking between Deleuze and Merleau-Ponty* (Athens: Ohio University Press, 2017), Judith Wambacq argues that Deleuze's and Merleau-Ponty's respective projects are best characterized as transcendental projects concerned with the immanence of thought in life. However, in his study, *Merleau-Ponty's Developmental Ontology* (Evanston: Northwestern University Press, 2018), David Morris argues that this problem is actually one of the complexity of an ontology that revolves around the production and expression of sense.

8 David Woodruff Smith and Barry Smith begin their contextualization of work on Husserl with a description of phenomenology as the reflective study of consciousness from a first-person perspective. David Woodruff Smith and Barry Smith, introduction to *Cambridge Companion to Husserl*, eds. David Woodruff Smith and Barry Smith (Cambridge: Cambridge University Press, 1995), 1.

9 Robert Sokolowski, *Introduction to Phenomenology* (Cambridge: Cambridge University Press, 2000), 4.

10 Lawlor, 'The End of Phenomenology', 15–16. See, for example, Merleau-Ponty's description of his project as an attempt 'to elucidate the primary function whereby we bring into existence, for ourselves, or take a hold upon, space, the object or the instrument, and to describe the body as the place where this appropriation occurs'. Maurice Merleau-Ponty, *Phenomenology of Perception*, trans. Colin Smith (New York: Routledge Classics, 2002), 178.

11 Gilles Deleuze, *Empiricism and Subjectivity: An Essay on Hume's Theory of Human Nature*, trans. Constantin V. Boundas (New York: Columbia University Press, 1991), 87. Deleuze's description of the given in Hume bears a striking similarity to Bergson's concept of images: '[The given is] the flux of the sensible, *a collection of impressions and images, or a set of perceptions*. It is the totality of that which appears, being which equals appearance; it also movement and change without identity or law.' Deleuze, *Empiricism and Subjectivity*, 87. Emphasis added.

12 In his classic *Introduction to Phenomenology*, Dermot Moran describes Husserl's reduction as an attempt to 'put the thumbscrews ... on transcendental *consciousness* itself, to get it to yield up its secrets as to how the world and its meanings are constituted' (London: Routledge, 2000), 148.

13 Deleuze and Guattari, *What Is Philosophy?*, 46.

14 Ibid., 46.

15 Deleuze, *Cinema 1*, 57–8.

16 Bryant, 'A Logic of Multiplicities', 4.

17 Deleuze argues that 'Spinoza was the philosopher who knew full well that immanence was only immanent to itself and therefore that it was a plane traversed by movements of the infinite, filled with intensive ordinates. He is therefore the prince of philosophers.' Deleuze and Guattari, *What Is Philosophy?*, 48.

18 Deleuze responds to Bergson's critique of cinema by posing a peculiar question: '[I]s not the reproduction of an illusion in a certain sense also its correction?' Deleuze, *Cinema 1*, 2. Deleuze argues that, while Bergson is correct to indict cinema for repeating the illusion that perception is composed of the juxtaposition of discrete units, cinema's juxtaposition of fixed shots through various editing techniques presupposes a heterogeneous, continuous whole and thus presents duration indirectly at first and then directly.

19 Gregory Flaxman, 'Cinema: Year Zero', in *The Brain Is the Screen: Deleuze and the Philosophy of Cinema*, ed. Gregory Flaxman (Minneapolis: University of Minnesota Press, 2000), 93.

20 Bergson, *Creative Evolution*, 304.

21 Jean Mitry, *The Aesthetics and Psychology of the Cinema*, trans. Christopher King (Bloomington: Indiana University Press, 1997), 214.

22 Ibid., 215.

23 Ibid.

24 Ibid., 209.

25 Ibid., 216.

26 Ibid., 209.

27 Deleuze, *Cinema 1*, 71.

28 Ibid., 74.

29 V. N. Vološinov, *Marxism and the Philosophy of Language*, trans. Ladislay Matejka and I. R. Titunik (New York: Seminar Press, 1973), 115. Given Vološinov's involvement in the Bakhtin Circle – a group of Soviet intellectuals in the early twentieth century – there have been habits of attributing works published under Vološinov's name to Mikhail Bakhtin. There is some debate around the issue, and Deleuze for his part attributes the work to Bakhtin. However, it seems easy to account for this discrepancy in Deleuze's case; the second footnote to chapter five of *L'Image-mouvement* suggests that Deleuze was working from the French text *Le marxisme et la philosophie du langage: Essai d'application de la méthode sociologique en linguistique* – published by *Les Éditions de Minuit* in 1977. Deleuze, *Cinéma 1*, 228; *Cinema 1*, 107. *Le marxisme* ... was primarily attributed to Bakhtin and only parenthetically to Vološinov.

30 Deleuze, *Cinema 1*, 73. Given this turn to Vološinov, it goes without saying that Deleuze's arguments in this field stretch much wider than just Mitry. Besides Mitry, two of his major influences are Vološinov and essays in Pier Paolo Pasolini's *Heretical Empiricism*, particularly 'The Cinema of Poetry'. In this chapter I focus on Mitry for the sake of clarifying the image constitutive of cinematic subjectivity; however, this will hopefully not undermine the importance of Vološinov on reporting and reported speech, and quasi-direct discourse, and Pasolini on free-indirect discourse. The genealogy of Deleuze's influences on this topic are much

more complex than I can present here; see Louis-George Schwartz, 'Typewriter: Free Indirect Discourse in Deleuze's *Cinema*', *SubStance* 34, no. 3 (2005): 107–35.
31 Deleuze, *Cinema 1*, 73.
32 Ibid., 74.
33 Ibid., 76.
34 Ibid.
35 Bogue, *Deleuze on Cinema*, 74.
36 Deleuze, *Cinema 1*, 80.
37 In the fifth chapter of *Cinema 1*, Deleuze argues that this liquid form of the perception-image gets its most in-depth treatment in the French school of the 1920s and 1930s.
38 Deleuze, *Difference and Repetition*, 74.
39 Deleuze, *Cinema 1*, 74.
40 Ibid., 13.
41 Ibid.: '[T]he frame serves as an opaque surface of information, sometimes blurred by saturation, sometimes reduced to the empty set, to the white or black screen.'
42 Bergson, *Matter and Memory*, 168. On the synonymy of memory and the whole, see Chapter 3's discussion of the second synthesis of time – that is, the passive synthesis of the whole of the past as the ontological condition of the passing present.
43 Ibid., 168.
44 Deleuze, *Cinema 1*, 65: 'There is inevitably a part of external movements that we "absorb", that we refract, and which does not transform itself into either objects of perception or acts of the subject; rather they mark the coincidence of the subject and the object in a pure quality.'
45 D. N. Rodowick, *Gilles Deleuze's Time Machine* (London: Duke University Press, 1997), 87.
46 Bergson, *Matière et mémoire*, 168.
47 Ibid., 28. John Mullarky argues that a central aspect of Deleuze's perversion of Bergson is the development of an ontology of the virtual that is not present in Bergson's own philosophy; while Deleuze treats it ontologically, the virtual for Bergson is, Mullarky argues, 'a *well-founded* perspectival and psychological phenomenon'. John Mullarky, 'Forget the Virtual: Bergson, Actualism, and the Refraction of Reality', *Continental Philosophy Review* 37, no. 4 (2004): 471. Consequently, Mullarky argues, the tendency of contemporary commentators to prioritize a concern with the virtual is a product of identifying too closely Deleuze's revitalization of Bergson's philosophy with Bergson per se.
48 Bergson, *Matter and Memory*, 210.
49 Deleuze, *Bergsonism*, 60.
50 Deleuze, *Difference and Repetition*, 211–12.

51　Ibid., 209.
52　Deleuze, *Bergsonism*, 64.
53　Deleuze, *Cinema 2*, 82–3.
54　Ibid., 99.
55　Deleuze, *Cinema 2*, 99.
56　Deleuze, *Bergsonism*, 52. 'Time has to split at the same time as it sets itself out or unrolls itself: it splits in two dissymmetrical jets, one of which makes all the present pass on, while the other preserves all the past. Time consists of this split, and it is this, it is time, that *we see in the crystal*.' Deleuze, *Cinema 2*, 81.
57　Deleuze, *Bergsonism*, 55; Gilles Deleuze, *Le bergsonisme* (Paris: Presses Universitaires de France, 1966), 50.
58　Deleuze, *Cinema 2*, 98.
59　Williams, *Deleuze's Philosophy of Time*, 51–2.
60　Deleuze, *Bergsonism*, 58–9.
61　'If the present is actually distinguishable from the future and the past, it is because it is presence of something, which precisely stops being present when it is replaced by *something else*.' Deleuze, *Cinema 2*, 100.
62　Williams, *Deleuze's Philosophy of Time*, 25.
63　Ibid., 26.
64　Deleuze, *Cinema 2*, 70.
65　Bergson, *Matière et mémoire*, 109; Deleuze, *Cinema 2*, 289.
66　Deleuze, *Cinema 2*, 26.
67　Ibid., 26–7.
68　'The material universe, the plane of immanence, is the *machine assemblage of movement-images*. Here Bergson is startlingly ahead of his time: it is the universe as cinema in itself, a metacinema.' Deleuze, *Cinema 1*, 59.
69　Deleuze discusses these two focuses in great detail in chapters nine and ten of *Cinema 1*. Chapter nine is concerned with the large-form of the action-image which moves from one problematic situation to a renewed situation by way of an action. Chapter ten deals with the small form of the action-image and its movement from one action to another through the intermediary of a situation disclosed or deduced through the initial action. For detailed commentary, see Bogue, *Deleuze on Cinema*, 85–92 and Rodowick, *Gilles Deleuze's Time Machine*, 68–72.
70　Deleuze, *Cinema 2*, 163.
71　Bogue, *Deleuze on Cinema*, 166. Bogue argues that we can find the Spinozist origin of this idea in the latter's *On the Improvement of the Understanding* where Spinoza argues that 'the soul acts according to fixed laws, and is as it were an *immaterial automaton*'. Benedict de Spinoza, *On the Improvement of the Understanding; The Ethics; Correspondence*, trans. and ed. R. H. M. Elwes (New York: Dover, 1977), 32. Emphasis added.

72 Deleuze, *Cinema 2*, 156.
73 Gilles Deleuze, 'On The Movement-Image', in *Negotiations 1972-1990*, trans. Martin Joughin (New York: Columbia University Press, 1995), 51.
74 Ibid., 49.
75 Deleuze, *Cinema 2*, 29.
76 Ibid.
77 'It is in difference that movement is produced as an "effect", that phenomena flash their meaning like signs.' Deleuze, *Difference and Repetition*, 57.
78 Deleuze, *Cinema 2*, 31.
79 Bogue, *Deleuze on Cinema*, 66.
80 Deleuze, *Cinema 2*, 31.
81 Ibid., 32.
82 John Mullarky, *Philosophy and the Moving Image: Refractions of Reality* (Hampshire: Palgrave Macmillan, 2009), 86.
83 Deleuze, *Difference and Repetition*, 139.
84 Williams, *Deleuze's Philosophy of Time*, 27.
85 Christian Kerslake argues that in the late nineteenth century Bergson, independently of Freud, discovered that the processes of consciousness are, in fact, far less interesting than the unconscious processes which ground them and, as such, the former do not warrant the privilege they often enjoy. Kerslake argues that Deleuze interprets this to mean that the transcendental philosopher must move away from the focus on consciousness in favour of an exploration of the syntheses of time which are characteristic of unconsciousness. What Deleuze calls consciousness is, Kerslake argues, 'almost entirely practical and focused on the *present*'. Christian Kerslake, *Deleuze and the Unconscious* (London: Continuum, 2007), 9. Deleuze argues that 'Bergson does not use the word "unconscious" to denote a psychological reality outside consciousness, but to denote a nonpsychological reality – being as it is in itself.' Deleuze, *Bergsonism*, 56. Following this suggestion, it is sufficient for our purposes to treat the past as synonymous with the unconscious and the present as synonymous with consciousness insofar as the former is pure ontology; that is, it is constituted as a series of passive, ideal syntheses which operate as the ontological conditions of consciousness conceived as actual, psychological presence. For a sophisticated account of Deleuze's interest in the unconscious as passive conditions for the present, as well as his interest in the subterranean history of this idea, see Kerslake's excellent genealogy *Deleuze and the Unconscious*.
86 As I have argued consistently, a central component of Deleuze's ontology is the making of sense, or, the expression of sensible propositions. Indeed, even in his reading of Spinoza, Deleuze describes finite, existing modes as expressions of the sense of this or that attribute's participation in the constitution of substance. For

another discussion of the importance of sense-making to Deleuze, see chapter seven, 'On Learning Good Sense of Murray Code', *Process, Reality, and the Power of Symbols: Thinking with A.N. Whitehead* (Hampshire: Palgrave Macmillan, 2007).
87. Deleuze, *Cinema 1*, 206.
88. Deleuze, *Cinema 2*, 69.
89. Ibid., 86.
90. Valentine Moulard, 'The Time-Image and Deleuze's Transcendental Experience', *Continental Philosophy Review* 35, no. 3 (2002): 328.
91. Immanuel Kant, *The Critique of Judgement*, trans. James Creed Meredith (Oxford: Oxford University Press, 1952), 94.
92. Ibid., 98.
93. Ibid., 97.
94. Ibid., 99.
95. Ibid.
96. Gilles Deleuze, *Kant's Critical Philosophy: The Doctrine of the Faculties*, trans. Hugh Tomlinson and Barbara Habberjam (London: The Athlone Press, 1984), 50.
97. Kant, *Critique of Judgement*, 99.
98. Daniel W. Smith, 'Deleuze's Theory of Sensation: Overcoming the Kantian Duality', in *Essays on Deleuze*, ed. Daniel W. Smith (Edinburgh: Edinburgh University Press, 2012), 93.
99. Kant, *Critique of Judgement*, 127.
100. Ibid., 119.
101. Smith, 'Deleuze's Theory of Sensation', 93.
102. Deleuze, *Kant's Critical Philosophy*, 50–1.
103. Ibid., 51.
104. Smith, 'Deleuze's Theory of Sensation', 34. Of course, these few paragraphs are only a small snapshot of Deleuze's relationship to Kant, a relationship that is both complex and ambivalent; indeed, he famously refers to Kant as an 'enemy'. Gilles Deleuze, 'Letter to a Harsh Critic', in *Negotiations 1972-1990*, trans. Martin Joughin (New York: Columbia University Press, 1995), 6. However, without Kant, Deleuze's philosophy would be significantly diminished. Two examples that are significant here are that, on the one hand, as Christian Kerslake observes, Deleuze's description of the virtual as a *problematic* field comes from a 'peculiarly *literal* reading' of Kant's argument that ideas are problematic. Kerslake, 'The Vertigo of Philosophy', 18. On the other hand, Deleuze's conception of the faculties and their interrelationships in the three syntheses of time owes a tremendous debt to Kant's three *Critiques*. Smith in particular explores the way that Deleuze moves from the disjunctive relationship between the faculties to a differential field beyond the norms of common sense and recognition' and an outside that forces us to think. See also Beth Lord, 'Deleuze and Kant', in *The Cambridge Companion to Deleuze*, eds. Daniel W. Smith and Henry Somers-Hall (Cambridge: Cambridge University Press, 2012).

105 Deleuze, *Cinema 2*, 98.
106 Ibid., 69.
107 Ibid., 82.
108 Ibid., 86.
109 Ibid., 87.

Conclusion

1 Deleuze, *Cinema 2*, 17.
2 Henri Bergson, *The Creative Mind: An Introduction to Metaphysics*, trans. Mabel L. Anderson (New York: Citadel Press, 1992), 74.
3 Deleuze, *Bergsonism*, 17.
4 An exciting discussion that has appeared over the last decade or so is concerned with the extent to which Deleuze's conception of differen*t/c*iation owes a debt to the historical development of the differential calculus and, particularly, the role of infinitesimals therein. Two important contributions to this debate are concerned with the place of Deleuze's interest in the history of mathematics in his reading of Spinoza, as well as how he marshals Spinoza against Hegel's problematic reading of Spinoza; see Simon Duffy's *The Logic of Expression* and Henry Somers-Hall's *Hegel, Deleuze, and the Critique of Representation: Dialectics of Negation and Difference* (Albany: State University Press of New York, 2012).
5 Deleuze, *Logic of Sense*, 21.
6 Ibid., 225.
7 Ibid., 6.
8 Ibid., 32.
9 Ibid., 33.
10 Jon Roffe, 'Deleuze's Concept of Quasi-Cause', *Deleuze Studies* 11, no. 2 (2017): 284.
11 Deleuze, *Logic of Sense*, 33.
12 Deleuze, *Difference and Repetition*, 183.
13 Ibid., 70.
14 Beistegui, *Deleuze – Immanence and Philosophy*, 105.
15 Deleuze, *Cinema 1*, 206. Emphasis added.
16 Deleuze and Guattari, *What Is Philosophy?*, 60.
17 Deleuze, *Cinema 1*, 73.
18 Deleuze and Guattari, *A Thousand Plateaus*, 286.
19 Haraway, *When Species Meet*, 29.
20 Ronald Bogue, 'The Companion Cyborg: Technics and Domestication', in *Deleuze and the Non-Human*, ed. Jon Roffe and Hannah Stark (Hampshire: Palgrave Macmillan, 2015).

21 Haraway, *When Species Meet*, 52.
22 Ibid., 232–45.
23 Ibid., 234.
24 Deleuze and Guattari, *A Thousand Plateaus*, 251.
25 Ibid., 240.
26 Gilles Deleuze, 'A as in "Animal"', interview by Claire Parnet, *Gilles Deleuze From A to Z*, Dir. Pierre-André Boutang, trans. Charles J. Stivale (Los Angeles: Semiotext(e), 2012).
27 Deleuze and Guattari, *A Thousand Plateaus*, 241.
28 Haraway, *When Species Meet*, 29.
29 Félix Guattari, *The Three Ecologies*, trans. Ian Pindar and Paul Sutton (London: Continuum, 2008), 30.
   Félix Guattari, *Les trois écologies* (Paris: Éditions Galilée, 1989), 37.
30 Félix Guattari, *Chaosmosis: An Ethico-Aesthetic Paradigm*, trans. Paul Bains and Julian Pefanis (Bloomington: Indiana University Press, 1995), 92.
31 Ibid., 92–3.
32 Brett Buchanan, Matthew Chrulew and Jeffrey Bussolini, 'ON ASKING THE RIGHT QUESTIONS: An interview with Vinciane Despret', *Angelaki* 20, no. 2 (2015): 165.
33 Vinciane Despret, *What Would Animals Say If We Asked the Right Questions?* trans. Brett Buchanan (Minneapolis: University of Minnesota Press, 2016), 161.
34 Ibid., 165.
35 Ibid., 163–4.
36 Uexküll, 'Sign Theory', 165.

Bibliography

Agamben, Giorgio. *The Open: Man and Animal*. Translated by Kevin Attell. Stanford: Stanford University Press, 2004.

Ansell-Pearson, Keith. *Philosophy and the Adventure of the Virtual: Bergson and the Time of Life*. New York: Routledge, 2002.

Badiou, Alain. *Deleuze: The Clamor of Being*. Translated by Louise Burchill. Minneapolis: University of Minnesota Press, 1999.

Barbieri, Marcello. 'A Short History of Biosemiotics', *Biosemiotics* 2, no. 2 (2009): 221–45.

Beistegui, Miguel de. *Immanence: Deleuze and Philosophy*. Edinburgh: Edinburgh University Press, 2010.

Beistegui, Miguel de. *Truth and Genesis: Philosophy as Differential Ontology*. Bloomington: Indiana University Press, 2004.

Bekoff, Marc. *Rewilding Our Hearts: Building Pathways of Compassion and Coexistence*. Novato: New World Library, 2014.

Bell, Jeffrey A. *Deleuze's Hume: Philosophy, Culture and the Scottish Enlightenment*. Edinburgh: Edinburgh University Press, 2009.

Bell, Jeffrey A. *Philosophy at the Edge of Chaos: Gilles Deleuze and the Philosophy of Difference*. Toronto: University of Toronto Press, 2006.

Bennett, Jane. *Vibrant Matter: A Political Ecology of Things*. Durham: Duke University Press, 2010.

Bergson, Henri. *Creative Evolution*. Translated by Arthur Mitchell. New York: Dover Publications Inc., 1998.

Bergson, Henri. *Key Writings*. Edited by Keith Ansell Pearson and John Mullarky. London: Continuum, 2002.

Bergson, Henri. *Matière et mémoire: essai sur la relation du corps a l'esprit*. Genève: Skira, 1946.

Bergson, Henri. *Matter and Memory*. Translated by Nancy Margaret Paul and W. Scott Palmer. Mineola: Dover Publications, Inc., 2004.

Bergson, Henri. *The Creative Mind: An Introduction to Metaphysics*. Translated by Mabel L. Anderson. New York: Citadel Press, 1992.

Bergson, Henri. 'The Possible and the Real'. In *An Introduction to Metaphysics: The Creative Mind*, translated by Mabelle L. Andison, 91–106. Patterson: Littlefield, Adams & Co., 1965.

Bergson, Henri. *Time and Free Will*. Translated by F. L. Pogson. Mineola: Dover Publications, Inc., 2001.

Berkeley, George. *Three Dialogues Between Hylas and Philonous*. Edited by Robert Merrihew Adams. Indianapolis: Hackett Publishing Company, 1979.

Bogue, Ronald. *Deleuze on Cinema*. London: Routledge, 2003.

Bogue, Ronald. 'The Companion Cyborg: Technics and Domestication'. In *Deleuze and the Non-Human*, edited by Jon Roffe and Hannah Stark, 163–79. Hampshire: Palgrave Macmillan, 2015.

Bogue, Ronald. 'To Choose to Choose – to Believe in This World', in *Afterimages of Gilles Deleuze's Film Philosophy*, edited by D. N. Rodowick, 115–32. Minneapolis: University of Minnesota Press, 2010.

Boundas, Constantin V. 'Deleuze-Bergson: An Ontology of the Virtual'. In *Deleuze: A Critical Reader*, edited by Paul Patton, 81–106. Boston, MA: Blackwell, 1996.

Bowden, Sean. *The Priority of Events: Deleuze's Logic of Sense*. Edinburgh: Edinburgh University Press, 2011.

Buchanan, Brett, Matthew Chrulew and Jeffrey Bussolini. 'ON ASKING THE RIGHT QUESTIONS: An Interview with Vinciane Despret'. *Angelaki* 20, no. 2 (2015): 165–78.

Brentari, Carlo. *Jakob von Uexküll: The Discovery of the Umwelt between Biosemiotics and Theoretical Biology*. Dordrecht: Springer, 2015.

Bryant, Levi R. 'A Logic of Multiplicities: Deleuze, Immanence, and Onticology'. *Analecta Hermeneutica* 0.3 (2011): 1–20.

Buchanan, Brett. *Onto-Ethologies: The Animal Environments of Uexküll, Heidegger, Merleau-Ponty and Deleuze*. Albany: State University of New York Press, 2008.

Burghart, Gordon M., ed. *Foundations of Comparative Ethology*. New York: Van Nostrand Reinhold Company Limited, 1985.

Burkhardt, Richard W., Jr. 'On the Emergence of Ethology as a Scientific Discipline'. *Conspectus of History* 1, no. 7 (1981), 62–81.

Burkhardt, Richard W., Jr. *Patterns of Behaviour: Konrad Lorenz, Niko Tinbergen, and the Founding of Ethology*. Chicago: The University of Chicago Press, 2005.

Burwick, Frederick and Paul Douglass. *The Crisis in Modernism: Bergson and the Vitalist Controversy*. Cambridge: Cambridge University Press, 1992.

Carroll, Lewis. *Alice's Adventures in Wonderland and Through the Looking Glass and What Alice Found There*. London: Vintage Books, 2007.

Code, Murray. *Process, Reality, and the Power of Symbols: Thinking with A.N. Whitehead*. Hampshire: Palgrave Macmillan, 2007.

Colman, Felicity. *Deleuze & Cinema: The Film Concepts*. Oxford: Berg, 2011.

Deleuze, Gilles. 'A as in "Animal"'. Interview by Claire Parnet. *Gilles Deleuze from A to Z*. Directed by Pierre-André Boutang, Translated by Charles J. Stivale. Los Angeles: Semiotext(e), 2012.

Deleuze, Gilles. *Bergsonism*. Translated by Hugh Tomlinson and Barbara Habberjam. New York: Zone Books, 1988.

Deleuze, Gilles. 'Bergson's Conception of Difference'. In *The New Bergson*, translated by Melissa McMahon and edited by John Mullarky, 42–64. Manchester: Manchester University Press, 1999.

Deleuze, Gilles. *Cinéma 1: L'image-mouvement*. Paris: Les Éditions de Minuit, 1983.
Deleuze, Gilles. *Cinema 1: The Movement-Image*. Translated by Hugh Tomlinson and Barbara Habberjam. Minneapolis: University of Minnesota Press, 1986.
Deleuze, Gilles. *Cinema 2: The Time-Image*. Translated by Hugh Tomlinson and Robert Galeta. Minneapolis: University of Minnesota Press, 1989.
Deleuze, Gilles. *Difference and Repetition*. Translated by Paul Patton. New York: Columbia University Press, 1994.
Deleuze, Gilles. 'Dualism, Monism and Multiplicities (Desire-Pleasure-*Jouissance*)'. Translated by Daniel W. Smith. *Contretemps* 2 (2001): 92–108.
Deleuze, Gilles. *Empiricism and Subjectivity: An Essay on Hume's Theory of Human Nature*. Translated by Constantin V. Boundas. New York: Columbia University Press, 1991.
Deleuze, Gilles. *Expressionism in Philosophy: Spinoza*. Translated by Martin Joughin. New York: Urzone, 1990.
Deleuze, Gilles. *Francis Bacon: The Logic of Sensation*. Translated by Daniel W. Smith. London: Bloomsbury, 2006.
Deleuze, Gilles. *Francis Bacon-Logique de la sensation*. Paris: Éditions de la Différence, 1981.
Deleuze, Gilles. 'Immanence: A Life'. In *Pure Immanence: Essays on A Life*, translated by Anne Boyman, 25–33. New York: Urzone, 2001.
Deleuze, Gilles. *Kant's Critical Philosophy: The Doctrine of the Faculties*. Translated by Hugh Tomlinson and Barabara Habberjam. London: The Athlone Press, 1984.
Deleuze, Gilles. *Le bergsonisme*. Paris: Presses Universitaires de France, 1966.
Deleuze, Gilles. 'Letter to a Harsh Critic'. In *Negotiations 1972–1990*, translated by Martin Joughin, 3–12. New York: Columbia University Press, 1995.
Deleuze, Gilles. 'Mediators'. In *Negotiations 1972–1990*, translated by Martin Joughin, 121–34. New York: Columbia University Press, 1995.
Deleuze, Gilles. 'Nietzsche'. In *Pure Immanence: Essays on A Life*, translated by Anne Boyman, 53–102. New York: Urzone, 2001.
Deleuze, Gilles. *Nietzsche and Philosophy*. Translated by Hugh Tomlinson. New York: Columbia University Press, 1983.
Deleuze, Gilles. '*On* The Movement-Image'. In *Negotiations 1972–1990*, translated by Martin Joughin, 46–56. New York: Columbia University Press, 1995.
Deleuze, Gilles. 'Responses to a Series of Questions'. *Collapse* 3 (November 2007): 39–43.
Deleuze, Gilles. *Spinoza et le problème de l'expression*. Paris: Les Éditions de Minuit, 1968.
Deleuze, Gilles. *Spinoza: Practical Philosophy*. Translated by Robert Hurley. San Francisco: City Lights Books, 1988.
Deleuze, Gilles. 'Sur *L'Image-Temps*'. In *Pourparlers*, 82–7. Paris: Les Éditions de Minuit, 1990.
Deleuze, Gilles. 'The Brain Is the Screen: An Interview with Gilles Deleuze'. In *The Brain Is the Screen: Deleuze and the Philosophy of Cinema*, translated by Marie

Therese Guigis and edited by Gregory Flaxman, 365–73. Minneapolis: University of Minnesota Press, 2000.

Deleuze, Gilles. 'The Concept of Difference in Bergson'. In *The New Bergson*, translated by Melissa McMahon and edited by John Mullarky, 42–65. Manchester: Manchester University Press, 1999.

Deleuze, Gilles. *The Fold: Leibniz and the Baroque*. Translated by Tom Conley. London: The Athlone Press, 1993.

Deleuze, Gilles. *The Logic of Sense*. Translated by Mark Lester. New York: Columbia University Press, 1990.

Deleuze, Gilles and Claire Parnet. *Dialogues*. Translated by Hugh Tomlinson and Barbara Habberjam. New York: Columbia University Press, 1987.

Deleuze, Gilles and Félix Guattari. *A Thousand Plateaus: Capitalism and Schizophrenia*. Translated by Brian Massumi. London: Continuum, 1987.

Deleuze, Gilles and Félix Guattari. *What Is Philosophy?* Translated by Hugh Tomlinson and Graham Burchill. London: Verso, 1994.

Descartes, René. *Meditations, Objections and Replies*. Translated and edited by Roger Ariew and Donald Cress. Indianapolis: Hackett, 2006.

Descartes, René. *Principles of Philosophy*. Translated by Valentine Rodger Miller and Reese P. Miller. Dordrecht: D. Reidel Publishing Company, 1983.

Despret, Vinciane. *What Would Animals Say If We Asked the Right Questions?* Translated by Brett Buchanan. Minneapolis: University of Minnesota Press, 2016.

Dosse, François. *Gilles Deleuze and Félix Guattari: Intersecting Lives*. Translated by Deborah Glassman. New York: Columbia University Press, 2011.

Drohan, Christopher M. *Deleuze and the Sign*. New York: Atropos Press, 2009.

Drouin, Jean-Marc. *A Philosophy of the Insect*. Translated by Anne Trager. New York: Columbia University Press, 2019.

Duffy, Simon. 'Albert Lautman'. In *Deleuze's Philosophical Lineage*, edited by Graham Jones and Jon Roffe, 356–79. Edinburgh: Edinburgh University Press, 2009.

Duffy, Simon. 'Schizo-Math: The Logic of Different/ciation and the Philosophy of Difference'. *Angelaki* 9, no. 3 (2004): 199–215.

Duffy, Simon. 'The Differential Point of View of the Infinitesimal Calculus in Spinoza, Leibniz and Deleuze'. *Journal of the British Society for Phenomenology* 37, no. 3 (2006): 286–307.

Duffy, Simon. *The Logic of Expression: Quality, Quantity, and Intensity in Spinoza, Hegel, and Deleuze*. Hampshire: Ashgate, 2006.

Durie, Robin. 'Immanence and Difference: Toward a Relational Ontology'. *The Southern Journal of Philosophy* 40, no. 2 (2002): 161–89.

Durie, Robin. *Time and the Instant*. Manchester: Clinamen Press, 2000.

Evans, Aden. 'Math Anxiety'. *Angelaki*. 5, no. 3 (2000): 105–15.

Faulkner, Keith. *Deleuze and the Three Syntheses of Time*. New York: Peter Lang Publishing, 2006.

Favareau, D., ed. *Essential Readings in Biosemiotics: Anthology and Commentary*, 2. Dordrecht: Springer, 2010.

Flaxman, Gregory. 'Cinema: Year Zero'. In *The Brain Is the Screen: Deleuze and the Philosophy of Cinema*, edited by Gregory Flaxman. Minneapolis: University of Minnesota Press, 2000, 87–108.

Gilbert, Scott F., Jan Sapp and Alfred I. Tauber. 'A Symbiotic View of Life: We Have Never Been Individuals'. *The Quarterly Review of Biology* 87, no. 4 (2012): 325–41.

Grosz, Elizabeth. 'Feminism, Materialism, and Freedom'. In *New Materialisms: Ontology, Agency, and Politics*, edited by Diana Coole and Samantha Frost. Durham: Duke University Press, 2010, 139–55.

Guattari, Félix. *Chaosmosis: An Ethico-Aesthetic Paradigm*. Translated by Paul Bains and Julian Pefanis. Bloomington: Indiana University Press, 1995.

Guattari, Félix. *Les trois écologies*. Paris: Éditions Galilée, 1989.

Guattari, Félix. *The Three Ecologies*. Translated by Ian Pindar and Paul Sutton. London: Continuum, 2008.

Guerlac, Suzanne. *Thinking in Time: An Introduction to Henri Bergson*. Ithaca: Cornell University Press, 2006.

Guattari, Félix. *When Species Meet*. Minneapolis: University of Minnesota Press, 2008.

Gutting, Gary. 'French Hegelianism and Anti-Hegelianism in the 1960s: Hyppolite, Foucault and Deleuze'. In *The Impact of Idealism: The Legacy of Post-Kantian German Thought*. vol. 1: Philosophy and Natural Sciences, edited by Karl Ameriks, 246–71. Cambridge: Cambridge University Press, 2013.

Haraway, Donna J. *Staying with the Trouble: Making Kin in the Chthulucene*. Durham: Duke University Press, 2016.

Hegel, G. W. F. *Phenomenology of Spirit*. Translated by A. V. Miller. Oxford: Oxford University Press, 1977.

Hoffmeyer, Jesper. 'A Biosemiotic Approach to the Question of Meaning', *Zygon* 45, no. 2 (2010): 367–90.

Holland, Eugene W., Smith, Daniel W. and Stivale, Charles J., ed. *Gilles Deleuze: Image and Text*. London: Continuum, 2009.

Hughes, Joe. *Deleuze's 'Difference and Repetition': A Reader's Guide*. New York: Continuum, 2009.

Hume, David. *An Enquiry Concerning Human Understanding*. Edited by Eric Steinberg. Indianapolis: Hackett Publishing Company, 1993.

Hume, David. *A Treatise of Human Nature*. Oxford: Oxford University Press, 1978.

Hyppolite, Jean. *Logic and Existence*. Translated by Leonard Lawlor and Amite Sen. Albany: State University of New York Press, 1997.

Jun, Nathan. 'Deleuze, Values, and Normativity'. In *Deleuze and Ethics*, edited by Nathan Jun and Daniel W. Smith, 89–107. Edinburgh: Edinburgh University Press, 2011.

Kant, Immanuel. *The Critique of Judgement*. Translated by James Creed Meredith. Oxford: Oxford University Press, 1952.

Kerslake, Christian. *Deleuze and the Unconscious*. London: Continuum, 2007.
Kerslake, Christian. *Immanence and the Vertigo of Philosophy: From Kant to Deleuze*. Edinburgh: Edinburgh University Press, 2009.
Kerslake, Christian. 'The Vertigo of Philosophy: Deleuze and the Problem of Immanence'. *Radical Philosophy* 113 (2002): 10–23.
Kuhn, Elizabeth. 'Toward an Anti-Humanism of Life: The Modernism of Nietzsche, Hulme and Yeats'. *Journal of Modern Literature* 34, no. 4 (2011): 1–20.
Lambert, Gregg. 'Expression'. In *Gilles Deleuze: Key Concepts*, edited by Charles Stivale, 31–41. Montreal: McGill-Queen's University Press, 2005.
Lampert, Jay. *Deleuze and Guattari's Philosophy of History*. London: Continuum, 2006.
Lawlor, Leonard. 'A Miniscule Hiatus: Foucault's Critique of the Concept of Lived-Experience (*Vécu*)'. In *Logos of Phenomenology and Phenomenology of the Logos. Book One: Phenomenology as the Critique of Reason in Contemporary Criticism and Interpretation*, edited by Anna-Teresa Tymieniecka, 417–28. Dordrecht: Springer, 2005.
Lawlor, Leonard. 'Is It Happening? Or, The Implications of Immanence'. *Research in Phenomenology*, 44 (2014): 347–61.
Lawlor, Leonard. *The Challenge of Bergsonism: Phenomenology, Ontology, Ethics*. London: Continuum, 2003.
Lawlor, Leonard. 'The End of Phenomenology: Expressionism in Deleuze and Merleau-Ponty'. *Continental Philosophy Review* 31, no. 1 (1998): 15–34.
Lehrmann, D. S. 'A Critique of Konrad Lorenz's Theory of Instinctive Behavior'. *The Quarterly Review of Biology*, 28, no. 4 (1953): 337–63.
Lord, Beth. 'Deleuze and Kant'. In *The Cambridge Companion to Deleuze*, edited by Daniel W. Smith and Henry Somers-Hall, 82–102. Cambridge: Cambridge University Press, 2012.
Lord, Beth. *Kant and Spinozism: Transcendental Idealism and Immanence from Jacobi to Deleuze*. Hampshire: Palgrave Macmillan, 2011.
Lord, Beth. *Spinoza's Ethics*. Edinburgh: Edinburgh University Press, 2010.
Lord, Beth. 'The Virtual and the Ether: Transcendental Empiricism in Kant's *Opus Postumum*'. *The Journal of the British Society for Phenomenology* 39, no. 2 (2008): 147–66.
Macherey, Pierre. 'From Action to Production of Effects, Observations on the Ethical Significance of *Ethics* I'. In *God & Nature: Spinoza's Metaphysics*, edited by Yirmiyahu Yovel, 161–80. Leiden: E.J. Bill, 1991.
Marks, John. 'Ethics'. In *The Deleuze Dictionary*, edited by Adrian Parr, 87–9. Edinburgh: Edinburgh University Press, 2010.
Mason, Richard. *The God of Spinoza: A Philosophical Study*. Cambridge: Cambridge University Press, 1991.
May, Todd. *Reconsidering Difference*. Pennsylvania: Pennsylvania State University, 1997.
McCarthy, Michael. *The Moth Snowstorm: Nature and Joy*. London: John Murray, 2015.

Meillasoux, Quentin. 'Subtraction and Contraction: Deleuze, Immanence and Matter and Memory'. *Collapse* 3 (2007): 63–107.
Merleau-Ponty, Maurice. *Phenomenology of Perception*. Translated by Colin Smith. New York: Routledge Classics, 2002.
Mill, John Stuart. *Utilitarianism*. Edited by George Sher. Cambridge: Hackett Company, 2001.
Mitry, Jean. *The Aesthetics and Psychology of the Cinema*. Translated by Christopher King. Bloomington: Indiana University Press, 1997.
Monbiot, George. *Feral: Searching for Enchantment on the Frontiers of Rewilding*. London: Allen Lane, 2013.
Moran, Dermot. *Introduction to Phenomenology*. London: Routledge, 2000.
Morris, David. *Merleau-Ponty's Developmental Ontology*. Evanston: Northwestern University Press, 2018.
Morton, Timothy. *The Ecological Thought*. Cambridge: Harvard University Press, 2010.
Moulard, Valentine. 'The Time-Image and Deleuze's Transcendental Experience'. *Continental Philosophy Review* 35, no. 3 (2002): 325–45.
Mullarky, John. 'Forget the Virtual: Bergson, Actualism, and the Refraction of Reality'. *Continental Philosophy Review* 37, no. 4 (2004): 469–93.
Mullarky, John. *Philosophy and the Moving Image: Refractions of Reality*. Hampshire: Palgrave Macmillan, 2009.
Nadler, Steven. *Spinoza's Ethics: An Introduction*. Cambridge: Cambridge University Press, 2006.
Nail, Thomas. 'Expression, Immanence and Constructivism: "Spinozism" and Gilles Deleuze'. *Deleuze Studies* 2, no. 2 (2008): 201–19.
Nietzsche, Friedrich. *The Will to Power*. Translated by Walter Kaufman and R. J. Hollingdale and edited by Walter Kaufman. New York: Vintage Books, 1968.
Patton, Paul. 'Freedom'. In *The Deleuze Dictionary*, edited by Adrian Parr, 117–19. Edinburgh: Edinburgh University Press, 2010.
Peirce, Charles Saunders. *Collected Papers of Charles Saunders Peirce*. Vol. 1: *Principles of Philosophy* and vol. 2: *Elements of Logic*. Edited by Charles Hartsthorne and Paul Weiss. Cambridge: The Belknap Press of Harvard University Press, 1960.
Plotnitsky, Arkady. 'Bernhard Riemann'. In *Deleuze's Philosophical Lineage*, edited by Graham Jones and Jon Roffe, 190–208. Edinburgh: Edinburgh University Press, 2009.
Rodowick, D. N. *Gilles Deleuze's Time Machine*. London: Duke University Press, 1997.
Rodowick, D. N. 'The World, Time'. In *Afterimages of Gilles Deleuze's Film Philosophy*, 97–114. Minneapolis: University of Minnesota Press, 2010.
Roffe, Jon. 'David Hume'. In *Deleuze's Philosophical Lineage*, edited by Graham Jones and Jon Roffe, 67–86. Edinburgh: Edinburgh University Press, 2009.
Roffe, Jon. 'Deleuze's Concept of Quasi-Cause'. *Deleuze Studies* 11, no. 2 (2017): 278–94.
Romanini, Vinicius and Eliseo Fernández, ed. *Peirce and Biosemiotics: A Guess at the Riddle of Life*. Dordrecht: Springer, 2014.

Sagan, Dorion. 'Introduction: Umwelt After Uexküll'. In *Uexküll, Jakob von. A Foray into the Worlds of Animals and Humans with A Theory of Meaning*, translated by Joseph D. O'Neil, 1–34. Minneapolis: University of Minnesota Press, 2010.

Sartre, Jean-Paul. *Being and Nothingness: An Essay on Phenomenological Ontology*. Translated by Hazel E. Barnes. London: Routledge, 2003.

Sauvagnargues, Anne. *Deleuze and Art*. London: Bloomsbury, 2013.

Schwartz, Louis-Georges. 'Typewriter: Free Indirect Discourse in Deleuze's Cinema'. *SubStance* 34, no. 3 (2005): 107–35.

Shaviro, Steven. 'The "Wrenching Duality" of Aesthetics: Kant, Deleuze, and the "Theory of the Sensible"'. *Scholarly Articles (in pdf format)*, November 10, 2007, accessed September 15 2016. http://www.shaviro.com/Othertexts/articles.html.

Shaviro, Steven. 'Transcendental Empiricism in Deleuze and Whitehead'. In *Secrets of Becoming: Negotiating Whitehead, Deleuze, and Butler*, edited by Roland Faber and Andrea M. Stephenson, 82–91. New York: Fordham University Press, 2011.

Shaviro, Steven. *Without Criteria: Kant, Whitehead, Deleuze and Aesthetics*. Cambridge: The MIT Press, 2009.

Smith, Daniel W. 'Deleuze and the Question of Desire: Towards an Immanent Theory of Ethics'. In *Deleuze and Ethics*, edited by Nathan Jun and Daniel W. Smith, 123–41. Edinburgh: Edinburgh University Press, 2011.

Smith, Daniel W. 'Deleuze's Theory of Sensation: Overcoming the Kantian Duality'. In *Essays on Deleuze*, 89–105. Edinburgh: Edinburgh University Press, 2012.

Smith, Daniel W. *Essays on Deleuze*. Edinburgh: Edinburgh University Press, 2012.

Smith, Daniel W. 'The Conditions of the New'. *Deleuze Studies* 1, no. 1 (2007): 1–21.

Smith, Daniel W. 'The Doctrine of Univocity: Deleuze's Ontology of Immanence'. In *Essays on Deleuze*, 27–42. Edinburgh: Edinburgh University Press, 2012.

Smith, Daniel W. and Henry Somers-Hall, ed. *The Cambridge Companion to Deleuze*. Cambridge: Cambridge University Press, 2012.

Smith, David Woodruff and Barry Smith. 'Introduction'. In *Cambridge Companion to Husserl*, edited by David Woodruff Smith and Barry Smith, 1–44. Cambridge: Cambridge University Press, 1995.

Sokolowski, Robert. *Introduction to Phenomenology*. Cambridge: Cambridge University Press, 2000.

Somers-Hall, Henry. *Hegel, Deleuze, and the Critique of Representation: Dialectics of Negation and Difference*. Albany: State University Press of New York, 2012.

Spinoza, Benedict de. *Complete Works*. Translated by Samuel Shirley and edited by Michael L. Morgan. Indianapolis: Hackett Publishing Company, Inc, 2002.

Spinoza, Benedict de. *Ethics*. Translated by Edwin Curley. London: Penguin Books, 1994.

Spinoza, Benedict de. 'Letter 12'. In *The Collected Works of Spinoza*. Vol. 1. Translated and edited by Edwin Curley, 200–205. Princeton, NJ: Princeton University Press, 1985.

Spinoza, Benedict de. *On the Improvement of the Understanding; The Ethics; Correspondence*. Translated and edited by R. H. M. Elwes. New York: Dover, 1977.

Stambaugh, Joan. *The Other Nietzsche*. Albany: State University of New York Press, 1994.

Uexküll, Jakob von A. *Foray into the Worlds of Animals and Humans with a Theory of Meaning*. Translated by Joseph D. O'Neil. Minneapolis: University of Minnesota Press.

Uexküll, Jakob von. 'The New Concept of Umwelt: A Link Between Science and the Humanities'. *Semiotica* 134 (2001): 111–23.

Uexküll, Jakob von. *Theoretical Biology*. Translated by D. L. MacKinnon. New York: Harcourt, Brace & Company, Inc., 1926.

Uexküll, Thure von. 'The Sign Theory of Jakob von Uexküll'. In *Classics of Semiotics*, edited by Martin Krampen, Klaus Oehler, Roland Posner, Thomas A. Sebeok and Thure von Uexküll, 147–79. New York: Springer, 1987.

Vološinov, V. N. *Marxism and the Philosophy of Language*. Translated by Ladislav Matejka and I. R. Titunik. New York: Seminar Press, 1973.

Wambacq, Judith. *Thinking Between Deleuze and Merleau-Ponty*. Athens: Ohio University Press, 2017.

Wasser, Audrey. 'Deleuze's Expressionism'. *Angelaki* 12, no. 2 (2007): 49–66.

White, Alfred North. *Process and Reality*. New York: The Free Press, 1978.

White, Alfred North. *Science and the Modern World*. New York: Pelican Mentor Books, 1948.

Williams, James. *Gilles Deleuze's 'Difference and Repetition': A Critical Introduction and Guide*. Edinburgh: Edinburgh University Press, 2003.

Williams, James. *Gilles Deleuze's Logic of Sense: A Critical Introduction and Guide*. Edinburgh: Edinburgh University Press, 2008.

Williams, James. *Gilles Deleuze's Philosophy of Time: A Critical Introduction and Guide*. Edinburgh: Edinburgh University Press, 2011.

Williams, James. 'Science and Dialectics in the Philosophies of Deleuze, Bachelard and DeLanda'. *Paragraph* 29, no. 2 (2006): 98–114.

Zepke, Stephen. 'Deleuze, Guattari and Contemporary Art'. In *Gilles Deleuze: Image and Text*, edited by Eugene W. Holland, Daniel W. Smith and Charles J. Stivale, 176–97. London: Continuum, 2009.

Index

the absolute 39
   internal differentiation 144–5
   as sense 30–1
   as substance 146
   the whole 43–5
action 104–5
   continuity with perception 100
   as 'effect-marks' and 'effect signs' 25–6
action-image 107–8
   large and small forms 152, 184 n.69
the actual 74
   reality as continuity 144–5, 150
actualisation through differentiation 74–5
The aesthetics and psychology of the cinema. See Mitry, Jean
affect 4, 8, 21, 107–8, 144–5
   as ideal singularities 111
affection 109–11
affection-image
   as bi-polar 109–12
   as close up, or the face 109
   as the coincidence of subject and object 107–8
analytic point of view 121, 152–3
animals
   with associated worlds 158
   domestic animals and inhuman relations 157
   encountering as strangers 156, 158–60
   Penny 157–9
   qualitative *vs.* quantitative distinction 155
anthropomorphism 154–6
anti-humanism 4–5, 29
   as non-human becoming 29
attributes
   as attribution 54
   as containing modal essences 62
   doubleness 65
   genetic elements of substance 57
   infinite in their own kind 59, 169 n.66
   as qualities 56
   as verbs 54

Bergson, Henri
   the artifice of *Matter and Memory* 98–9, 176 n.25
   critique of non-being 145–6
   critique of possibility 74–7
   critique of representation 98–9
   significance for a Deleuzian ethology 14, 152
biosemiotics 34–5
body 101–2
   as the being of the special image 101
   as embodiment 4
   as relatively closed system 4, 91–2, 102

caesura. *See* radical cut
camera consciousness 123
causation
   and association 171–2 n.25
   correspondence without causation 82–3
   emanative 51–3
   immanent 51–3
   our expectations of 146
   relationship to determination 144, 178–9 n.91
   scepticism 110
   transitive 51–3, 150
choice 115
   and the formulation of problems 115–16
Cinema
   Cinema books 11–12
   Cinema's great advantage 118
   Cinema studies 9–10
cinematographical illusion 96, 118–19, 175–6 n.14
clichés 116, 141

Index 199

close up   109–10
crystal-image   137–40, 160

Deleuze's methodology   11–12
deliberation   126–8
descriptive point of view   121, 152–3
Despret, Vinciane   158–9
dialectic of problems   77–9
    as opposed to Kantian or Hegelian
        dialecticism   77
difference in itself   50
different/ciation   78, 88
differential relations   3. See also
        mathematics
dualism
    Spinoza and Bergson against   99
duration   89, 102, 128

epoché/reduction   117–18
ethics   6, 8
ethology   1–2, 6, 18–21
    contra vitalism and mechanism   18
    the conversion of ethics and ontology
        9, 15
exceptionalism
    of consciousness   117–20
    of humans   118–19
experience and the formulation of
        problems   116–17
experimentation   141–2
expression   54
    attributive   57
    modal   62
    substantive   62

faceification   109
framing   125–6
free-indirect discourse   123–4
functional circle
    and an object's significance   22–3
    as the reciprocity of an individual and
        its environment   21–2

habit   83–4
Haraway, Donna
    criticism of anthropomorphism   154
    rejection of Deleuze and Guattari
        154–6
Heretical empiricism   182–3 n.30. See also
    Pasolini, Pier Paolo

holism   12–14, 23–4, 90–2
Hume, David
    critique of representation   98
    importance for repetition   84, 150
    problem of induction   173–4 n.41
Hyppolite, Jean   2–3, 29–31

idea
    immanence to its object   30, 59–60
    in God   59–60
    as multiplicity   80
    organism as biological idea   108
    as problem   44, 80–2, 151
    as transforming direction   159–60
    virtuality of   108
image   99–100
    image = movement   100
    mise en scène of perception   100
    referred to a system of reference
        99–100
immanence   54
    four features of   52
immanent cause   52–3, 58
    God as   52–3, 58–9
indetermination   86–7, 107, 178 n.66
individual
    as expression of differentiation in
        Being   50–1
    as expressions of degrees of power
        50–1
    relational constitution   21
    as transformation of moving-matter
        108

Jezebel (film)   121–2

Kant, Immanuel. *See* the sublime

the law of association   120
Lorenz, Konrad
    innate behaviour as animals' capacities
        18–19
    Lehrman's criticism   163, n. 4

Marxism and the philosophy of language
    182 n.29. See also Vološinov, V. N.
mathematics   166–7 n.18, 187 n.4
matter   89–90
memory   128
    L'en soi of being   130

Mitry, Jean   120–2
modes
   as degrees of power   63–4
   essence distinct from existence   65
   essences as events   89–90
   as expressing the constitution of substance   62–3
   as expressions of the absolute   66
   infinite because they rely on absolute infinity   67
   as intrinsic to being   66–7
   the relationship between essence and existence   145–7
montage   133
movement
   reality as continuous movement   97
   three theses   95–7
movement-image   103
   cardinal relationship of the avatars   104
   three avatars   104–5
multiplicity
   continuous multiplicity   79–80 (*see also* duration)
   as manifold   172 n.28
   simultaneity with the terms of its actualization   81–2
   as structure   79 (*see also* idea)
   as substitution for the one and the multiple   79
   three conditions of emergence   80–1, 173 n.34

narrative   133
numerical distinction   56

object
   existing for multiple subjects   26–7, 33–4
   as feature carrier   26–7
   as meaning carrier   33–4
   neutral objects   33–4
one and the many   54–5, 102. See also multiplicity
ontology   5, 7, 9, 14
   against anthropology   7, 30

Pandora and the flying Dutchman (film)   123

Pascal's wager   115
Pasolini, Pier Paolo   124
Peirce, Charles Saunders
   significance for Deleuze   34–5
perception   104
   as bi-polar   120, 124–5
   continuity with object   101, 105–6
   as degree-zero   36–7, 104–5
   as marks/signs   24–6
   as problem   106
   relation with action   100
   as subtraction   27, 38, 106
perception-image
   three moments   124–5
phaneroscopy   35
phenomenology   117–20, 180–1 n.7
problems   39
   determination of   78
   dialectical relationship to solutions   77–8
   dialectic as temporal   128
   as transcendent   77
propositions
   as expressions of sense   41, 60–1
   and the internal differentiation of sense   42
   repetition of   61, 169–70 n.72

quasi-cause   148–51

radical cut   87
real distinction   56–8
   as formal distinction   62
reciprocal determination
   of individuals and their environments   1–2, 3–4, 15, 144–5
   of sense and affect   144–5
   of the virtual and the actual   12, 78, 127–8
reported speech   123–4
the rule of limitation   75–6
the rule of resemblance   75

semiotics
   firstness, secondness, thirdness   35–8, 104
semisubjective image   120–2
semisubjectivity and the differentiation of two subjects   122–4

sense
    as the absolute   30–1
    as direction   38–9
    against essentialism   6–7, 30
    internal differentiation   144–7
    making sense   9, 38–40
    as tripartite process   38–9
sensory-motor schema   131–4, 152, 160
    breakdown   136–41, 142 (*see also* sublime)
signs   24–6, 34–5, 134–6
Spinoza, Benedict de
    Deleuze's criticism   72–3
    as grammarian   60
    significance for Deleuze's ethology   13–14
    substance monism   13–14
subjects
    as objects in other worlds   28–9
the sublime   14, 136–40, 153
    as breakdown of the sensory-motor schema   136–41
    'Too big for me'   87
substance   44, 47. *See also* the absolute
    absolutely infinite   169 n.66
    differential constitution of essence   54

three syntheses of time
    first synthesis   84–5, 109, 131
    second synthesis   85–6, 129–30
    third synthesis   86–7, 131–2

time
    contraction towards the future   131
    as object of experience   128–9
    passing present   130–1
    past in general   85–6
    subjects internal to   128–9
    three syntheses (*see* three syntheses of time)
transcendental empiricism   31

Uexküll, Jakob von   21–9, 33–4
    Kantianism   19
umwelt   19–20
    divesting the everyday of its familiarity   158
    influence on coding   21–2
    semiotic structure   20
    suprasystem   20, 160
univocity   48–51

the virtual   74
    and the fallacy of misplaced concreteness   40
    as opposed to possibility   74–9
    as structure   74
    as transcendental conditions of experience   40
Vološinov, V. N.   123–4

the whole   96–7
    as temporal   129
    as virtual   128–9

www.ingramcontent.com/pod-product-compliance
Lightning Source LLC
Chambersburg PA
CBHW072237290426
44111CB00012B/2126